The Last Door

VIOLENCE IN LATIN AMERICAN HISTORY

Edited by Pablo Piccato, Federico Finchelstein, and Paul Gillingham

1. *Uruguay, 1968: Student Activism from Global Counterculture to Molotov Cocktails,* by Vania Markarian

2. *While the City Sleeps: A History of Pistoleros, Policemen, and the Crime Beat in Buenos Aires before Perón,* by Lila Caimari

3. *Forgotten Peace: Reform, Violence, and the Making of Contemporary Colombia,* by Robert A. Karl

4. *A History of Infamy: Crime, Truth, and Justice in Mexico,* by Pablo Piccato

5. *Death in the City: Suicide and the Social Imaginary in Modern Mexico,* by Kathryn A. Sloan

6. *Argentina's Missing Bones: Revisiting the History of the Dirty War,* by James P. Brennan

7. *In the Vortex of Violence: Lynching, Extralegal Justice, and the State in Post-Revolutionary Mexico,* by Gema Kloppe-Santamaría

8. *Nicaragua Must Survive: Sandinista Revolutionary Diplomacy in the Global Cold War,* by Eline van Ommen

9. *The Last Door: A History of Torture in Mexico's War against Subversives,* by Gladys I. McCormick

The Last Door

A HISTORY OF TORTURE IN MEXICO'S
WAR AGAINST SUBVERSIVES

Gladys I. McCormick

UNIVERSITY OF CALIFORNIA PRESS

Content Warning: Chapters 1, 3, and 5 contain detailed discussions and recollections of torture that may be disturbing or triggering.

University of California Press
Oakland, California

© 2025 by Gladys I. McCormick

Sections of this book are reprinted by permission of the University of Arizona Press, from "Torture and the Making of a Subversive during Mexico's Dirty War," in Jaime M. Pensado and Enrique C. Ochoa, editors, *México Beyond 1968: Revolutionaries, Radicals, and State Repression during the 1960s and 1970s*, © 2018 by The Arizona Board of Regents.

Sections of this book are reprinted with permission from "The Last Door: Political Prisoners and the Use of Torture in Mexico's Dirty War," *The Americas*, Vol. 74, Issue 1, January 2017.

Library of Congress Cataloging-in-Publication Data

Names: McCormick, Gladys author
Title: The last door : a history of torture in Mexico's war against
    subversives / Gladys I. McCormick.
Other titles: Violence in Latin American history 9.
Description: Oakland, California : University of California Press, [2025] |
    Series: Violence in Latin American history ; 9 | Includes
    bibliographical references and index.
Identifiers: LCCN 2024045144 (print) | LCCN 2024045145 (ebook) |
    ISBN 9780520404182 cloth | ISBN 9780520404205 paperback |
    ISBN 9780520404212 ebook
Subjects: LCSH: Torture—Mexico—History—20th century
Classification: LCC HV8599.M6 M33 2025 (print) | LCC HV8599.M6
    (ebook) | DDC 364.6/750972--dc23/eng/20250210
LC record available at https://lccn.loc.gov/2024045144
LC ebook record available at https://lccn.loc.gov/2024045145

GPSR Authorized Representative: Easy Access System Europe,
Mustamäe tee 50, 10621 Tallinn, Estonia, gpsr.requests@easproject.com

34   33   32   31   30   29   28   27   26   25
10 9 8 7 6 5 4 3 2 1

Contents

List of Figures and Maps   viii

Acknowledgments   ix

Organizations and Abbreviations   xii

Introduction: The Open Secret   1

1. The Torture   21

2. The Making of the Subversive   52

3. The Torturers   79

4. The Making of the Political Prisoner   110

5. The Family   138

6. Three Prisoners   168

    Conclusion: Torture in the Age of Impunity   194

Archives and Archival Abbreviations   213

Notes   215

List of Interviewees   245

Periodicals   248

Bibliography   249

Index   269

Figures and Maps

FIGURES

1. Mural of Los Vikingos in the San Andres neighborhood
   of Guadalajara   77

2. A plaque with six tiles sits on a pedestal across the street from
   Circular de Morelia 8   207

3. Circular de Morelia 8, headquarters of the Dirección Federal de
   Seguridad in the 1970s and 1980s   210

4. Interior of the Sitio de Memoria in the basement of Circular
   Morelia 8   211

MAPS

1. Mexico, with the seven states frequently discussed in the
   book highlighted   xvi

2. The center of Mexico City   xvii

3. The state of Guerrero   xviii

Acknowledgments

This book arose from a conversation with Hugo Velazquez Villa many years ago. He and I became friends while working with the declassified intelligence files of the Dirección Federal de Seguridad (DFS; Federal Security Directorate) housed at the Archivo General de la Nación (AGN; General Archive of the Nation) in Mexico City. He asked me why no one was studying torture, especially given how prevalent it must have been at the hands of the police and the military. I was researching what had happened to political prisoners in the 1970s, and we knew of other scholars studying guerrilla groups and student movements at a similar moment. Yet the subject of torture had not been analyzed on its own terms. His question lingered and led me to reread the files I had gathered on political prisoners. Gracias, Hugo. As time went on, I learned that Camilo Vicente Ovalle, a fellow historian, was researching the topic of disappearances of so-called insurgents. My work on torture, I realized, would contribute to an emerging scholarship on what happened to those caught up in the cycle of counterinsurgency in the 1970s—detention, interrogation, torture, imprisonment, or disappearance. I owe a debt of gratitude to Adela Cedillo for encouraging me, especially at the start of this project, and sharing the wealth of her personal library. She introduced me to Francisco

Ávila Coronel, whose commitment to honoring the memory of the victims of state terrorism, in particular, those who followed Lucio Cabañas, is truly to be commended. I thank him for his support, his humor, his generosity, and his inspiration. Through him, I came to know Eneida Martínez Ocampo, who also supported this project and added to my understanding of what took place in the state of Guerrero. Hugo, Francisco, and Eneida helped me with collecting the interviews for this book, and they introduced me to many people who left their imprint on the pages that follow. My gratitude to each of these individuals is immense, and I am honored to watch their dedication to ensuring a full accounting of what took place across the 1970s.

Many others have supported this project over the years. Thank you to my editor at the University of California Press, Enrique Ochoa-Kaup, both for his comments on the manuscript and for his careful shepherding to bring the book to fruition. I am grateful for the meaningful financial support of the University of California's First Gen Program. I especially appreciate the generous and immeasurably valuable feedback from Jaime Pensado and Alexander Aviña on the manuscript at a critical moment; while all errors are my own, both of them made my analysis and reading of the sources much stronger. I am also appreciative of the support (and humor) of Gema Kloppe-Santamaría and Victor Macías-Gonzalez, who fielded an array of questions that fine-tuned my understanding of violence. Ray Craib helped me refine my presentation of political prisoners many years ago; his advice still rings true. Maureen Meyer's astute insights into the uses of torture in Mexico today also had an impact on my thinking. I thank Al McCoy for generously allowing me to ask so many questions about how his studies on torture elsewhere in the world compared to what I was finding in the case of Mexico. I also want to thank the many others who volunteered comments and cheered me on in my writing.

I have benefited from a rich and supportive intellectual community at Syracuse University and the Maxwell School of Citizenship and Public Affairs. While there are many colleagues I would like to thank, I want to single out Norman Kutcher, Andrew Cohen, Susan Branson, Michael Ebner, and Denisa Jashari for their generosity. David Van Slyke, Carol Faulkner, and Jaime Winders proved pivotal in their intentional mentoring these past few years. I am forever grateful for their unflagging encouragement and for believing in me. I would like to express my deepest appreciation to Jay and Debe Moskowitz for giving me the necessary intellectual and professional space to bring this book to fruition. I am honored to have been the recipient these past few years of the professorship they endowed at the Maxwell School at Syracuse University. I hope they see this book as a testament to their dedication to furthering our understanding of Mexico. Many graduate students supported this project in innumerable ways. In particular, I thank Alex Vazquez, Rachel Scalisi, Valeria Urbina, Stephanie Prochaska, Lluvia Hernandez, and Jorge Valdebenito for their professionalism and commitment to making this book possible. Bridgette Werner proved instrumental in giving me the vision to tie together all the disparate pieces.

I want to thank Steve Stern and Florencia Mallon for giving me the intellectual tools to study such a challenging topic and nurturing the ethical commitment to ensure I tell this story from a place of deep respect that honors the experiences of the victims and their families. Ileana Rodriguez-Silva, Solsiree del Moral, and Brenna Wynne were by my side at every stage. Now to my own family. Thank you to my sister-by-choice, Jaymie Heilman, for never giving up on prodding me with her formidable intellect, her kindness, and her enormous capacity for humor. Thank you to Bill Moore for his humor and unfettered support, for keeping me grounded, and for bringing Lauren and Maddie into my world. Suzette Melendez, Eboni Britt, Jorge Castillo, Kris and Malcolm Patel, Jim Crawford, and Paul Heinz proved instrumental in keeping me going. Para Lucía y Amelia: como siempre, niñas, las adoro con todo mi corazón y les dedico esta obra que es un testamento a la fuerza y el amor de la familia.

Organizations and Abbreviations

GOVERNMENT, STATE-AFFILIATED, AND POLITICAL PARTY ORGANIZATIONS

Name in Spanish	Name in English
6/a Brigada de Servicios Especiales de la División de Investigaciones para la Prevención de la Delincuencia	6/a Brigade of Special Services of the Division of Investigations for the Prevention of Delinquency
Brigada Blanca	White Brigade, also known as the Special Brigade
Batallón Olimpia	Olympic Battalion
Brigada Quince de la División de Investigaciones para la Prevención de la Delincuencia (DIPD)	Fifth Brigade of the Investigation Division of the Prevention of Delinquency
Centro de Investigación y Docencia Económica (CIDE)	Center for Economic Research and Teaching
Centro de Investigación y Seguridad Nacional (CISEN)	Center for Investigation and National Security

Centro de Readaptación Social (CERESO) — Social Rehabilitation Center

Comisión para Acceso a la Verdad, Esclarecimiento Histórico e Impulso a la Justicia de violaciones graves a derechos humanos de 1965–1990 — Commission for Access to the Truth, Historical Clarification, and Promotion of Justice for grave human rights violations, 1965–1990

Comisión Nacional de Derechos Humanos (CNDH) — National Human Rights Commission

Dirección Federal de Seguridad (DFS) — Federal Security Directorate,

Dirección General de Investigaciones Políticas y Sociales (DGIPS) — General Directorate of Political and Social Investigations

Federación de Partidos del Pueblo Mexicano (FPPM) — Federation of the Mexican Peoples' Political Parties

Fiscalía para Movimientos Sociales y Póliticos del Pasado — Special Prosecutor for Social and Political Movements of the Past

Grupo Sangre — Blood Group

Los Halcones — The Hawks

Instituto Politécnico Nacional (IPN) — National Polytechnical Institute

International Police Academy (IPA)

Movimiento de Liberación Nacional (MLN) — National Liberation Movement

Partido de Acción Nacional (PAN) — National Action Party

Partido Comunista Mexicano (PCM) — Mexican Communist Party

Partido de la Revolución Democrática (PRD) — Party of the Democratic Revolution

Partido Revolucionario Institucional (PRI) — Institutional Revolutionary Party

Partido Revolucionario de los Trabajadores (PRT) — Revolutionary Workers Party

Partido Socialista (PS)	Socialist Party
Partido Socialista de Trabajadores (PST)	Workers' Socialist Party
	School of the Americas (SOA)
Secretaria de la Defensa Nacional (SEDENA)	Ministry of National Defense
Secretaría de Gobernación	Ministry of Interior
Servicio Secreto	Secret Service
Grupo Especial de Investigaciones C-047	Special Investigations Group C-047
Universidad Nacional Autónoma de México (UNAM)	National Autonomous University of Mexico

GUERRILLA AND CIVIL SOCIETY ORGANIZATIONS

Note: There were about thirty separate guerrilla organizations during the period covered in this book. The list below includes only those that are mentioned in the text. Likewise, there were many civil society organizations involved in issues relevant to the book. These include international human rights organizations, church groups, and solidarity movements inside and outside Mexico. Only those mentioned in the text are included below.

Name in Spanish	Name in English
Asociación Cívica Revolucionaria	Civic-Revolutionary Association
Asociación de Padres y Familiares de los Presos Políticos	Association of Parents and Family of Political Prisoners
Brigada Roja	Red Brigade
Comité Eureka de Desaparacidos	Eureka Committee of the Disappeared
Ejército Zapatista de Liberación Nacional (EZLN)	Zapatista Army of National Liberation
Los Enfermos	The Sick Ones

Frente Estudiantil Revolucionario (FER)	Revolutionary Student Front
Frente Revolucionario Armado del Pueblo (FRAP)	Armed Revolutionary Front of the People
Frente Urbano Zapatista (FUZ)	Zapatista Urban Front
Fuerzas Armadas Revolucionarias (FAR)	Revolutionary Armed Forces
Fuerzas Armadas de Liberación (FAL)	Armed Liberation Forces
Fuerzas de Liberación Nacional (FLN)	National Liberation Forces
Los Lacandones	The Lacandones
Liga Comunista 23 de Septiembre (LC23S)	September 23 Communist League
Liga Comunista Espartaco	Spartacus Communist League
Movimiento de Acción Revolucionaria (MAR)	Movement for Revolutionary Action
Partido de los Pobres (PDLP)	Party of the Poor
Los Procesos	The Processes
Los Vikingos	The Vikings

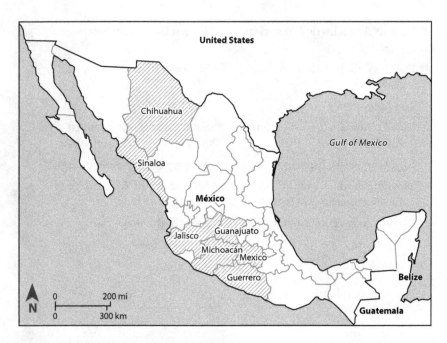

Map 1. Mexico, with the seven states frequently discussed in the book highlighted. Cartographer: Joseph Stoll

Map 2. The center of Mexico City. The Zócalo is the main square at the very heart of the city. The six other locations marked on the map housed clandestine detention and torture centers employed during the 1970s. Not included in the map is Campo Militar-1 because it is farther afield. Cartographer: Joseph Stoll

Map 3. The state of Guerrero. The four highlighted cities are especially important locations discussed in the book. Cartographer: Joseph Stoll

Introduction

Though his name is Ricardo Velasco, he asked me to call him Richard, with no explanation given. We sat at the back of a coffee shop located off the main square in the working-class neighborhood of San Andrés in Guadalajara, a large city in the state of Jalisco, Mexico. It was midafternoon, and we were the only people in the establishment. He sat across the table from me and clutched a plastic shopping bag to his chest. Richard had been a member of an armed guerrilla group in the early 1970s, and the bag contained photographs, pamphlets, and other memorabilia from this period of his life. He later showed me its contents, which included newspaper clippings of events he and other survivors from San Andrés organized to commemorate the lives of comrades killed by government forces. We laid a big sheet of brown paper on the table in front of us, on which I drew a rough sketch of the city and jotted down notes. I asked Richard to list the clandestine torture centers he knew about in Guadalajara during the 1970s and show me where they were on the map I had drawn. For the first time since we sat down to talk, he smiled, then burst out laughing at my choice of words. "Everybody knew where they were because there was nothing clandestine about them. Their location was an open secret."[1]

The tension between "open" and "secret" hung in the air between us. What made these spaces clandestine was not that they were hidden from the public's view. If anything, as Richard explained to me, it was the opposite: the public was supposed to know about them, and that knowledge was intended to instill fear. What made them clandestine was that they were shielded by official impunity and that the rule of law ceased to matter once an individual entered them. In Richard's words, "The officers could do anything." These were spaces of pain, degradation, and vulnerability, possibly culminating in an excruciating death. They were sites of torture. Behind closed doors, the Mexican government could unleash its unfettered wrath on any alleged member or supporter of a guerrilla group, holding fast to the idea that these individuals were determined to overthrow the political order through armed revolution. Guerrilla groups such as the Partido de los Pobres (Party of the Poor), Frente Revolucionario Armado del Pueblo (FRAP; Armed Revolutionary Front of the People), and, most notably, the Liga Comunista 23 de Septiembre (LC23S; September 23 Communist League) rose up at this time as more moderate paths to fight for social change were closed.[2] As the government took on a more hard-line response, torture—one of the ultimate forms of punishment—became the central element in its fight against suspected insurgents.

This book explores the Mexican government's use of torture in its counterinsurgency program during what is referred to as the long 1970s, the period from the late 1960s to 1982. These years saw the authoritarian government, in part fueled by growing Cold War anxiety throughout Latin America, become increasingly paranoid about all domestic challenges. The book considers the counterinsurgency program's routines, tracing how its agents profiled and detained so-called subversives. It follows these individuals into clandestine prisons and from there into torture chambers. It then traces what happened to these tortured individuals at the end of their time in clandestine prisons: they were either released, or relocated to a formal prison for longer detention, or disappeared. To tell this story, the first few chapters take the reader through the whole experience of arrest, torture, and detention, detailing the rituals of the sessions and the roles of different people who were present during this process. I track the adaptation of torture methods used inside these spaces as they became customary and routine practices among members of the military and police institutions. As was the case in Mexico and elsewhere, these modern forms of torture blended physical and psychological forms of torment into one practice. These new forms of torture began developing in the 1950s, during the earliest moments of the Cold War.[3] Solitary confinement, the use of medications to prolong pain, the application of tools carrying electrical currents, threats, extended hanging from limbs, and simulated drownings were all state-sanctioned forms of violence employed by military and police officers.[4] In the Mexican case, as this book finds, torture also routinely involved loved ones and family members in the experience.

Torture has a long history in Mexico. Across time, law enforcement officers routinely used brutal beatings in their investigations while court officers turned a blind eye to questions of how information was gathered. Nevertheless, torture became a more sophisticated part of policing and statecraft across the 1970s, spurred by an urge to modernize the practice in light of counterinsurgency innovations. This modern practice of torture became normalized and ultimately sat at the very center of the government's security apparatus, explaining its pervasiveness today. To demonstrate that throughline from the 1970s to the present, I make two key arguments. The first argument is that this type of modern torture worked in the most ruthless ways. It destroyed the individual and, by extension, their social and familial networks. In fact, it was so successful that counterinsurgent forms of torture became a quotidian practice of state making in Mexico above and beyond the war against subversion and well past the 1970s. Torture worked because it was the ultimate exercise of power. If a state could resort to torture, both physical and psychological, and institutionalize it as a law enforcement practice in perpetuity, why would it opt to return to the guardrails that proscribed it before? Torture worked because it allowed for the impossible to be possible: for impunity to thrive in a system supposedly abiding by the rule of law. Torture also—as we will see in the many accounts in this book—left lasting trauma for survivors and their loved ones.

The second argument rests on impunity. Torture worked as well as it did because police and military officers could employ it without reservation or fear of repercussion. With the world split between the United States and the Soviet Union as warring superpowers in the Cold War, the Mexican

government proved especially paranoid about any challenges to its authority from internal constituencies, no matter their cause. From the 1970s
forward, cohorts of officers trained and came of age during a time of war
that placed them above and beyond civilian oversight. Because military
and police officers employed torture in the name of national security and
under the banner of the rule of law during exigent times, they could ostensibly sidestep accountability for their excesses. Under the cover of impunity, officers acted outside the parameters of citizen oversight and could
resort to unfettered repression without providing explanation and without
fear of retaliation. The corroding effects of torture seeped through the
institutions meant to protect Mexican citizens by normalizing the impunity necessary to sanction extrajudicial tactics. To question the reach of
their coercive arm would be to question patriotism, since these individuals
were at the front lines of protecting the nation from ambiguous and faceless enemies referred to as "subversives" during the 1970s and as "narcos"
in the counter-narcotics era that followed in the 1980s and beyond.

COLD WAR POLITICS IN 1970S MEXICO

Pointing to the contemporary cases of Cuba, Vietnam, Argentina, and
Chile, to name a few examples, Mexican government officials throughout
the 1970s argued that guerrilla groups posed an unprecedented threat to
national security.[5] Across the 1960s, these same officials closed moderate
paths to social change and, as the decade progressed, responded more violently to challenges calling for democratization—most egregiously, the
October 2, 1968, massacre of several hundred peaceful protesters in
downtown Mexico City on the eve of the Olympics. In the aftermath of this
and other massacres, activists faced a choice to either cease mobilizing or
opt for more extreme tactics, including joining a guerrilla group and calling for outright revolution to overthrow the government. Most Mexicans
understood that the war between the government and guerrilla groups
took place in both conventional and unconventional spaces and similarly
drew on conventional and unconventional tactics that became the norm
during the Cold War. Conventional warfare conjured up men in uniforms
fighting with guns in remote rural regions, such as the jungles of Vietnam,

the mountains of Cuba, or closer to home in the states of Guerrero and Chihuahua. Less clear to average Mexican citizens was what exactly unconventional warfare was—an uncertainty that stemmed from the fact that unconventional warfare did not take place on battlefields but rather in urban or rural centers using an amalgam of premodern and modern tactics. In these places, soldiers, police officers, and others acting at the behest of the government operated with no state oversight or accountability. Regardless, this unconventional warfare fed off the illusion that the alleged enemy could be anyone hiding in plain sight, requiring plain-clothes officers to infiltrate meetings or show up in a nondescript Ford Falcon to forcefully abduct an individual in broad daylight.

Mexico's dirty war displayed many of the same dehumanizing techniques employed in other such conflicts throughout Latin America at the time. First, members of the military and the police used the category "subversive" to create an imagined enemy that could be anywhere and anyone—an enemy so threatening that they ceased to be human. Propaganda disseminated through government-controlled media channels ensured the creation of a siege mentality that favored official narratives. Second, these agents capitalized on this siege mentality to suspend the rule of law in the name of national security, granting themselves total impunity for the torture and murder of so-called subversives. Third, the Cold War afforded these agents the necessary language, techniques, and resources to deflect attention from the fact this was an internal war. Agents could nest their actions against civilians within an international conflict to avoid criticism or sanctions. The fact that students carried placards with the face of Che Guevara and that guerrillas expressed support for the Cuban Revolution made such official justification easier.[6] And fourth, the aim of this dirty war was to teach sectors of society the folly of their challenges to the establishment.

Across the long 1970s, the Mexican government—led first by Gustavo Díaz Ordaz, then by Luis Echeverría Álvarez, and then by José López Portillo—set up clandestine prisons in areas close to guerrilla activity, from nondescript houses in middle-class neighborhoods in Guadalajara to the basement of the Dirección Federal de Seguridad (DFS; Federal Security Directorate) office building in the Roma neighborhood of Mexico City and the military base at Pie de la Cuesta a few miles north of Acapulco on the Pacific coast of the state of Guerrero.[7] Borrowing from Giorgio Agamben's idea of a state of exception, these clandestine prisons were spaces of exception, where members of law enforcement acted outside the law, in a sort of "juridical void" for the sake of the nation.[8] Due process, among other legal protections, no longer applied to anyone designated "subversive." Inside clandestine torture centers, the prisoner's civil rights ceased to exist as police and military officers set aside whatever patriotic oath they had made to protect and serve. The threat was supposedly so extreme that officers had to resort to "dirty" tactics against unarmed civilians in order to uphold their patriotic duty.

Torture became a central part of the Mexican government's strategy against so-called subversion and was not always for the purpose of extracting information. Torture could also be strictly punitive: it was about inflicting punishment on a faceless transgressor the government designated as its "enemy." A subversive could be a known guerrilla member or one of their family members, a young woman challenging gender norms, a leader in a peasant movement, a labor activist, or a university student voicing dissatisfaction with the political order. This enemy could be wearing fatigues or jeans, listening to rock 'n' roll or reading Karl Marx, and living in the countryside or the city. Subversives could be anyone, anywhere, willing to possibly resort to extreme tactics that did not respect the confines of a battlefield or traditional norms of warfare. That ambiguity surrounding the identity of this faceless enemy magnified the threat so-called subversives posed to Mexico's social fabric. While it was unclear precisely what harm could come at the hands of subversives, they represented an unfamiliar threat to Mexicans' familiar way of life and traditional norms guarding against social chaos.

Just as the existence of clandestine detention centers was an open secret, information about what happened inside these centers seeped outside their walls. Media outlets disseminated the government's messages about the threat posed by guerrilla groups. Family members sought information on their loved ones' whereabouts, clamoring outside government offices. This war, with its provisional and exceptional measures, thus extended beyond the clandestine prisons to include family networks and society at large, thereby nurturing a self-reinforcing and durable culture of fear.[9] The unspoken purpose of such a culture was to train society not to question what the government did in the name of national security; to educate citizens to trust that their government—covertly or overtly—acted for the collective good; and to illustrate what would happen to social actors who questioned the government's prerogative during these exceptional times. Mexico's dirty war reeducated the nation's citizenry, normalizing and rendering permanent the weakening of the rule of law. Even the absence of the detained, imprisoned, or disappeared individual—along with the individual's grieving and fearful family—communicated to the community at large the consequences of association, deliberate or accidental, with guerrillas.

The primary subjects of this reeducation, developed in chapter 2, were young people who made demands on the political order, demands that Mexican officials deemed unreasonable. Government actors stripped these citizens of their humanity, thereby rendering them a faceless other. Categorized simply as subversives, these individuals were no longer deserving of the government's protection and, because they supposedly posed an immediate threat, had to be punished by torture. The secondary subjects of this reeducation, as chapter 5 argues, were family networks, who were just as suspicious if not culpable in the eyes of the security forces. This layered approach to categories of guilt broadened the reach of the pervasive culture of fear and social complicity. Most citizens tacitly endorsed political violence by not challenging the government's narrative that it engaged in violence, conventional or unconventional, for the greater good.

A MEXICAN-STYLE DIRTY WAR

The French military pioneered "antirevolutionary war" tactics in battles to retain its colonies in Vietnam and Algeria during the 1950s. These same tactics, nested within a framework of counterinsurgency, came to be called "dirty war" when militaries employed them against civilian populations in Latin America starting in the late 1960s.[10] The seeming need for this type of warfare emerged from earlier failed attempts to institutionalize reforms to assuage new political constituencies, such as growing working and middle classes, demanding access to power. When populist leaders failed to deliver on promises made to these new constituencies, some resorted to calls for revolution, which led to violent reactions from conservative sectors demanding a return to the status quo. They also, as in Mexico, followed a perceived need to rein in a reform-greedy populace that demanded more than what those in power were willing to concede for the sake of national security. Government agents, almost always the military but also police forces, addressed this popular dissatisfaction through intimidation, violence, and the infantilization of civil society. It was called dirty war because, rather than an external enemy, the enemy was internal and hidden among civilians, which required military and police forces to resort to methods it would not usually employ. The enemy played dirty, so went the logic, thereby forcing the hand of law enforcement to do the same. This was more than a repressive state using the idea of a dirty war to justify political violence or as a tool of dictatorship. This type of war normalized the use of modern forms of state terror in Mexico, and torture was at the very heart of the security apparatus. While there were similarities with other dirty wars of the period, there were also features unique to the Mexican case. One of the key differences was the systematic inclusion of families—sons, daughters, fathers, mothers, siblings, grandparents, cousins—in the torture experience as witnesses, subjects of threats, and victims of state terror.

While the notion of the dirty war in Mexico may appear new to those outside the country, many Mexican scholars, journalists, activists, and direct participants have written and debated about it extensively for decades. More recently, Verónica Okión Solano, Adela Cedillo, Fernando Calderón, Ariel Rodríguez Kuri, and others have tackled the question of what to call what transpired across the long 1970s as they unearthed the history of the many guerrilla groups active at the time, the role of women in them, and the development of a human rights framework.[11] Camilo Vicente Ovalle cautions against using the term "dirty war" out of concern that it is too homogenizing and not ample enough to capture the complexity of what took place in Mexico at this time.[12] In their work on Guerrero, Claudia Rangel and Evangelina Sánchez posit that what took place here and elsewhere in Mexico was both a "dirty war" and a campaign of "state terror."[13] I side with Rangel and Sánchez by using the term "dirty war" to reckon with the government's campaign of terrorism—upheld by the rule of law and carried out by state agents—against its civilian population.

By keeping "dirty war" in the conversation alongside "state terror," we can push back on narratives of exceptionalism in Mexico that claim what happened here is not the same as what happened elsewhere in Latin America, in particular, in the Southern Cone, in the 1970s. Doing so is especially important because of the quantity of pro-government narratives, many written in the 1970s, that justify state repression. As Cedillo and Calderón meticulously detail, several survivors of the 1968 massacre at the Tlatelolco housing project in Mexico City on the eve of the Olympics wrote that their activism was a foolish action on their part.[14] Former guerrilla members of LC23S, such as Gustavo Hirales, and one of the founders of the Socialist Party, José Woldenberg, condemned these movements and claimed others, including the agents of the US Central Intelligence Agency (CIA), with ulterior motives, led them astray. These apologist narratives have made way for much more precise and well-documented studies. That change has resulted from the opening up of archives, including those of the DFS, a growing interest in understanding what happened during this period, the widespread discourse of human rights, and an openness of families and survivors to discuss their experiences.[15]

There have been attempts to officially document what happened in Mexico's long 1970s, such as the investigations by the Comisión Nacional de Derechos Humanos (CNDH; National Human Rights Commission) in the 1990s and the Fiscalía para Movimientos Sociales y Políticos del Pasado (FEMOSSP; Special Prosecutor for Social and Political Movements of the Past) in the mid-2000s.[16] The reports produced by both of these bodies did not go beyond partially documenting what happened and did not lead to any prosecutions. President Andrés Manuel López Obrador established a truth commission in June 2022 with much fanfare and declared that the Mexican people would finally have a true accounting of human rights abuses perpetrated by government officials between 1965 and 1990, years of intense state violence straddling the period covered in this book.[17] Yet even while this new body has further opened archives and deepened our knowledge of the period, it lacks the legal instruments to enforce change.[18] There have been no effective justice frameworks attached to any of these efforts to devise accountability mechanisms, such as trials of perpetrators or reparations to victims and their families. This is not to say that families, survivors, and human rights activists have not tried for decades to push for more concerted forms of justice. Without a genuine reckoning about what happened, as well as who was responsible, the open wound of collective trauma remains unhealed. The ranks of torture victims continue to grow, as Mexicans have endured human rights abuses throughout the period from the dirty war to the present. Despite efforts to have some forms of reckoning, the particular brand of government repression implemented across the 1970s normalized impunity throughout Mexican society. This then explains why contemporary forms of impunity appear so profoundly intractable. As this book demonstrates, the roots of today's security crisis are found in how the government legitimated its counterinsurgency actions during the 1970s.

PERIODIZING STATE VIOLENCE

The Partido de la Revolución Institucional (PRI; Institutional Revolutionary Party) was in control of Mexico from 1927 until the 2000 presidential elections, making it one of the most successful cases of authoritarianism in Latin America.[19] This meant that members of the PRI held virtually every public office, including the presidency, until Vicente Fox from the Partido de Acción Nacional (PAN; National Action Party) was elected president in 2000. The PRI's brand of authoritarianism incorporated a range of flexible state-society relationships that served to reinforce the power of the central executive.[20] The range and specificity of these relationships allowed the central executive to give the appearance of democratic processes even while it naturalized one-party rule. The governing regime's monopoly of resource management and control of modern Mexico's founding narratives guaranteed its position as the interlocutor between different social sectors, which helped it fend off challenges at the polling booth. During periods of political crisis, when the governing regime came under threat from popular sectors within its bases of support, PRI officials co-opted leaders and selectively deployed violence against those who continued challenging it.[21] Challenges from popular movements periodically resisted the power of patron-client networks and divide-and-conquer tactics. In these cases, the PRI-led state did not hesitate to deploy top-down and selective coercive force to protect the system's integrity and intimidate those social sectors making what its agents deemed unreasonable demands.[22]

Political violence proved central to how the governing regime maintained its power for as long as it did. From the late 1960s to the early 1980s, torture, imprisoning political opponents, and an assortment of other counterinsurgency tactics gained greater importance in response to challenges from popular sectors. The government's security apparatus operated in a liminal space where its leaders, agents, informants, and allies could selectively apply the rule of law in service of their own agendas under the guise of ensuring national security. In short, the PRI was successful because it could draw on an array of corrective measures—albeit with varying degrees of success—when one of its own or an outsider threatened its control. I thus echo Wil Pansters, who posited that so much attention has been focused on distinguishing Mexico's "moderate authoritarianism" from other cases of repressive regimes in Latin America that scholars have "unintentionally contributed to underestimating or masking violence and coercion—the 'dark side'—in state-making."[23]

That "dark side" could appear fragmented and partial because it happened in far-flung places or involved both state-affiliated and non-state actors.[24] Pansters explains how these points of contention and resistance across Mexico—from street vendors to industrial workers, students, and rural peoples mobilizing to express their dissatisfaction—gathered momentum and collided with the Cold War–inflected language of protest to challenge political elites. In response, and most tellingly in the 1968 Tlatelolco massacre, Mexican elites turned a blind eye to the sources of discontent and leaned into Communist paranoia to explain their failures at dampening protest and to justify their hard-line response.[25] As a result, the military and police detained, tortured, imprisoned, and disappeared enemies of the state. Some victims belonged to urban or rural guerrilla groups, while others were family members, student or labor activists, members of criminal groups, rural peoples, or innocent bystanders. Regardless, they fell into the category "subversive"—an internal, unconventional enemy so threatening to the social fabric that the government had to undermine the established rule of law to deal with it. The threat these so-called subversives posed imbued members of the police and military with the necessary authority to set aside due process in pursuing them.[26]

We can periodize modern Mexico's state-sponsored political violence into three stages. The first, between 1946 and 1962, is linked to both a birth and a death. The death occurred in the massacre of several dozen civilians in León, Guanajuato, who were protesting the official imposition of a candidate.[27] The birth happened soon after, in 1947, with the formation of the Dirección Federal de Seguridad as the "operative" branch of the federal government's surveillance agencies. During this first stage, the government experimented with different forms of repression at the hands of state agents, primarily in the countryside and far from the public eye.[28] It had diffused political threats from opposition candidates, such as Miguel Henriquéz Gúzman in the 1952 presidential elections, and tackled large-scale social mobilizations, including those of railroad workers and, most tellingly, the 1959 teachers' strikes in Mexico City.[29] The second stage, between 1962 and 1968, began with the brutal assassination of Rubén Jaramillo and his family in Morelos for mobilizing rural peoples. Jaramillo's murder foreshadowed the arrival of more openly repressive tactics to an urban audience. It encompasses the beginning of the radical armed insurgency, especially after the September 23, 1965, assault by guerrilla groups on army barracks in Ciudad Madera, Chihuahua, and the military's heavy-handed reaction that left many dead.[30]

The third and most violent stage is the focus of this book. It began with two brutal massacres that spurred activists to take more radical paths to social change. The first of these massacres, in May 1967, was of rural peoples in the community of Atoyac, located in the highlands of Guerrero, who were clamoring for the release of a teacher imprisoned for calling for better living conditions.[31] The second mass killing followed the rise of the student mobilizations in Mexico City during the spring and summer of 1968, culminating with their massacre at Tlatelolco on October 2.[32] The events surrounding these two massacres dramatically upped the ante of the internal war, spurred on by a deepening Cold War ethos, increasing dissatisfaction with a restricted political order, and, most dramatically, the state's implementation of counterinsurgency tactics against internal threats—in other words, the advent of dirty war modalities and logics. That the mobilizations and the ensuing massacre unfolded against the backdrop of the Olympics internationalized 1968, tying domestic turmoil to events taking place across the globe, namely, in the United States, France, Yugoslavia, and other global theaters of the youth movement.[33]

Although they came from the same political party, the PRI presidents of the 1960s and 1970s left their own imprint on the nature of state-sponsored repression. President Gustavo Diaz Ordáz (1964–70) is perhaps the most well known because of his hard-line response to opposition, most notoriously, the Tlatelolco massacre. Subsequent administrations pulled away from such overt displays of violence. Luis Echeverría Álvarez (1970–76), Diaz Ordáz's successor, opted for more covert forms of repression. Unofficially, his administration delegated violence to gangs of thugs on the government's payroll, using them to brutally quell public protests such as the 1971 Corpus Christi massacre in Mexico City. Officially, the military and the DFS employed counterinsurgency methods to destroy urban and rural guerrilla groups. While Echeverría Álvarez sponsored these covert forms of repression, he deflected criticism by maintaining relations with the Cuban revolutionary government, and welcoming political exiles fleeing for their lives from brutal military dictatorships such as Chile's.[34] Echeverría Álvarez's embrace of these exiles picked up on the rhetoric of earlier presidents, in particular, Adolfo López's Mateos (1958–64), to capitalize on the government's bona fides as a leftist revolutionary bastion in the aftermath of the Cuban Revolution.[35]

José López Portillo (1976–82) adapted the mechanisms of state-sponsored repression to the needs of the time. With much of the so-called guerrilla and Communist threat virtually eliminated when he took office, he declared an amnesty for guerrilla members in 1982, marking the end of the "dirty war." His government pivoted to a new form of an internal enemy to justify ongoing sponsorship of its sizable security apparatus. Setting aside "subversives," the government rallied around the threat posed by "narcos" and drug traffickers to stoke fears of social corruption and galvanize support against a new internal enemy. As the economy cleaved after decades of mismanagement and corruption, López Portillo used the distractions afforded by drug traffickers to ease the way for a more technocratic era of neoliberalism and new collaborations with the US government, including its recently created Drug Enforcement Agency (DEA).[36]

Far from monolithic, the PRI's system of political rule was flexible— and imperfect—enough to accommodate new mechanisms of state repression and a certain degree of messiness in recalibrating existing practices. On the surface, the changes across the presidencies appear much like a pendulum swinging between a more populist and a more hard-line approach that sustained a constant center in the political spectrum. Nevertheless, a closer look at the presidencies of Diaz Ordáz, Echeverría Álvarez, and López Portillo, spanning the period 1964–82, defies that narrative. Officials in each of these administrations became increasingly paranoid as they surveyed the impact of the Cold War in Latin America. In taking stock of Mexico's popular demands for a political opening as well as later guerrilla activity that called for the overthrow of the state, these officials opted for empty concessions. Under Diaz Ordáz, officials ramped up state repression that nurtured a culture of fear, while officials under Echeverría Álvarez adopted covert tactics to conceal the increasing brutality. In doing so, the presidents themselves along with police and military officers far below them chipped away at the very institutions responsible for the rule of law. Clandestine operations and paramilitary gangs existed outside a system of accountability, where in the name of national security officials overseeing them answered to no one. The resulting institutional weakness enabled organized crime to infiltrate the government from within and made neoliberal economic policies—so antithetical to the idea of "institutionalizing" the revolution—officials' preferred solution for growing financial instability. Neoliberalism and drug cartels thereby became the hallmarks of the closing years of López Portillo's presidency.

This third and most violent stage had its own ebbs and flows. Between 1970 and 1972, the government experimented with quelling emerging urban and rural guerrilla movements.[37] In urban settings, police covertly infiltrated popular movements and sabotaged them from within and, when necessary, resorted to paramilitary violence to stop their activities. One of the most extreme acts of such violence occurred in the June 10, 1971, Corpus Christi massacre in Mexico City when a group of paramilitary thugs known as the Halcones (Hawks) on the government's payroll killed fifty peaceful student demonstrators.[38] The majority of these young people were students at the Universidad Nacional Autónoma de México (UNAM; National Autonomous University of Mexico) and part of a broader effort of university students to call on the government of

Echeverría Álvarez to follow through on his promises of a "democratic opening" to correct for his predecessor's hard-line approach to student activism.[39] The violence was even more pronounced in the countryside, specifically, the state of Guerrero. There a professionalized paramilitary group used a combination of standard and new counterinsurgency tactics to issue a fearsome response to the rise of two guerrilla groups: one led by Genaro Vázquez and another led by Lucio Cabañas.

Between 1973 and 1975, the Mexican torture program came into its own under the guiding hand of Miguel Nazar Haro, a key figure in the DFS's leadership, and others like him as they targeted their biggest threat to date: the LC23S. This guerrilla group straddled urban and rural areas and was responsible for over sixty direct action operations, including the failed kidnapping and killing of the business leader Eugenio Garza Sada in 1973. The techniques employed during this period revealed a mature security apparatus capable of reaching and coordinating threats throughout Mexico with precision. Between 1976 and 1979, the use of torture declined in favor of the more expedient disappearance of so-called insurgents as well as the near-complete obliteration of any guerrilla threat. During the post-1979 period, the government's amnesty for guerrilla members marked the end of traditional counterinsurgency and the beginning of state attempts to control the emerging drug trade.

After the PRI was voted out of office in the 2000 presidential election, President Vicente Fox established the FEMOSPP to investigate what happened during the long 1970s; it concluded it was not possible to ascertain precise numbers of victims before funding was cut off and the office was dissolved in 2007.[40] Some scholars have proposed rough numbers of Mexicans victimized by the state between 1964 and 1982: approximately 7,000 people tortured, at least 3,000 detained as political prisoners, and more than 3,000 disappeared or killed.[41] However, there are still outstanding questions and a lack of concrete documentation to cite definite figures.

THE DFS AS THE ARCHITECT OF PAIN

Under the guise of counterinsurgency, the Mexican government's security apparatus, principally through the DFS and branches of the military and police, shaped the narrative about the national security threat and then rolled out Cold War counterinsurgency tactics against it. Propaganda went hand in hand with intelligence gathering, aided by the emergence of new forms of surveillance technology developed during the Cold War.[42] Sophisticated recording devices, infiltration tactics, and misinformation strategies developed in counterinsurgency campaigns and transported to Mexico by the US government accompanied traditional surveillance methods, including the nurturing of a vast web of informants. It was easy to justify this type of incursion into civilian life because so many different kinds of people could be the enemy: sons and daughters of government leaders susceptible to the ideological scourge of Communism or greedy government officials who demanded too many payoffs and risked jeopardizing the balance of institutionalized corruption. For the public, the impression of an immutable and paternalistic state presence conferred a sense of stability in a chaotic world threatened both by guerrilla insurgents attempting the forcible takeover of the social order and by sexually liberated university students who challenged traditional values. For government officials, such unruliness would make Mexico vulnerable to attacks from external and—more ominously—internal enemies that could undermine their authority and challenge the political order.

The DFS was joined by other agencies, including various police branches and the military, in the "dark side" of state making. The DFS, however, was the most notable agency to operate in this liminal and "exceptional" space—most notable because of its brutally effective operations against so-called subversives. The agency maintained surveillance of thousands of organizations and individuals, amassing an impressive archive of valuable material on subversives.[43] Targets for surveillance included leftist activists, reformist politicians, and union leaders maneuvering inside the corporatist system. The DFS complemented its surveillance activities with more aggressive strategies to co-opt and subvert dissent against the government. This meant that the DFS helped the executive branch manage electoral competitions and watch over the many branches of government; and, when necessary, it intervened to rein in an overly ambitious leader or place supporters in key posts. Early in its history, DFS agents exaggerated the threat posed by subjects of surveillance to justify the agency's mandate and budget. Nevertheless, as the Cold War gathered steam, the DFS no longer needed to resort to exaggeration because of government agents' genuine paranoia and fear—especially within the executive branch—of Communist infiltration or a successful guerrilla takeover.

The DFS was dissolved in 1985 as a result of its implication in the killing of Enrique "Kiki" Camarena, an agent of the US DEA.[44] Many of the former agents were hired back by the new version of the DFS, the Centro de Investigación y Seguridad Nacional (CISEN; Center for Investigation and National Security), after 1989. The practices of detention, torture, imprisonment, and disappearance continued across this period because they had become central to the government's toolbox for maintaining control. Brutal violence was now a de facto part of policing in Mexico. At the same time, impunity allowed DFS agents and others involved in counterinsurgency to collaborate with the emerging drug-trafficking organizations of the period. In the absence of government oversight, DFS agents slipped into illegal practices that first began in their official capacity, such as inside torture chambers, but grew to facilitate drug trafficking. This ambiguous space inhabited by the DFS agents transformed into what Al McCoy refers to as the "covert netherworld": a place where secret services and criminal syndicates acted without restrictions, their activities nurturing the rise of drug trafficking.[45] From the 1970s to 1985, the DFS's activities helped entrench impunity and make it durable in Mexico, and that durability carried over from counterinsurgency activities into connections with narcotrafficking and organized crime.[46]

THE SUBVERSIVES IN PRISON

Before 1968, the Mexican government had a long track record of imprisoning dissidents, such as the railroad leader Demetrio Vallejo and the muralist and known Communist David Alfaro Siqueiros.[47] This practice ramped up after 1968. In December 1969, former president Lázaro Cárdenas sent a letter to political prisoners in the Lecumberri federal penitentiary in Mexico City, assuring them that he would continue to lobby for their release.[48] In October 1973, Michoacán university students marching in front of the state government building in Morelia held up placards demanding the release of political prisoners.[49] On June 29, 1974, Lucio

Cabañas, guerrilla leader of the Partido de los Pobres in the mountains of Guerrero, released a communiqué in which the group's first demand was the release of political prisoners.[50] In its founding document of March 1973, the LC23S made it clear that political prisoners were one of the costs of carrying out a revolution and, as such, would not distract from its broader mission.[51] Taken together, the many references to political prisoners suggest imprisonment was a common reality in the lives of those challenging the authoritarian government in the 1960s and 1970s. As chapter 4 shows, a certain contradictory looseness characterized prison life.[52] On the one hand, if they could afford bribes, prisoners could cook their own meals; receive extended visits from family, friends, and prostitutes; and take part in educational workshops. On the other hand, the same accommodating guards could be arbitrarily tough, vengeful, and brutal.

The frequency with which political prisoners were addressed among groups opposing the PRI is jarring when read against the official common sense of the time—that the Mexican government, while violent in its response to the 1968 student movement and when battling guerrilla groups in the 1970s, did not resort to repression in the same way as military dictatorships elsewhere in Latin America did. This attitude is evident in a confidential report sent by the US embassy to the US State Department in March 1976, acknowledging the existence of "a pattern of human rights violations in Mexico." The report acknowledged that torture was part of this pattern but denied that these abuses rose to the level of "gross violations." The report concluded that torture and other human rights abuses were standard practice in Mexico and would "be overcome only as the country gradually modernizes."[53] This would have us believe that Mexican state-sponsored violence of this period was not on par with what was happening in Chile or Argentina. If anything, it lined up with what some scholars have referred to as "dictablanda"—a softer, yet effective version of authoritarianism.[54]

In the 1970s, PRI state officials used a mix of methods to maintain control, including co-opting intellectuals and promoting an international image as a progressive haven for foreign exiles. These well-studied "softer" methods increasingly relied on the strategic deployment of "harder" methods, including the wide-scale use of torture and imprisonment to nurture a culture of fear. In other words, the PRI-led state calibrated its repressive measures to fit the realities of a society making greater demands on political spaces. This book thus finds that the Mexican government regularly utilized extreme violence, to the extent that it amounted to a campaign of terror against its own citizens. Tracing what happened to those who were targeted in this campaign of terror, this book shows how the government learned to use these two repressive tools—imprisonment and torture—to intimidate society at large. Crucially, government officials learned that they could easily resort to violence to maintain control during moments of vulnerability, such as in the face of attacks by guerrilla groups, popular movements, or organized crime. Invoking national security gave government officials impunity to do as they saw necessary, without having to answer to an oversight body, divulge evidence justifying their actions, or disclose precisely what occurred.

A NOTE ON SOURCES

The book's evidentiary backbone is oral histories with approximately sixty individuals associated with the events in question.[55] Their stories are difficult and painful to read, and, as such, I treat them with respect in service of understanding the broader arguments. Because of the volume of interviews, I chose not to provide notes when I quote or refer to a given person; readers are encouraged to refer to the list of interviewees at the end of the book for more information.[56] After identifying individuals, I use first names when writing about them to indicate they are interviewees. Because of the highly sensitive subject matter, I privileged including interviews with individuals who had told their stories before, whether to other scholars, to journalists, or to one of the attempted truth commissions. Several of them, such as Carlos Salcedo, Lourdes López Uranga, Antonio Orozco Michel, and José Luis Moreno Borbolla, have published memoirs and testimonios detailing what happened to them during Mexico's long 1970s.[57] Others have gone on to become scholars of the period in their own right, most notably, Enrique Condés Lara. Many of the individuals interviewed for this project shared unpublished memoirs, collections of documents, and personal papers. These are listed in the bibliography. The book also draws on a range of archival documentary collections, including declassified intelligence reports of security forces in Mexico and the United States. These include the collections of the Dirección Federal de Seguridad and the Dirección General de Investigaciones Políticas y Sociales.[58] Finally, I use information from the various iterations of reports documenting what happened during the 1970s, including those from the Comisión Nacional de Derechos Humanos, the Comisión para la Verdad del Estado de Guerrero, and the Fiscalía Especial para Movimientos Sociales y Políticos del Pasado.

1 The Torture

Members of the military came in the middle of the night for Lucio Cabañas's uncle, Alejandro Arroyo Cabañas, and great-uncle, Sostenes López Cienfuegos, in June 1972 at their home in San Vicente, a small community located in the municipality of Atoyac in Guerrero.[1] They were hooded and taken to the nearby military base, where officers began torturing them. Alejandro's son, José Luis Arroyo, recalled that his father told him there was "an American [*gringo*] adviser giving the instructions to the person torturing him and that's when he started receiving electric shocks all over his body. They would put him inside a sink and apply the electric cables. Stick needles inside his nails, hang him, beat him, kick him." Alejandro was tortured repeatedly by different officers. "He would wake up, after they left him for dead, and he didn't remember where he was, who he was. A guard would talk to him, offer him a cigarette," José Luis explained. "He was afraid of the cigarette because sometimes when he was tortured they would put the lit end of the cigarette inside his mouth."

At one point, officers covered Alejandro's eyes and put him and his father in what Alejandro thought was the trunk of a car. On the long drive, the soldiers stopped periodically, brought them out, and threatened to kill them. They were taken to Mexico City, then sent back to a prison in Acapulco, where they managed to send word to their families that they were alive. Alejandro's wife went to find them in Acapulco, only to be told that her husband and father had been transferred to the federal prison in Tecpan de Galeana, not far from Atoyac. When she was allowed to see them there, they had been beaten so badly they were unable to walk. At her father's urging, she scraped together the money to pay their exorbitant bail by selling their cows to the owner of a slaughterhouse who handled the exchange discreetly. Alejandro's son recalled how hard it was for her to find anyone who would help her or buy anything from her because "the whole place was filled with the military. Anyone who was seen lending money for that would be detained, taken away, and disappeared." On the day the men were released, they all packed their belongings and fled to Mexico City.

Right after their release, the family took Alejandro and his father to a doctor and a psychologist. The doctor concluded that both men had ample signs of having suffered torture, Alejandro, who at the time was in his fifties, more than Sostenes, who was in his seventies. Both medical professionals concluded that Alejandro would suffer long-term physical and psychological effects from the torture he endured. He was not the only one: thousands of Mexicans endured similar experiences of detention, torture, and imprisonment from the mid-1960s to the early 1980s and carried with them lasting scars. Scholars, activists, victims, and their families are now trying to understand the cumulative effects of state terror and reckon with their lasting impact on civil society.

In his pathbreaking book on the practice of forced disappearance in Mexico, Camilo Vicente Ovalle uses the concept *circuito* (circuit) to describe the steps victims went through from apprehension and detention to either temporary or permanent disappearance at the hands of the government's security forces.[2] It is in the second stage of the circuit—detention—that officials used torture, ostensibly to extract information. I build on Vicente Ovalle's arguments to suggest that gathering actionable information was a secondary purpose of interrogation. The primary purpose of torture was twofold: to punish so-called subversives by breaking down their sense of self and to forge a common purpose among those who participated. Al McCoy describes this primary purpose as a "transactional experience that simultaneously destroys the victim and empowers the perpetrator."[3] Each of the stages in the circuit Vicente Ovalle describes functioned in tandem to reinforce the power of state terror. While Vicente Ovalle looks at the culmination of that circuit in forced disappearances, I explore the earlier stage of detention and torture to argue that the roots of impunity in Mexico run deep. Like he does for the practice of forced disappearances, I propose that the strategies of counterinsurgency changed how security forces used torture as part of their interrogation procedures to be much more than just information gathering. Vicente Ovalle describes "the bureaucratization of counterinsurgency, the institutionalization of forced disappearance, the perfecting of their techniques; this is to say we can observe the processes of how the state administers violence."[4]

This chapter lays the foundation for understanding this institutionalization of torture as part of the state security apparatus, from the perspective of the victims. At times necessarily graphic, it details the different interrogation tactics officials employed, spanning from the physical to the psychological infliction of pain. I argue that officials resorted to these counterinsurgency interrogation tactics—and, when necessary, adapted and extended them—because they worked, in the cruelest way possible. They worked because at their core these tactics were uniquely domestic in nature, even though officers learned some of them while training abroad as part of the Cold War. They worked because torture destroyed and forever changed so-called subversives and, by extension, their social and familial networks. They worked because news of what happened inside the torture chamber and clandestine prisons leaked beyond the confines of these spaces and served as cautionary tales messaging obedience. The messages were sent, as the next chapter discusses, through media outlets showcasing weapon caches seized by authorities and through rumors on the streets and in neighborhoods about suspicious activities of rebellious teenagers. The messages also reinforced the dangerous work that select military and police officers carried out in liminal spaces in the name of national security. Beginning the book with a reckoning of precisely what was done in the interrogation room establishes a clear and incontrovertible baseline of brutality that illustrates why torture persists today.

THE LOGIC OF PAIN

In *A Lexicon of Terror*, Marguerite Feitlowitz traces the effects of Argentina's dirty war on the population at large and pays special attention to how a new vocabulary emerged to describe the collective experience of living through this period. She argues that the "terrorist state created two worlds—one public and one clandestine, each with its own encoded discourse."[5] She includes a list—what she calls a lexicon—of words that took on new meanings as a result of the military junta's aim to remake Argentine society. *Submarino* no longer referred to the naval vessel or a hot chocolate drink; it now also stood for waterboarding.[6] *Quirófano* was used to name the torture chamber instead of the operating room.[7] Mexico also has its own lexicon of terror that emerged from its dirty war. Some of the words overlap with Argentina's and are commonly known forms of torture. *Picana*, for example, is the electrical prod used to touch or penetrate a prisoner's sensitive areas such as the genitals. *Paquete* describes both a package and the name given to detainees. *Trasladar* means the act of transferring a prisoner to be killed. Yet there are contributions to this lexicon that are unique to Mexico. The *tamalito* is the act of wrapping a person in cardboard and forcing a hose down their throat. Regardless of the variations, Feitlowitz's analysis of the lexicon of terror in Argentina carries over to Mexico. She shows how "language helps to ritualize torture; it lends a structure, provides a 'reason,' an 'explanation,' an 'objective' . . . where euphemisms created psychological distance between the doer and his act."[8]

The term "to disappear," *desaparecer*, slowly came into popular awareness in Mexico. As Álvaro Mario Cartagena López, also known as El Guaymas, said of the early 1970s, "We were laughing the first time we were taken to prison because we didn't know about disappearances." The families of the disappeared gradually realized that the authorities deliberately stonewalled their search for a reason: their son or daughter was nowhere to be found. That gradual awareness reflected how government forces adapted their use of disappearing victims. Vicente Ovalle shows how this practice occurred before the 1970s, but it was during this decade that it became used systematically against so-called subversives. He points to 1974–75 as a turning point when the odds of an individual being channeled into the prison system after interrogation dropped in favor of being disappeared.[9] Federal officials set up "specialized infrastructure" supported by trained personnel dedicated to the task of eliminating all traces of victims.[10] Families picked up on these changes in counterinsurgency techniques and began using the language of disappearance in their activism.

The uses and modalities surrounding torture developed and changed too. Mexican security forces drew on interrogation practices tried out in other conflicts throughout the world. Using the Algerian conflict to frame her study, Marnia Lazreg analyzes how liberal democracies, in this case, France and the United States, adopt torture as a tool against enemies of the state, including those labeled insurgents or terrorists.[11] Said another way, Lazreg traces the patterns of broad-scale use of modern torture methods to understand how torture has been a cornerstone of geopolitical power struggles since the mid-twentieth century. Despite appearing antithetical to their supposedly civilized political values, liberal democratic states turned to torture when their leaders felt their security or way of life was threatened.[12] These states created legal frameworks to allow for torture in terms of a crisis that supposedly threatened national security. The notion that exceptional times call for exceptional measures—that using torture was the only path to protect the nation—implied that there would be a return to an earlier, more democratic, pre-crisis moment when government officials would not need to resort to the practice. In Mexico, thus, torture was an exceptional tool deployed under extenuating circumstances to save all Mexicans, especially those who had fallen prey to the enemy and who the government labeled "subversives" intent on undermining national security. Moreover, officials used torture and imprisonment in their calculus to decide whether to dispose of Mexicans who, in the officials' judgment, were beyond saving by disappearing them.

Lazreg argues that colonial powers, such as France, Britain, and the United States, developed and refined modern forms of state-sponsored torture to resist decolonization and crush resistance, what she refers to as the "ideology of subjugation."[13] Though I agree with Lazreg, I prefer the notion of culture of fear to underscore the end goal of the Mexican government's security forces' use of torture to quell dissent. A culture of fear has permanence beyond an ideology and allows us to see the ways it spilled into other social sectors. While I explore the framework of dirty war in the introduction, the logic underlying counterinsurgent forms of torture suggests a manifold purpose to arrive at social subjugation. This logic is underscored by the awareness that physical torture may not generate actionable information on an insurgent group. Individuals will say anything to stop extreme forms of pain. If the information gathered might be unreliable, what purpose did torture serve? It could serve as a cautionary example to others. Simply put, to state actors, the ends justify the means because the government is dealing with an irredeemable enemy under exigent circumstances. In this context, the traditional rules cease to apply because the enemy is everywhere and poses a threat to the social fabric. Inflicting pain may rend the moral fabric of a civilized society, but it is ultimately for the larger social good. Because members of this society may find it repugnant to know that torture is carried out in their name and for their protection, paternalistic logic dictates that it must be carried out in a secret world of clandestine prisons by specially trained officers versed in its conventions. It follows that since torture in ostensibly democratic regimes takes place in a covert world, hidden from public view, only a few can have access to this secretive but necessary performance. These few individuals who could withstand the moral travails of using torture had special training in counterinsurgency techniques. Superiors with similar training and greater experience oversaw—and, when necessary, taught— the procedural aspects of torture.

All of these individuals employed in the security forces used torture with the certainty of its place in a broader bureaucratic arsenal for protecting national security. That bureaucratization protected perpetrators from feeling guilty about inflicting extreme pain or questioning the morality of side-stepping the rule of law. Lazreg argues that even the notion of torture as being a "necessary evil" draws on the ambiguous idea that the ends justify the means: "evil" is necessary to protect the greater good.[14] She proceeds to argue the hypocrisy of justifying torture with the language of morality because if torture "is moral, on what grounds is an act of terror that functions in the same manner considered amoral when committed by others?"[15] Hypocrisy here is inscribed in who gets to decide what is a moral act and which self-serving standards justify it. The larger goal of such heinous acts is to protect or defend the collective; it is not driven by an individual's needs. Security officials then stood above and outside traditional norms that would police their actions and, in their minds, belonged to a specialized group of individuals protecting the nation at all costs, including from the enemy within.

IN THE TORTURE CHAMBER

In Mexico, torture was a group activity with a veneer of legitimacy. Officers wore their uniforms to the torture session and respected the institutional hierarchy. One officer oversaw the process and gave orders to the other two or three officers. When necessary, the senior officer would order a subordinate to call in a nurse or doctor, on standby for such proceedings, to assist in a particular practice or to gauge the victim's ability to withstand further torture. The designated actors, the space it took place in, the routine it followed, the timing of different tactics, and the endpoint when the victim no longer served a purpose were all decided before the torture session began. Those orchestrating the session had few decisions to make because they were following protocol. Torture was intended to transform the individual into a submissive subject. If released back into the population, the submissive subject acted as a deterrent to other potential insurgents. This broken individual, now a shadow of their former self, ran up against notions of activists willing to go to any length for their cause. Romantic notions of being a guerrilla member and willingly opting to take on the deprivations of a clandestine life contrasted with the reality of being targeted as an insurgent by government forces intent on destroying this threat. Idealistic young men and women encountered torture for the first time and experienced the ways in which it remade an individual.

Like others detained in the mountains of Guerrero, Humberto Rivera Leyva's torture took place in the clandestine prison located in the basement of the town of Iguala's Municipal Palace. He could not recall who tortured him because he was always blindfolded during his sessions. "It was more than anything physical torture. They'd punch me in the stomach, throw me on the floor, and twist my hands until the bones cracked," he recalled. "I lost consciousness several times." They knew he belonged to the Partido de los Pobres, a guerrilla group affiliated with Lucio Cabañas, and they wanted the names of his contacts in Iguala, Chilpancingo, and in the nearby state of Morelos. He never gave them up. "The colonel who interrogated me kept slapping my cheeks and telling me to stop being so stupid." Humberto's story is like that of many who began traveling the circuit of state terror. Detention was the first step in a process that often culminated in an individual's imprisonment or disappearance.[16] Officials used the element of surprise to kidnap individuals, sometimes in broad daylight or a nighttime raid of their homes, and worked in groups of up to thirty to guarantee the detainee's successful capture.[17] From there, prisoners were transported, usually in an unmarked vehicle, to a detention center, where they endured physical and later psychological violence.

There are scant written records that document the precise steps interrogators followed when torturing an individual. Officers related much of what they did orally to other, less experienced officers. Much as Feitlowitz found in Argentina, officials in Mexico relied on the strategic and pervasive use of euphemism to describe torture across this period.[18] As Marnia Lazreg describes, torture was "an elusive practice semantically hiding behind various euphemisms that sought to protect its existence."[19] Institutionalizing torture as an accepted practice depended on a "vocabulary developed to code the meaning of terror-inducing methods" that altered language to create a "psychological distance between practitioners of terror and their practices."[20] This distancing further depended on the use of coded language to render ambiguous the meanings of the words used to identify the infliction of pain. The DFS documents adopt an ambiguous tone regarding how agents acquired information, saying that agents "applied pressure" or that guerrilla group members "provided" or "manifested" information after a preliminary interrogation.[21] A member of the FEMOSPP noted that Mexican officials preferred to "use phrases such as the 'detained were interrogated,' but you only have to look at photographs after these interrogations to know how this was carried out."[22]

What we know about torture comes primarily from testimony given to human rights organizations, such as the CNDH, as well as interviews with survivors. These testimonies tell us that there was a certain art to interrogating an individual and that torturers drew on a growing arsenal of counterinsurgency techniques.[23] Carlos Salcedo is one of these individuals who was willing to talk about what happened to him. He was one of about twenty militants belonging to an urban guerrilla group who were rounded up in October 1972. Police picked him up as he was walking on a Mexico City university campus at 8:00 a.m. He was carrying a gun, and on realizing that plainclothes police were following him, he drew his weapon. Afterward, he said he did not shoot because it was a new gun and he did not know how to release the safety. The young officer following him most closely threw himself on the ground to avoid being shot. Another officer shot Carlos in the leg, and he fell to the ground. Four officers then dragged him into a waiting vehicle. They kicked and punched him. One slammed the butt of his gun into the bridge of Carlos's nose, breaking it. Another officer, in a strange act of kindness, cleaned up some of the blood pouring down his face. "They didn't ask anything. Just threatened me and told me I was going to meet hell," Carlos said. Once he arrived at the clandestine prison, he explained, "they brought in other comrades, all completely naked, dripping water, in terrible conditions, holding them up because they couldn't stand on their own. They slapped them and at that moment I felt great tenderness for my comrades because they were torn to pieces."

Carlos's torture lasted ten days, with most days including three sessions. He shifts tenses from the past to the present, back to the past in his narration. This interplay of tenses gives the listener the illusion that he is still enduring torture in some version of the present. Carlos described his torture sessions as always being under the command of a senior officer, called the "vampire," who mostly gave orders and asked questions, with three, sometimes two, other officers present. "Strapped to a board, sitting down, completely tied up, blindfolded, and that's when the questions started. At the start, who are you, what did you do, in what did you participate." At the beginning, the questions were general; as the sessions progressed, they became more pointed. "That's when people fall." At the beginning, torture was a physical experience, according to Carlos, "to soften you, to take you down because, in hurting the body, you lower everything and especially a person's morale. They denigrate you with beatings, with torture, by making you feel pain and feel penetrated with terror." As the session advanced, "they [the torturers] become more refined, the questions are more concrete, and they start leading their investigation where they want to go." For Carlos, this was the point when he met the DFS's Miguel Nazar Haro, who started asking questions, not about the organization Carlos belonged to, but about the relationships among its members. "The torture now was different. They are more precise in the fibers that they touch because they get to know where you are tough and where you are weak. Maybe you can withstand beatings, but you can't take the *pozo* [lit. "well," referring to water immersion]. Maybe you can put up with some of the *pozo*, but you can't resist electrical currents." They started fine-tuning their treatment, and once they discerned a prisoner's weaknesses, they doubled that part of the treatment with almost surgical precision.

Nazar Haro, one of the best-known torturers, figures prominently in survivors' accounts. He had a long career inside Mexico's security establishment, primarily in the DFS, which he headed from 1979 to 1982. As part of his duties, he commanded tactical military units targeting guerrillas for elimination. These included the White Brigade in the 1970s, which decimated the Liga Comunista 23 de Septiembre, an umbrella guerrilla group that at the time was considered to pose the biggest threat to the government. As discussed in greater detail in chapter 3, Nazar Haro oversaw the torture sessions of many of the activists during this period. Eladio Torres, an LC23S member captured by the White Brigade in summer 1975, recalled that Nazar Haro and his agents showed him pictures of guerrilla members in an attempt to get him to identify them. They continued to use the language of photography in his torture session. They referred to the blows as "photographs," and their intensity corresponded to the size and purpose of a photograph: passport, certificate, children's photograph.

José Arturo Gallegos Nájera, a member of the Partido de los Pobres in Guerrero, experienced Nazar Haro's techniques firsthand.[24] Security forces arrested him and several others in Acapulco in November 1971, transported them to Campo Militar-1 (CM-1; Military Base Number 1) in Mexico City, and interrogated them multiple times over the course of eight days. It was winter, and Gallegos Nájera recalled the intense cold they felt, having come from Acapulco without proper clothing. The cells in CM-1 were laid out so that prisoners could see one another across the hallway but not those who were in the cells on either side.[25] Soon after arriving, Nazar Haro paid them their first visit. He handed out blank pages and told the prisoners to "write your whole story, don't leave anything out, and I'll come back later."[26] One of his comrades started with his date and place of birth and went on to outline his studies, including at the *normal* teacher-training school in Ayotzinapa, Guerrero, from which he and forty-six fellow students were expelled in 1966 for their political activism.[27] When Nazar Haro returned, he looked at what they had written. "Garbage, this is all garbage," he exclaimed, "the bravest one here is the one who sings," and ordered them sent to the torture chambers. Nazar Haro embodies the venerable, confident, and trained official intent on subjugating subversives threatening national security. On display for both victims and other officers present was his assuredness that he was doing the right thing.

Gallegos Nájera explained that the reality of being tortured was so much worse than anything he could put into words: "To know you're in the hands of the enemy, defenseless and without any chance of escape, makes one feel like the most vulnerable being in the universe."[28] The torture he was subjected to was psychological at first. But when the officers were dissatisfied with his answers, they proceeded with physical torture. When he described this part of his experience, Gallegos Nájera's writing changes to a dissociative tone: "first punches, electrical currents to the wet bodies, bare feet, placement of plastic bags on the head, tied up by the neck, which forces the victim to enter a state of desperation because the bag is inhaled into the mouth and nose when the person breathes in."[29] Gallegos Nájera's dissociative tone parallels Carlos's shifting verb tenses when describing the torture. Below, I describe what was done to these men and many other individuals by government officials.

From the perspective of the victim, it was difficult to determine the length of a torture session. Carlos described losing his sense of time. José Luis Moreno Borbolla recalled that the guard had a radio at full volume tuned to a program called "La Hora" (The Hour), which announces the time each minute with a distinct chime between advertisements. "As time goes on, you get all mixed up and all you hear is that damn chime. It's a way to break you." Creating confusion through such tactics as manipulating or heightening time further weakened an individual's ability to hold onto their sense of self during detention.

A single torture session would often include different psychological and physical techniques, used to inflict pain with surgical precision. José Luis's weakness was hanging, what prisoners referred to as the *pollo rostizado* (rotisserie chicken). "They hung me from my arms and one of the soldiers took down my right arm and leaves me hanging from my left hand and he left me like that for days." He suffered long-term injuries from prolonged hanging. The pozo was a common waterboarding technique. Alberto Ulloa Bornemann described how "several agents submerged my head backwards in the cold and dirty water of the basin."[30] Some prisoners did not survive the pozo. Ulloa Bornemann recalled that "they brought a young, educated man—as his speech revealed—from somewhere else to the basement [of CM-1]. I never saw him, but I know that they submerged his head several times in a steel drum full of water until they drowned him."[31] One of Elena Poniatowska's informants recalled that the picana "was inserted in men's anuses, women's anuses and vaginas. It's also applied to testicles, nipples, lips, gums, in all soft parts."[32] Often the picana would follow or be used in combination with the pozo. Using water augmented the effects of electricity on the body. The prisoner would be blindfolded with hands or feet restrained, sometimes naked, soaking wet, or standing in a pail of water. Ulloa Bornemann described how torturers used this technique on a young boy: "They dunked him several times for increasingly long periods. When he began to lose consciousness, they revived him by shocking his wet body with an electrical wire with the insulation peeled off at the end."[33]

Doctors were often around to ensure a prisoner could withstand continued torture, to aid the torturers in pushing the body to its limits without resulting in death, not to ensure their health or safety.[34] After Carlos was picked up, a doctor was brought in to assess the gunshot wound on his leg and gave him what he imagined was an antibiotic. Carlos received no additional care for the wound. Prisoners spent so much time blindfolded that many who were detained have a scar on the bridge of the nose, where the tight blindfold rested. As Jesús Morales, a former political prisoner, recounted in his interview with Sergio Aguayo, "They never took it off and you're screwed because they get you wet, they shove your head in toilets and then it dries, it gets sore, infected."[35] José Luis's blindfold only came off when his eyes became severely infected from being closed for so long. Domingo Estrada Ramírez remembered that the only time they removed the bandage from his eyes was so that he could sign a confession, which he was not able to see.[36] The blindfold also features in Saul López de la Torre's account of his torture: "They would bandage my eyes so tightly that I could feel the blindfold encrusted in my skin."[37]

Near the end of his ten-day detention and while still blindfolded, Carlos was dragged onto a helicopter. The torturers had been asking him if he knew anything about a plane, to which he truthfully replied he did not. The topic of the plane came up over and over again, until they put him aboard a helicopter. Carlos could not think there was a connection between the plane they asked about and the helicopter he was on. The helicopter went up in the air, and they persisted in their questioning. After realizing his answer was not going to change, the torturers strung up his hands and hung him out the door. Carlos remembered feeling the wind on his body and the sensation of hanging, but because he was blindfolded, he could not see what was happening.

Detainees experienced different patterns of detention, imprisonment, and torture. After he was picked up, José Luis was relocated to several different prisons, clandestine and official. Instead of an intense ten-day session, he was tortured every third day for approximately four weeks. Another former prisoner recounted what happened to him after he was picked up in Ciudad Juárez, Chihuahua, and transferred to a clandestine prison in Mexico City in May 1978: "Mineral water through the nose, immersion of our head in a pail of water, electric shocks to private parts, blows in series of ten for each question that we answered that we didn't know, given methodically with a rubber bar or other objects to the shoulders, head, face, chest, back, legs, sitting down, rear end, knees, shins, feet, arms, elbows, hands, and toenails. Other days the torture was different. Some persuasion, psychological torture, like simulated killings, death threats to our families."[38] In all cases, the torture was brutal.

The testimony of Francisco Juventino Campaña López, a leader of the FRAP, captures the array of torture techniques commonly used in the counterinsurgent campaign.[39] He was detained on August 6, 1973, on the highway en route to Mazatlán, allegedly for transporting subversive literature in his car. He was then taken to Guadalajara's police headquarters. For two days, the officers interrogated him by having him kneel on a broomstick with his arms extended and bright lights shining on his face. Between sessions, they placed him in a cell with someone who turned out to be an undercover informant entrusted with plying him for information.[40]

On August 8, Francisco was transported to the DFS headquarters in Mexico City, where he first met Miguel Nazar Haro.[41] Nazar Haro began by commiserating with Francisco over his brutal treatment at the hands of the Guadalajara officers, declaring that it was unnecessary if one just answered the questions.[42] When it became clear that Francisco was not going to divulge information, Nazar Haro changed tactics and ordered that he be strapped to parallel bars to begin his torture. Agents deliberately applied electric shocks to the bruised areas of his body and submerged Francisco in water to the point of drowning. When it appeared he had passed out, they threw him in a corner, and Nazar Haro came over to stand on his body. Later, Nazar Haro told him, "This is a war that you have lost."[43]

Francisco's torture continued for approximately twelve days. Medical personnel briefly attended to him but with little effect. As noted above, doctors were not there to make torture bearable but to ensure that prisoners did not die while they were still useful. Francisco recalled the pain of the tight blindfold, which constantly pressed against his eyes and dug into the bridge of his nose. After begging for days, a guard finally loosened it enough for Francisco to catch glimpses of his surroundings.[44] He grew to know his torturers and noted that "they were not all the same." According to him, some of them enjoyed inflicting pain and frequently boasted of raping women prisoners. Others appeared to not want to be there. Some talked about being students at the UNAM and others about their stints at training bases in the United States and Panama.[45] On August 19, his torture ended. After receiving medical treatment, he was transferred to the Oblatos Penitentiary in Guadalajara.

What Francisco endured is echoed over and over in survivors' testimonies. Armando Rentería remembered that the torture session always began with a combination of beatings and psychological threats, followed by electrical shocks and submersion in dirty water. Rentería affirmed that the torturers "must have been trained to commit all sorts of irregularities."[46] Lourdes Quiñones said torturers reduced her husband, Rigoberto Lorenze López, "to *chocho*" after they were detained in November 1974. *Chocho*, slang in this context, means being reduced to something small and insignificant. "It's being naked in your cell and you're whittled away until you are the size of a *chocho* because they keep throwing buckets of cold water all night." Descriptions such as these of the end results of a torture session convey a particular kind of defeat: an annihilation of self.

Agents tied El Guaymas down and put his head between two boards. They put a hose in his mouth and shot water into it to simulate drowning.[47] "I knew they were going to destroy me with torture," he said.

In his testimony, El Guaymas returned several times to the fact that "nobody can withstand torture" and that he managed to trick his torturers with incorrect information. He stressed that he "felt [his] consciousness [was] strong" because he had not given real information that led to the capture of other guerrilla members.[48] This contrasts with Carlos's account, in which he noted that there was an understanding that everyone broke down under torture. Evidently, prisoners faced contradictory rules as the torture session began. On the one hand, they had to try to survive what was coming; on the other, they had to protect their comrades. In view of this contradiction, Carlos explained that survival was primordial: "All that psychological and physical aggression is documenting the total collapse of morality and consciousness. You have to remake yourself in every moment, assimilate, get a grip on your identity." Some of the prisoners gave up the names of innocent people under torture. Josafath Hernández Ríos remembered, "Because the pummeling they gave made any *machito* [little man] double over. Just to make them stop beating you, you give up anything. 'I know this guy who is doing such things with those over there.' All torture victims gave up the names of many innocent people." This assertion that everyone gave up names, including those of innocent people, illustrates how unreliable torture was for obtaining actionable intelligence.

Guerrilla members had unwritten rules to deal with disclosing information under torture. Carlos and José Luis noted that they had to wait at least twenty-four hours before breaking down and naming names to give their comrades enough time to avoid capture. José Luis remembers that the initial questions were about meetings and safe houses so that officers could round up more comrades before word got out and they fled. A month after his initial detention and well into a torture session, Ulloa Bornemann described the vehicle of two of his comrades, believing they would have gotten rid of it by that time. They had not, and soon after Ulloa Bornemann divulged their names and vehicle description, they were picked up and brought into CM-1. He talked of listening to one of them being tortured and the extreme guilt he felt at having been part of his capture.[49]

STORIES FROM THE MOUNTAINS OF GUERRERO

"I became politically active when I realized that my parents were exploited." Desidor Silva Valle grew up in Atoyac and recalled that his high school teacher would give him reading materials that he had picked up from the Cuban embassy, including magazines from the Soviet Union and Cuba. He was a member of the Communist youth group in Atoyac and helped run meetings to recruit others to the cause. He was picked up by the authorities on a number of occasions for pasting political posters on the walls at night but released when his teacher would come to get him out. After the 1967 massacre in Atoyac, he became even more politically active and started taking supplies up the mountains to Lucio Cabañas. He joined the Partido de los Pobres and spent time with Lucio in Ayotzinapa in 1970. From here, he was assigned to the guerrilla cell in the communities of Costa Rica and later Chilpancingo.

Desidor was detained in Guerrero and put in the trunk of a car and taken to two different clandestine prisons. "One of them was all for questions and the other was all about beatings, beatings, beatings, and 'You better get up because I'm going to kick you,' and you'd get up however you could. Then you get to that point where you think they lost, that they're going to kill you, that's when your blood boils. You don't ask for pity or 'Please forgive me.' When they say, 'We're going to kill you,' I'd say, 'Go ahead.'" This first place, he thought, was near a bus station because you could hear the buses pass by. He was held here for two days. "They recorded everything. Back then, they used a big tape recorder, and you could hear it going 'tas, tas, tas' as it recorded." They kept asking questions about everything. "They asked over ten hours of questions. Where did you study? Who are your parents? Elementary? High school? In the other place, they would hit me and 'Stand up' only to be hit again and then kicked."

He was held at the second clandestine prison for another day or two, where he was brutally tortured. Once they were done, they told Desidor that they were going to kill him. "They put me in a car at night and drove. They threw me in a ditch, and 'We're going to kill you.' One of them got close and loosened my hand ties. I waited for the gunshot, and after some time I untied myself. I walked and found a taxi to take me home." Once there, he went to see a doctor to treat his injuries. "My mother gave me a lot of vinegar to drink. You know what they say about vinegar and a mother's beliefs, they heal internal injuries." Desidor repeated how he got to the point where he wanted to die from the beatings. "All about the kicking, they'd stand you up, and again you'd fall down over and over again. I've never talked about this, never wanted to say it, but now I'm saying it to you because I'm soon going to a graveyard."

Like Desidor, Josafath Hernández Ríos and his father, Julio Hernandez Hinojosa, were taken to the military barracks in Atoyac, Guerrero, in May 1970. Only sixteen years old at the time, Josafath recalled, "They made me drink water, put me on a barrel, and then jump on me. I would spit up with the water mixed with blood." They would beat him and a comrade named Chabelo together. Then the officers would separate them and say that the other was talking. "Then they would say that they had killed him and that they would kill me too if I didn't start talking. Every time I remember that moment, it hurts. I relive it." Within a day of their capture, the officers had beaten Josafath's father to death. "They killed him behind my cell. I could hear him agonizing in pain as they took him away."

METHODOLOGIES OF TORTURE

At first, Adolfo Godoy remembered, they interrogated him and his brother repeatedly for several days at CM-1 in Mexico City. Later on, "when the officers realized they had gotten all they could, hardly ever." The rest of the prisoners around him, however, were interrogated more frequently. "Sometimes, when they had finished interrogating them, I could see the [officers] taking them away in gurneys, covered up, and more than likely dead."

Pablo Cabañas Barrientos's physical torture happened at the clandestine prison in the military camp in Novajoa, Sonora. It stopped after he was transported to CM-1. Pablo described how they would leave him in his cell alone or take him outside, with his hood on, telling him, "You are all finished, you have all died here." As Pablo described it, at CM-1 "it was psychological torture." "They would make me stand in a corner and I can sense that there are people there. I'm not tied, but I have a hood on. 'Stay standing there.' The radio is full volume. I can't remember what was on the radio."

After Pablo was transported to CM-1, Baltazar, a politically active teacher at the same school, started urging Pablo to tell interrogators that he was "the chief because they're going to kill us." Pablo refused and kept denying leadership in the group they were organizing in Sonora. "Baltazar was the one who sunk me by telling them I was chief." Pablo spent ten days at CM-1 before being transferred to a prison in Hermosillo, Sonora, along with several other political prisoners from the area.

Pablo's and Adolfo's experiences outline the methodologies of torture routinely employed by both police and military forces in Mexico at this time. We see the interplay of physical and psychological interrogation techniques from the perspective of the victim. Though with variations, sexual humiliation, the threat of or infliction of pain, and physical discomfort are common experiences discussed in virtually every interview. What is clear is that this array of techniques, especially when deployed in succession, worked at breaking down individuals and annihilating their sense of self. Interviewees also spoke of lack of sleep, prolonged standing or hanging, time confusion, cold, hunger, intense noise, blindfolding, and intense smells. These were just some of the psychological techniques that allowed officers to penetrate the victim's mind. They assaulted a person's five senses and weakened their ability to resist interrogation. Though the techniques' power to destroy an individual was evident, they did not leave physical scars, allowing officials to obfuscate what was done to them. In his analysis of counterinsurgency torture sessions in the Philippines during the 1970s, McCoy writes that these sessions have a similar plot.

> The interrogator begins with a few questions, meets resistance, and next applies coercion, psychological then physical, to elicit cooperation. Thespians all, the torturers assume the role of omnipotent inquisitor, using the theatricality of the torture chamber to heighten the victim's pain and disorientation. Within the script, there is ample room for improvisation. Each interrogator seems to extemporize around a guiding image that becomes embedded in the victim's recollection of the event.[50]

Similar plots and choreography were found in Mexico's torture sessions across the same period, suggesting that the guiding principles of counterinsurgency traveled around the world.

Prolonged stress positions, such as hanging by the arms or standing, accompanied by blindfolding appeared to be commonplace for many victims of torture. After being tortured at the horse barracks, "they took us to a house that was still under construction," Hugo David Iriarte Bonilla said. "The whole time we were blindfolded. Our eyes covered. You could talk and your hands tied behind your back. Not too tight because my hands didn't fall asleep. There were several rooms, but I didn't know if someone was next to me because we weren't allowed to talk." The inability to see what was happening fueled the victim's imagination and contributed to the psychological torture. José Arturo Gallegos Najera described another torture used at CM-1. Soldiers would tie the detainee by the feet and hands and, forcing them to lean forward, insert a metal bar under the victim's elbows. Soldiers would then raise the ends of the bar and in turn elevate the prisoner in the position of tension and swing the bar. "This action produced a wave of nausea, but even though you want to throw up you can't because you feel like you're drowning."[51] As he described his torture, David Iriarte Bonilla noted the intensity of being punched, followed by "threats that they were going to bring our mothers, sisters, brothers." He described being pummeled over and over.

> They'd use a very special technique where, for example, they'd beat you and then interrogate you, followed by another beating, and then they'd stick you in a corner. And that's where you'd stay. All the while you'd be blindfolded and tied up, so you didn't know where you were and you couldn't see anything. They wouldn't feed you other than to give you a little water. They didn't feed us for five days.

What is clear from these stories is the role of the victim's imagination in enhancing the effectiveness of torture. Feeding the imagination was efficient and required less effort than inflicting direct physical pain. It was less messy, left fewer physical scars, and gave the veneer of modernity because it drew so heavily from the new counterinsurgency techniques employed in Cold War theaters throughout the world. Below I unpack these techniques to show them as stand-alone practices that when taken together show what made torture distinct during this period. It was no longer merely inflicting physical pain; it now drew on sophisticated forms of terrorizing the subject.

WATER AS A SOURCE OF PAIN

Officers routinely used water to enhance torture. In the words of Gallegos Najera, "They immersed a person in an oil drum filled with 200 liters of water. The person would be standing in it and they would forcefully submerge him ... the victim would try to get out as they asphyxiated but it was impossible because their legs would get stuck against the sides of the barrel."[52] Torturers might dunk a prisoner—either just the head or the whole body—in a pail, trough, or well. Prisoners might be submerged in water or a mixture of water and human or animal excrement. Torturers might lay a prisoner on their back, either flat or tilted at an angle, their face bare or covered with a cloth, and dump water on them. Regardless of the precise method, the intent was to simulate drowning and stimulate a deep-seated, visceral fear of impending death. The interrogators, at times assisted by medical personnel, gradually learned to gauge how much waterboarding individual prisoners could take, perhaps sixty seconds, perhaps two minutes, before they passed out or their brain function became compromised. The prisoner would be revived or given just enough time to catch their breath before the interrogators resumed the torture. However long a prisoner could withstand waterboarding, it was highly effective at breaking down an individual with little effort on the officers' part.

El Guaymas described the especially brutal form of waterboarding called el tamalito.

> They wrap you up in cardboard and tie you up with a rope, one, two, three times. With my hands [at my sides], they stuck a piece of wood here, a piece of wood there, and I couldn't move. . . . They made me swallow this surgical hose. They'd hit my face while yelling at me, 'Open your mouth, son of a bitch. Open!' It was a doctor who put the hose in. I couldn't see because my eyes were covered. They started putting water through the hose. My stomach. Now I understand how pregnant women feel. . . . I lasted fifteen minutes that felt like an eternity. Feeling like you're drowning and having all that water was a desperate feeling despite the fact that I was a swimmer all my life.

Simulated drowning through waterboarding was highly effective. Nobody could withstand it for a prolonged period. Moreover, it required little effort on the part of officials and left no visible scars on the victim.

ELECTRICITY AS A SOURCE OF PAIN

According to El Guaymas, "You vibrate all over like a bull when they shove it into a truck. It's called a picana, and it's a machine that has like ten batteries that can turn it into 220 or 120 voltage, I'm not sure, but it's really high. I peed myself. I knew nothing about torture."

Electricity was also frequently employed along with water or on its own in torture sessions and, like waterboarding, required little effort on the part of officers. "The first time they tortured me," El Guaymas recalled, "they strip you naked, throw you all wet on a patio, and they start shocking you. That's when you say, 'Just kill me, I can't take it anymore.' They shock you all over your body." Torturers used electricity differently on men and women, often using the picana as a prod to penetrate women. As he remembered how his torturers used the picana on him—how they forcibly restrained him to reach his testicles—El Guaymas fell back into using the second person, creating narrative distance in his retelling. "The shocks are super *cabrones* [brutal] and everything vibrates." El Guaymas explained how everyone had different reactions to the shocks, some defecated, while others, like him, urinated. He paused and after a minute finished detailing the effects of electric shocks. "I didn't know what torture was. I think that if I had been told before, 'If they detain you, we are going to torture you and this and this and this is going to happen.'" He stopped here and took a break to get a cup of tea before resuming. "You know you'd think about it, of course. But you don't really know what torture is like and, even though you think 'to the death!', but you don't really think about what is death." In other words, there was no way to convey what torture inflicted on him and others, let alone make an informed choice about whether it was worth the risk.

WITNESSING AS A SOURCE OF PAIN

Water and electricity did not necessarily leave visible scars or require extensive effort on the part of the officers, and the same can be said about psychological forms of inflicting pain. These no-touch forms of torture involved guilt, as well as threats. As McCoy describes it, this is "self-inflicted pain . . . that causes the victims to feel responsible for their own suffering and feel subservient to their inquisitors."[53] While water and electricity played a fundamental role in the previous two sources of pain, the victim's imagination was center stage in this one.

Yolanda Isabel Casas Quiroz talks about the guilt she felt because her comrades were tortured so much worse than she was. "What did I do so that they didn't torture me as badly as they did others?" To her, it was like a type of rape because "the first thing I felt was guilt, then acceptance, then that I must have done something to deserve it, that's what this type of torture felt like. I don't know how I escaped so much of the pain, cruelty, and misery that my [women] comrades endured. They did a lot less than I had, and some barely had done anything at all."

Yolanda chalked up her relatively light experience in the torture chamber to the officers' believing her when she said she was not a guerrilla. Yet what becomes clear when talking with Yolanda is that she defined torture as pain, as rape, as physical violation, when in reality she was the victim of extreme psychological torture. The guilt she endured over not having been raped was one manifestation of it; another was the type of interrogation she was subjected to. "They don't let you sleep. They keep you tired, everything to make you weak. That's when they would tell me, 'Look you bitch, we have others like you. We're going to show you to them and if they recognize you, you're going to regret it.' I was so afraid." Then Yolanda described the real torture she endured. "The hardest thing for me was when they took me in front of Jesús [her partner]. He was destroyed. They had tortured him so much, and they had given him electrical shocks on his testicles, different parts of his body." The officers undressed Yolanda when she stood before Jesús and asked who she was. They were trying to get Jesús to incriminate Yolanda in guerrilla activities as well as ensure their complete humiliation in both her nakedness and what she had witnessed being done to Jesús.

Lourdes Quiñones tells a similar story of torture. The DFS detained her and her husband, Rigoberto, in November 1974 when a comrade from the Partido de los Pobres gave up their names. She recalls leaving her daughter in the care of her mother and being blindfolded in a car while the DFS agents screamed at her. Once in Mexico City, the officers entrusted with interrogating her did not inflict physical pain but instead used psychological torture. She chalked up the absence of pain to the political connections of her brother-in-law, who was a military doctor and close ally of top figures in the government. She explained, "They couldn't touch me, but these were disgusting, vile people who humiliated, killed, and raped people who had done nothing." As for the psychological torture she endured, she said that the two men told her that they had her "mother, my children, my husband, all detained." One of the men was an army colonel, and the other "look[ed] like my grandfather. Very nice looking with a face like that of a university professor, well dressed, well spoken, well behaved." As McCoy explains, "Psychological torture could transmit intolerable pain directly to the brain through means that eliminated any need for physical abuse."[54] Lourdes believed the officers did not touch her, but in a way they did. She knew what they were capable of and believed they would act on the threats against her family.

Manuel Molina Salazar likewise spoke of witnessing as a source of pain. He recalled that it was the killing of one of his comrades who got shot in the back as the two of them were walking down the street in Guadalajara that "catalyzed my becoming a guerrilla." He summed up his feelings by stating that "you have to kill the bastards who are trying to kill us." Each wing of the Frente Estudiantil Revolucionario (FER; Revolutionary Student Front) had its own cells with members living a clandestine life and in charge of their "expropriations." Manuel laughingly described his "damn inexperience" in holding up a bank. The first time the judicial police "caught me on February 3, 1972. All of my comrades, eleven of them, had already been caught. I was number twelve." The next time was in Sinaloa in 1973, when they took him to CM-1. "The torture was to the death. They'd kill you and then revive you. That's why there was always a doctor there. In case your heart stopped, they'd make you keep going. 'Who are your comrades?'"

Like others, Manuel repeated it was understood that everybody talked under torture. "If you hadn't shown to a meet-up, the others knew they had picked you up." As for the pain, he started by saying that "that [type of] torture was not easy. It's death and you go, you go, you go." Manuel's demeanor changed when describing what was done to him after the officers transported him to the CM-1. He proceeded to look down and quickly mumble, "Always tied, always blindfolded, and they stick a folded rag in your mouth so you don't scream so much, always tied from behind, and that's how it starts." This time in Mexico City was different from other times he had been tortured in Guadalajara. "They did something to me that nobody had ever done before and it was pretty fucked up [*bien cabrona*]. It doesn't leave a single trace. They tie you up to some wires, string you up by the hands, water, a fucking pail of water dumped over your head, and they connect it to the lights. You're sitting on a metal chair. Imagine that." Manuel cringed as he remembered what was done to some of his women comrades. "They'd tie them up with their legs up in the air. Pour boiling oil inside their vaginas." For the men, he said that "they would dump your marbles," referring to his testicles. "They make us kneel on the chair, sitting on our heels, needles beneath the nails, with electrical current running into our teeth, in the ears, until you die. They did this until we died."

Antonio Orozco Michel was a member of a guerrilla group in Guadalajara when its leadership decided to become a part of LC23S in 1973. He recalled the amount of reading the leaders of LC23S sent them to catch up on to ensure they understood the new organization's political program: "old copies of the *Madera* newspaper [organ of LC23S], documents detailing Mexico's history since the revolution, and those discussing how to start the struggle for socialism and the overthrow of the bourgeois government." Less than a year later, in 1974, the judicial police detained Antonio. "It was a violent experience. We couldn't take on the police because they surrounded us and we were overcome. It was useless to resist. We didn't want to die there. We were so young and just learning how to be guerrillas. They blindfolded us and transported us to a safe house. The blindfold stayed on, but they took our clothes off. That's where they started hitting us. The electrical charges." Antonio was brutally tortured for approximately an hour while they grilled him on the details of the organization. "The problem was that we were left hanging by the Liga, completely isolated since the fall of Enrique Pérez [another comrade] in January. We did not have any connections to the Liga."

Antonio never actually saw his torturers. "There were at least ten of them. Two or three of them were the ones who hit us. There was a lot of noise from all the people where we were. It was like separate little rooms and we could hear each other screaming, the questions, the answers."

Antonio explained that they used the electric prod when asking questions, starting with the phrase, "We're going to kill you if you don't collaborate." At first the questions were basic: name, address, mother, father. Later they asked, "What actions have you participated in? holdups? car thefts?," and so on. He described how a torturer who was wielding a gun during an interrogation accidentally shot a round into a prisoner's head. Antonio could hear the guard yelling, "I shot the son of a bitch in the head!"

GENDER

In Mexico across the 1970s, the group activity aspect of torture magnified the gender dynamics of the session. Men performed hypermasculine acts, including rapes and beatings, before an audience of their peers, who responded with appreciation and validation of their prowess. The victims, irrespective of their sex, assumed a passive posture in relation to their torturers. In their impotence, the victims' gender was highlighted as torture sessions were tailored to sexualize their weaknesses. Forced nudity and tools applied to genitals magnified pain depending on the victim's gender. Outright gang rape—as reported by victims—was used more frequently against women than men. A victim's gender identity also became malleable in these settings. Torturers feminized male prisoners and enabled their rape either by another man or an object before a group of their peers. In these performances, rape was a punishment meted out to a lesser man through his emasculation in front of his same-gendered peers. Existing gender conventions of chivalry ceased to exist when men brutalized alleged insurgent women using the rationale that they were not women after all. Men were feminized through torture, while women were masculinized.

Women figured on the lists of those detained, tortured, and disappeared across the 1970s.[55] We do not yet have a precise accounting of how many suffered this fate, but they were there. A DFS list of political prisoners from August 1978 includes the names of 117 individuals, organized according to their guerrilla group and including the location of their detention.[56] The list contained the names of 27 women belonging to fifteen guerrilla groups. Adela Cedillo confirmed that 43 women were disappeared, at least 20 assassinated, 89 incarcerated, and 7 exiled.[57] According to Carlos, the guerrilla group he belonged to had between 5 and 10 percent female members. Some of the first members of his group to be captured were women. José Luis also noted that three of the sixteen people he was originally imprisoned with were women. In her study on women guerrilla members in the 1970s, María de Jesús Méndez Alvarado uses numerous interviews to explore the specific forms of torture women endured.[58] She details the physical and psychological forms of torture discussed in the previous pages but tracks the experience to their imprisonment and eventual release. A heavily gendered form of degradation appears key to their torture, meaning that their bodies, even when pregnant, their minds, and their roles as mothers and wives were fair game for destruction. The more overt presence of women in the ranks of guerrilla members meant they now featured as torture victims in unprecedented ways.

The DFS detained Elia Hernández Hernández and her husband at a safe house in Mexico City on February 28, 1971. Around 2:00 p.m., the agents let themselves into the house with a key and took a knife out of Elia's hand. They started telling her things about herself; she recalled thinking that "they knew a lot." They put her and her husband in a car and drove around the city for hours, periodically stopping to beat them or pretend to shoot them. She recalled there was beer in the car, and she thought the agents were drunk. They took her and her husband to a detention center near the Monument of the Revolution and kept them there for two or three days, where they were fingerprinted. They were then relocated, handcuffed and blindfolded, to Campo Militar-1. That was when the torture began. Elia recalled being taken blindfolded to an interrogation room. Nazar Haro led the interrogation, and she could hear someone typing what was being said. She explained that there was not really a routine at CM-1 other than to wait for nightfall and for the interrogation to begin. "They would hit me in the stomach, below the stomach. They would threaten to kill me. They would put the gun at me and then not pull the trigger. With hanging too. They would put on a rope, threaten to pull, and then not do it." They would also threaten to kill and rape her family. Elia recalled there were bad cops and good cops. Carlos Quinto gave her a chocolate and said, "But you're so young. Look at you messing around with these things."

Torture was a different experience for women than for men because sexual forms of violence, including keeping them in a constant state of nudity and penetrating their genitals, was a common feature in their sessions.[59] A former woman guerrilla member explained, "Besides the beatings and waterboarding and all else, one had to endure very severe sexual aggression which leaves indelible marks . . . I still wake up screaming."[60] Another woman recalled, "They took me in front of my husband, who was also naked, and they were applying electrical shocks to his testicles. They threw me on the ground in front of him and hit me, then hung me by my nipples. Later they introduced a metal prod into my vagina and started applying electrical shocks to my vulva and nipples."[61] As Lazreg explains, sexual assault, particularly rape, afforded torturers an efficient and reliable way of breaking down victims by systematically inflicting pain and humiliation while de-sexing them.[62] In other words, sex-oriented torture techniques were a routine part of the interrogators' arsenal—one that gave the interrogator a clear sense of domination over the victim. In addition to the way sexual forms of torture positioned the torturer, it destroyed the victim—both physically and emotionally—in a unique way.

As with other victims of sexual violence, these men and women experienced long-term heightened forms of anxiety and fear tinged with self-blame, shame, and fear of intimacy. For these reasons, the marriage of psychological and physical pain took on a deeper meaning when officers engaged in intimate forms of torture. Nowhere is this more apparent than in the practice of castration. More than one interviewee had a testicle removed without anesthesia. This happened to Carlos Salcedo and José Arturo Gallegos Nájera.[63] Gallegos Nájera was strapped naked to a table as the torturer held his testicles firmly in his hands. "If you don't talk, I'm going to get rid of your balls to make you less macho [machín]."[64] The torturer wrapped a piece of string around one of his testicles and started pulling up. Gallegos Nájera arched his back as far as he could, trying to alleviate the pressure on his testicle before passing out from the pain. Julio Hernandez Hinojosa, who died under brutal circumstances, was also castrated at the military base in Atoyac, Guerrero, in 1970. His remains were so badly beaten that it was unclear whether the castration took place before or after his death. Castration, as part of the arsenal of torture techniques employed against dissidents, is perhaps the most visceral way in which agents remade these young men. After all, state agents stripped them of their masculinity and punished their insubordination by making a farce of the leftist pretension to become a "new man" akin to Ché Guevara's interpretation of a social-ist society. Castration thus violated the romantic archetype of the *barbudo*—the bearded guerrilla leader wearing fatigues and hiding out in the jungle. Castration, moreover, was a direct punishment for the alternative masculin-ity that was so prevalent in leftist ideology at this time.

Once a subversive was detained, their body belonged to the officers to do with what they would. This extended to their death. After José Luis Alonso Vargas and others robbed a bank, the police eventually captured one of his comrades, Ramiro. They tortured him for three days, and then they killed him. They hung his body on a fence and claimed he had com-mitted suicide by hanging. The photograph the authorities released to the press, José Luis Alonso recalled, showed Ramiro's feet touching the ground, which suggested that the hanging had been staged. José Luis Esparza explained why staging deaths was so important for the govern-ment authorities: promoting the idea that a guerrilla died in a confronta-tion with the police implied that there was no legal recourse and that the guerrilla was ultimately at fault for their own death. Setting up the murder scene gave the authorities authorship of the narrative of the death, which served the broader purpose of making the police appear to be defending themselves. By extension, they were defending the Mexican people from a dangerous enemy that only responded to violence in kind. It bears return-ing to Ramiro's feet touching the ground in the photograph released to the press of his apparent hanging. Why were authorities so careless in their staging of the "suicide," neglecting to even hang the body high enough to support their narrative? It was a mistake, but after all, there would be no repercussions. In the throes of a dirty war where national security was under threat, members of the press, let alone the public, would not quibble over inconsistencies in the government's version of the truth.

THE PLACE OF THE UNITED STATES IN MEXICO'S TORTURE PROGRAM

Some of the techniques employed in torture sessions in Mexico shared characteristics of those used by US-backed forces elsewhere in the region at a similar moment. How much was the United States involved in Mexico's

battles against its own insurgents? While the US government had a profound impact in Mexico's diplomatic, cultural, and economic arenas, it
played a more limited role in Mexico's counterinsurgency operations and
what transpired in its clandestine detention centers.[65] The CIA had officers on the ground in Mexico, including at the US embassy in Mexico City,
who gathered information from a vast array of informants. These agents
monitored and reported back to Washington, DC, on what was happening
in Mexico, as well as elsewhere in the region. We need only review the
many now-declassified reports filed by CIA analysts to understand that the
US government kept a watchful eye on what was happening in Mexico.[66]
The CIA, however, had significantly less of a presence outside the confines
of the embassy because there was an understanding that the Mexican government was sufficiently efficient in its use of repression to, for the most
part, effectively deal with its guerrilla and dissident issues. This is borne
out in the evidence for this book: the American adviser present in Alejando
Arroyo Cabañas's torture session, mentioned at the beginning of this chapter, is the only reference to an on-the-ground US officer in the accounts of
interviewees. In other words, the Mexican government accommodated the
needs of the US government in many areas that did not necessarily include
hands-on and significant participation from their American counterparts
in clandestine counterinsurgency operations. Indeed, it is presumptive to
assume that the Mexicans were not adequately prepared to handle opposition without direct oversight of its neighbor to the north.

The low level of direct US involvement in covert operations in Mexico,
in contrast to other countries in the region, owed to a long-held understanding of mutual respect between the two nations. This understanding
had roots in the Good Neighbor policy of previous decades and the fact
that the Mexican government had pushed back against the US government's hegemony, compelling its northern neighbor to limit its interven-
tions in Mexico in order to preserve their strategic partnership.[67] Had the
US government taken a more assertive stance on Mexico's counterinsurgency efforts, actively intervening to support or curb those efforts, it would
have risked destabilizing its partnership with Mexico.[68]

Certainly, the US government had an active role in training Mexican
police and military officials in counterinsurgency operations. A select
group of Mexican law enforcement officers, including one of the key

architects of Mexico's torture program, Miguel Nazar Haro, took part in training at the Office for Public Safety in Washington, DC. This training also extended to paramilitary groups. The historian Renata Keller has documented the details surrounding the US-sponsored training program for Mexican security officials led by Colonel Manuel Díaz Escobar in early 1971. The purpose of the training was "police work and crowd control."[69] Several months after the brutal massacre of students on Corpus Christi, the US embassy complained to the Mexican government that Díaz Escobar, along with three other officers who had taken part in the training, were leaders of the Halcones paramilitary group that carried out the massacre. US officials complained because the Mexican government had offered assurances beforehand that there would be no such participation by individuals trained in the program. Foreign Secretary Emilio Rabasa assured the US ambassador that they would conceal the US connection.[70]

A review of available sources shows a light footprint of interrogation techniques coming from abroad into Mexico. These would have been disseminated in Spanish-language interrogation manuals the CIA shared with many Latin American governments at the time.[71] To date, scholars have not located any of these manuals in Mexico. The techniques would have also been taught in training sessions at the School of the Americas (SOA) at the US military's base in Panama and later at Fort Benning, Georgia, where several Mexican military officers received training.[72] Importantly, however, the number of Mexican military students at SOA during the 1970s was relatively low in comparison to other countries in the region. Venezuela, Colombia, Argentina, El Salvador, Honduras, and Guatemala, to name a few, sent considerably more students to train at SOA. It was not until the 1980s, with the twin threats of Central America's instability and the emergence of drug cartels, that US officials increased the participation of the Mexican military in its counterinsurgency and counternarcotics training program.[73]

CONCLUSION

In 1963, the CIA started distributing the *Kubark Counterintelligence Interrogation* handbook to sympathetic governments. McCoy documents that several hundred of these handbooks made their way into Latin America over the coming decades.[74] A key point made in the handbook is that "effective questioning, both coercive and non-coercive, involves 'methods of inducing regression of the personality to whatever earlier and weaker level is required for the dissolution of resistance and the inculcation of dependence.'"[75] The handbook goes on to make the case that the "threat to inflict pain . . . can trigger fears more damaging than the immediate sensation of pain."[76] In other words, mental pain was more effective than physical pain at rendering the victim pliable, vulnerable, and willing to collaborate with officers. The manipulation of time, the inclusion of water, electricity, and stress poses, sexual violence, and threats are detailed in the *Kubark Counterintelligence Interrogation* handbook.

While we have yet to find copies of this handbook in Mexico, we know that it—as well as revised versions of it—were taught throughout the 1960s at the Office for Public Safety courses in Washington, DC. Nazar Haro attended these courses and used them to design what would become the Mexican government's own torture program. We thus see how the Mexican military and police developed their own tool kit of torture techniques without outsized assistance from foreign actors. They did draw on some of the psychological innovations developed from the Cold War's experimentation with cognitive science. From victim testimony, as is amply discussed in this chapter, we know that Mexican officials used self-inflicted pain from prolonged stress positions and the manipulation of the prisoners' environment, targeting their senses with sound, light, temperature, and altering their perceptions of time. Yet victims also tell how officers used techniques unique to Mexico. These included the overt sexualization of torture, such as rape, against both men and women, as well as torturing—not just threatening to torture—family members, explored in greater detail in later chapters. Mexican officials thus adapted techniques learned elsewhere, but theirs was still a profoundly domestic program.

2 The Making of the Subversive

The year 1968 saw dramatic political mobilizations in France, the United States, Czechoslovakia, and many other countries around the world. Protesters spoke out against a variety of issues, such as the war in Vietnam, the political status quo, and economic inequality. With a legacy of political protests against the ruling PRI in the preceding years, Mexico entered 1968 with many of its citizens feeling an increasing sense of dissatisfaction with the authoritarian regime that had been in place for almost forty years. From rail workers calling for improved working conditions to peasants demanding greater access to market opportunities and students protesting in support of the new Cuban regime, dissident political actors pushed the boundaries of a system of control imposed by a monolithic state apparatus.

Political violence was an integral part of maintaining that apparatus—with the PRI at its pinnacle—and advancing the country's economic modernization. Nevertheless, cracks emerged in the governing regime's ability to control dissent beginning in the late 1940s, coming to a crisis point by the 1970s. By the middle of 1968, a student movement based in two of the largest universities in Mexico City, the Universidad Nacional Autónoma de México and the Instituto Politécnico Nacional, rose up in spontaneous protest, demanding greater democratization, political dialogue with the governing regime, and a stop to political repression. The student movement's demands resonated with many citizens, and its ranks quickly expanded to include Mexicans from all walks of life— housewives, teachers, professionals. From June through October, massive protest marches involving hundreds of thousands of people and led by the student movement made the voices of dissident citizens heard in the governing palace of the capital city. As the marches grew in size, official responses to the movement became more violent, leading to brutal confrontations with the police and the arrest of the movement's leaders.

As the student movement took shape, Mexico City prepared to host the 1968 Summer Olympics, scheduled for October 12 to 27. It was the first time an underdeveloped nation had hosted the Games, and for political elites it was a testament to the success of Mexico's version of authoritarian modernization. To counteract perceptions of an underdeveloped country prone to civil unrest, as Mexico had been depicted in many Hollywood movies, the government was anxious to present to the world an image of a modernized nation with a stable democracy and content populace.[1] As officials prepared for this momentous event, the mostly peaceful protest movement gathered force across the summer months. By September, however, the crowds had started falling away, and the movement showed signs of waning. But, unable to ignore the threats to its authority and concerned with the need to produce order in the capital city before the opening ceremony of the Olympic Games, President Gustavo Díaz Ordáz's government chose a brutal and swift solution. On October 2, army troops and police started shooting indiscriminately at hundreds of unarmed civilians peacefully assembled for a rally in the Plaza de las Tres Culturas located in the Tlatelolco housing unit in Mexico City. Chaos ensued, and when the shooting stopped, the toll from the Tlatelolco massacre left several hundred Mexicans dead, many more injured, and even more illegally detained and tortured. In the aftermath of the massacre, the student movement was effectively crippled, and a government-led campaign of censorship and cover-ups silenced word of the massacre in time for the opening day of the Olympics. Ten days later, the Olympics were inaugurated to much fanfare and no mention of the massacre that had taken place a little over a week before.[2]

The trauma and pain unleashed by the government's violent response—and ensuing cover-up—left an indelible stain on the country's historical memory in the long run. In the short term, the massacre fueled a change in tactics among the survivors, many of whom came to believe that only direct action would achieve large-scale social change. The trauma of that day thus marked a turning point in the lives of many Mexicans who had participated in the mobilizations. Some retreated out of fear, exhaustion, and disillusionment. The cost was too high and the rewards too low to justify continuing down the path of fighting for social change. Others went on to take up arms against a government that refused to negotiate with peaceful protesters. For them, there was no other option against a political order willing to resort to such repression.

The massacre also marked a turning point for government leaders coming to terms with the "utility" of employing extreme forms of violence in the name of national security. Officials, especially those in the military and specialized police forces like the DFS, understood that leaning into paranoia worked to justify their use of state terror. They had mobilized approximately three thousand officers to Tlatelolco and, after the dust settled, had only located a handful of guns and ammunition.[3] Nevertheless, they saw the need to professionalize and modernize—along the lines of the counterinsurgency—how they would employ political violence moving forward. Just as activists learned they had to change course after the 1968 massacre at Tlatelolco, the government did as well. Indiscriminate and highly visible displays of repression could generate too much pushback and take extensive resources to manage damage control. They thus saw the appeal of clandestine counterinsurgency tactics, many of which were being touted by military governments elsewhere in Latin America and in Cold War proxy conflicts throughout the world. These tactics included how to make the category "subversive" salient to the public at large and more effective interrogation strategies in service of social control. Building on the previous chapter's analysis of the torture methodologies used in Mexico during the long 1970s, this chapter unpacks what made these individuals subjects of torture by studying how they were labeled "subversive." Though inflected with international significance, the making of this label was a uniquely Mexican process that involved both victims and victimizers.[4]

If the primary purpose of torture was to annihilate the victim and empower the government's security forces, we need to understand how the government cast these victims as enemies of the state. How was the government able to strip these individuals of their humanity to the point where it was fair game for military and police agents to destroy them and, in many cases, their families? The tension between the senselessness of this violence and the cold, calculating cruelty of state agents who carried it out leads us to a painful crux of this chapter: this ruthless violence worked in part because of the effective othering of Mexican citizens. As this chapter shows, this alleged enemy could take many shapes and be present anywhere. The government capitalized on this omnipresence to adopt extralegal tactics that Mexicans should or could not question for risk of being labeled unpatriotic. The making of the subversive is a cornerstone of the siege mentality supporting the government's counterinsurgency tactics across the 1970s.

To build this category of a common enemy, officials blended it with other transgressive social identities, such as counterculture hippies or criminal drug producers, and popularized euphemisms that signaled fear of an unknown enemy that could be lurking anywhere. The category reflected gendered, class, and generational norms to make it identifiable and legitimate in the eyes of the Mexican public and security forces. Young people and the rural poor were now suspect solely because of the threat they *potentially* represented. Last, government officials embedded the category of subversive into a legal framework that gave it the veneer of legitimacy and assigned culpability to the victim without due process. According to this logic, the victim was at fault for having forced the government to resort to extreme measures in this time of crisis.[5]

Certainly, there were some who resisted and publicly condemned state repression—at great personal cost. Independent journalists, human rights activists, and members of progressive Catholic groups joined in the chorus of voices denouncing abuses. Despite their courage, their efforts proved limited in garnering domestic or international attention to their causes or staving off the violence. The chapter concludes by probing what was a possible end game for the use of the subversive label. In referencing a "cure," the final section explores the cases of individuals who went on to become collaborators with the security forces to showcase the complexity behind such an identity.

THE INTERNAL ENEMY

Before moving on to explore the making of the subversive, let us briefly recap the profile of guerrilla movements, considering how they varied in response to the government's increasing use of terror to quell any opposition, including the 1967 massacre in Atoyac, Guerrero, and the 1968 massacre in Tlatelolco, Mexico City.[6] Guerrilla members debated how liberation theology—a Catholic ideology spurring activism among its adherents[7]—and variants of Marxism and Maoism provided road maps to armed revolutionary change. They looked to parallel movements in Cuba, Colombia, Guatemala, Vietnam, and North Korea, to name a few countries, for inspiration and tactics they could employ to stave off government repression. Militants traveled to Moscow to study at the Patrice Lumumba People's Friendship University or spent time in training camps in North Korea learning guerrilla warfare. At their height, there were just shy of two thousand guerrilla members in Mexico divided across at least thirty groups.[8] The FEMOSPP investigators concluded that number was closer to forty organizations.[9] While sizable, the number of active guerrillas was not as large, or as threatening, as the government would have the Mexican public imagine across the 1970s. Regardless of size, these movements were focused on domestic issues and argued for radical change that conformed to the realities of Mexico.

These movements existed in both urban and rural locales.[10] Rural movements in the states of Guerrero, Oaxaca, and Chihuahua, for example, drew on a pipeline of activists graduating from the government-funded *escuelas normales*, teacher-training colleges established during the presidency of Lázaro Cárdenas. They fought for redress of political marginalization, unmet promises of agrarian reform, and endemic poverty.[11] Genaro Vázquez and Lucio Cabañas emerged as teachers from these schools in the highlands of Guerrero. Both men went on to spearhead militant guerrilla groups—respectively, Asociación Cívica Revolucionaria (Civic-Revolutionary Association) and Partido de los Pobres—and both were killed: Genaro in 1972 and Lucio in 1974.[12]

While the state of Guerrero, as scholars have made amply clear, stands out for the military's extreme forms of political violence unleashed in retaliation for activism, it was not alone.[13] In the case of Chihuahua,

Padilla has studied what she refers to as the "layered dimensions of nor-malistas rurales' identity—one that blurred the lines between campesinos, students, and professionals," which explains the unique and lasting brand of radical activism that emerged from these schools and influenced guer-rilla movements there.[14] In his study on forced disappearances across the 1970s, Vicente Ovalle compares and contrasts guerrilla activity and the government's response in Oaxaca, Sinaloa, and Guerrero. He shows that guerrilla groups, such as the Unión del Pueblo (UP; Union of the People), which was founded in the 1960s by agronomy students and faculty in Chapingo outside of Mexico City, straddled the urban-rural divide in their activism.[15]

Urban movements, such as those in Mexico City, Monterrey, and Guadalajara, fed off long-standing forms of *barrio* (neighborhood), worker, and student activism. Inspired by increasingly militant forms of Marxism calling for armed struggle, these groups fought for more equita-ble socioeconomic conditions for all Mexicans and greater access to politi-cal voice. The 1968 massacre was a watershed moment for guerrilla mem-bers recognizing a narrowing of channels for achieving change, but it was just one of several moments that pushed activists to take up direct action.[16] Outside of Mexico City, working-class activists established alliances with students. As Fernando Calderón has shown, "students from the University of Guadalajara were instrumental in redefining student militancy after the 1968 student movement."[17] It was in this city that radicalized univer-sity student organizations, with a history of battling more conservative student organizations and the university administration, organized guer-rilla groups after the 1968 massacre in Mexico City. They established the Federación Estudiantil Revolucionario (FER; Revolutionary Student Federation), which had strong ties to the working-class neighborhood of San Andrés. Several members also formed more radical guerrilla groups, such as Los Vikingos (the Vikings), Los Lacandones, Los Enfermos (the Sick Ones), and the Movimiento de Acción Revolucionaria (MAR; Movement for Revolutionary Action).[18] Guadalajara was also the birth-place of the Liga Comunista 23 de Septiembre, in March 1973. As the next chapter details, LC23S brought together several disparate, primarily urban guerrilla groups under one umbrella. From Guadalajara, LC23S extended to Mexico City, Oaxaca, Guerrero, Sinaloa, Chihuahua, and other places to establish a national presence. In addition, Guadalajara was the scene of the May 1973 kidnapping of the US consul general by the FRAP. In response, President Echeverría Álvarez negotiated the release of thirty political prisoners as a concession. His approach changed radically when the same group kidnapped his father-in-law in 1974. Instead of negotiating, the president sent in the military to arrest approximately seven hundred people to signal that the guerrilla group had gone too far.

The above realities shaped how government officials categorized the internal enemy in the equation of counterinsurgency. While there were some women, the individuals at the heart of this analysis are predominantly young men and, as such, the chapter incorporates a gendered and generational perspective on what drove them to their activism, why the government targeted them, and how they experienced torture. For government officials, especially those in the security establishment, the guerrillas and the countercultural *jipis* (hippies) were on the same continuum of social degenerates. People who engaged in alternative and countercultural lifestyles not only challenged authority, traditional notions of masculinity, and sexual and religious norms but also, according to political elites, posed a threat to the established social and political order. Their challenge to societal norms and values rendered these young men dangerous—even subversive—and made them potential subjects of repression.[19] The fact that guerrillas and so-called jipis inhabited many of the same social circles on university campuses and often expressed a similar ethos of rebellion made it difficult for authorities to discern differences between counterculture youths and insurgent ones. For already anxious government officials, the threat posed by this ambiguous insurgency only worsened as transnational youth and guerrilla mobilizations gained traction throughout the region.[20] Said another way, jipis' countercultural activities remained in the realm of challenging social norms, not the structures of government. But the state had difficulty distinguishing the differences—and did not care to.

In the aftermath of the 1968 massacre at Tlatelolco, the government targeted young Mexicans and made them subjects of unfettered torture when the line between jipi and insurgent blurred—a blurring that both government officials and guerrilla members engaged in. Louise Walker alludes to the conflation of these identities when she discusses fissures among urban middle-class youth: those who believed the government's commitment to reform, those who belonged to the counterculture, and those who were invested in radical options for bringing about large-scale social change.[21] Nevertheless, as Walker notes, "the lines dividing moderates, hippies, and radicals were not rigidly drawn: most of them came from the same middle-class world, and individuals often engaged in different kinds of protest."[22] In practice, this meant that Molotov cocktails and marijuana "were often found side by side at house parties in the 1960s and 1970s."[23] Roger Bartra echoes this in his recollections of gatherings at his house during the 1970s where "those in search of artificial paradises" joined "those seeking to overthrow oppressive systems."[24]

Individuals used the blurring of the line between all these identities to their advantage, regardless of whether they belonged to a guerrilla movement, hunted down insurgents, or wanted to challenge social conventions.[25] That blurring made it all the more alluring and all the more difficult to precisely identify who was the enemy of the state. From the government's perspective, jipis and insurgents were one and the same because they shared a counterculture lifestyle. From the perspective of guerrilla members, the lack of a rigid line between counterculture youths and insurgents helped them live in clandestinity. As Carlos Salcedo, a former guerrilla member, explained, "The fundamental objective of a safe house was to not draw attention and give the impression that its inhabitants have a normal life. We looked like students and we were students. We went to university. We were good young men. You ask what is a good young man? One who studies, focuses on his things, doesn't party, doesn't make a racket, doesn't get drunk." Carlos goes on to modulate what "good" meant in clandestine life.[26]

> We were part of that generation of the sixties and the first to engage the counterculture of that age. Some [used drugs] but it was a luxury that we criticized and challenged but not like a holy inquisition. . . . Alcohol was frowned upon because if you're in a struggle where your life and ideals are at risk—how would it look if you started talking because you were drunk? We considered it a great indiscretion. But we didn't completely reject it because we lived in a place where that was a part of being young. We would drink beer in front of the university halls. There was a lot of pot smoked at CU [Ciudad Universitaria, the main campus of the national university in Mexico City]. Some of us had our hippie girlfriend that taught us what we know.

Carlos's statement that guerrilla members did not reject the counterculture movement on university campuses at the time is of critical importance to my analysis because it shows how the blurriness was deliberately used by both guerrilla members and the government.

Masculinity looms large in the construction of the subversive for both the guerrillas and the government's security forces, despite the fact that women participated in both armed groups and countercultural movements. For José Luis Esparza, women played three roles in his memory of this period. The first was that of the caring and strong mother figure, such as his mother-in-law. The second was that of an object of suspect affection, relegated to the periphery of action, because of the distraction or danger they posed. As an example of this distracting female role, he explained that male guerrillas could not associate with prostitutes because it would distract them from the mission, thereby posing a danger to the organization. The third role for a woman, according to José Luis, was as a comrade in the guerrilla movement. Even as he discusses women's contributions to the movement, José Luis conflates the distracting role of women with their usefulness. He brings up the case of his girlfriend in the movement and the complications posed by her competing relationship with another member of the group. In male narratives like José Luis's, women exist primarily as objects of affection and distraction, secondarily as equal comrades in arms.

Government officials shared this sexist view of women, most evident in how they included them in the interrogation process. As chapter 5 discusses, officials viewed family members as suspect and as an extension of the category of subversive. By including women—mothers, sisters, daughters, partners—in the torture process, officials emasculated male guerrillas and reified their own masculinity by possessing suspect women, often by rape. Aside from capitalizing on them as objects of affection, law enforcement denigrated women's participation by connecting their dissident politics to what they most likely viewed as deviant sexual practices. When police paraded detainees in front of the media, they would humiliate them. In reference to Ana María Parra Ramos, police stated, "this woman, who looks like a dyke [*tortillera*], was actually a dangerous terrorist."[27] The only way women could have agency in an insurgent movement, according to officials, was to resort to sexualized tropes that denied their identity and highlighted them as transgressive subjects. In resorting to this trope, government officials messaged that they had to stop these deviant women from perpetuating their wanton acts for fear of infecting other, presumably innocent women.

The place of women in the category of subversive must be analyzed in relation to women's actual role in guerrilla movements.[28] For this, I turn to their own words to see the parallels with their male counterparts. Like men, women experienced the 1968 Tlatelolco massacre as a turning point in their radicalization. A student and then a teacher in Nezahualcoyotl, Elia Hernández Hernández stopped working after the massacre to dedicate herself exclusively to her work as a guerrilla. María de la Luz Aguilar Torres told a similar story: she had been a student in 1968 and active in the student movement and went on to become a guerrilla after the massacre. Though she had been politically active since 1962, Yolanda Isabel Casas Quiroz pointed to 1968 as the moment when she abandoned a nonviolent perspective, opted to take up arms against the government, and joined Lucio Cabañas's guerrilla organization. Lourdes Quiñones described 1968 as a moment of awakening, a conjuncture that convinced her that the only way to create change was by joining an armed guerrilla movement. Her mother had raised her to "be an anti-imperialist," so it was not surprising that Lourdes studied political science at UNAM in the early 1960s and went to night school to train as a teacher. After Tlatelolco, she and her husband, Rigoberto Lorenzo López, dedicated themselves entirely to guerrilla movements and ended up moving to the countryside to fight for change alongside Cabañas.

These four women—Elia, María de la Luz, Yolanda, and Lourdes—were all actively involved in their respective guerrilla organizations. All four, when asked about the gender dynamics, tell a similar story. "There were feminists against *machistas*," Lourdes remembered. "We were equal. We shot the same. It was a very military-centered type of equality. This doesn't mean that machismo didn't continue to exist outside the group, but I didn't feel it inside." She then laughingly finished by saying, "I was the only woman with five men, so this was really weird." There is a dissonance between how women remembered their experiences inside versus outside a guerrilla movement. To use Lourdes's phrasing, the "military-centered type of equality" gave the illusion they were on the same footing as men, whereas outside the movement machismo continued. That dissonance belies the fact that there was a difference between the theory of gender equality espoused inside guerrilla groups and the lived reality that continued to exclude or condemn women as dissidents.

The making of the subversive must be understood from the perspective of how the "subversives" fashioned themselves: their political identities, their icons like Ché Guevara, their ideas about masculinity and armed struggle, and their habits in clandestinity and when blending into the broader counterculture movement of the 1960s and 1970s. To be young, according to DFS's Miguel Nazar Haro, made an individual susceptible to "brainwashing" by the "Soviet conspiracy."[29] Officials could selectively weave parts of how these young people saw themselves to fit the narrative of an internal enemy intent on destroying the national fabric. Said another way, the making of the subversive was not solely a top-down construction. It involved a range of individuals invested in using it for self-serving and competing purposes. Precisely because it served the government's purpose of securing social control, there was little incentive to carefully parse the categories of hippie, activist, and guerrilla insurgent. Law enforcement criminalized them as one and the same under a state of emergency and created the torturable subject.

Most Mexicans supported this characterization, thanks in part to diligent efforts by Mexican officials. The historian Jaime Pensado has shown President Díaz Ordaz understood that popular support for the government's repression of the student movement was contingent on the government "portraying the students as 'misguided,' 'bitter,' 'utopian,' 'insecure,' and/or 'dangerous' pawns manipulated by external enemies of Mexico."[30] Loyal *porros* (government-paid infiltrators) and journalists played key roles in this work, as did apocryphal propaganda. In addition, several of the intellectual authors of the 1968 student movement went on to collaborate with the Echeverría Álvarez administration's rewriting of both the massacre and the ensuing insurgency to whitewash—and justify—the government's brutality.[31] If these facts rationalizing the government's actions came from the very architects of the 1968 student movement, then they must be true. Pensado goes on to argue that popular frustration with the student movement and the tarnish it brought to Mexico on the eve of the much-heralded Olympics far outweighed dissatisfaction with the political order.[32] Díaz Ordaz's misinformation campaign in the aftermath of 1968 bore fruit and found receptive audiences to explain away other massacres, most egregiously the June 10, 1971, massacre of students on the eve of Corpus Christi in Mexico City.[33]

Groups on Mexico's political right actively stoked popular fears about revolutionary activity. These groups, especially those affiliated with conservative Catholic movements, used a range of channels—such as the distribution of posters, letter-writing campaigns, and public meetings—to publicly condemn the government for not taking a more hard-line response to the pervasive "moral sickness" afflicting Mexican society.[34] They spoke out against Socialist education policies that taught about Karl Marx or Ché Guevara and healthcare that promoted birth control and promiscuity. Conservative student groups organized around alternatives to the counterculture movements on campus.[35] The Mexican press compounded these concerns, reporting extensively on Mexicans who traveled to places like Cuba, the Soviet Union, and North Korea to receive training in guerrilla warfare.[36] In these popular portrayals, the guerrilla members stood at the far end of the spectrum of what was to be the most feared result if these practices continued unabated to influence young people. That fear—as heard in the many rumors and conspiracy theories circulating at the time—found an audience among officials and society at large.[37]

MAKING THE ENEMY DANGEROUS

Key to making the subversive a torturable subject was communicating that they were dangerous to the public at large. To do so, government officials drew on a variety of strategies that messaged fear to the broader population and justified their brutal retaliatory response. One of these strategies—as the previous section showed—was to selectively weave countercultural elements into the portrayal of the subversive as a threat to national security. Other strategies included relying on legal pretense, disseminating propaganda through media channels, and calling on neighborhood watch groups. These strategies could also be region-specific. In the same way that countercultural jipis tended to gather in urban centers, officials blurred the line between insurgent and criminal groups in rural areas—specifically, those involved in growing marijuana and poppies in Guerrero and surrounding states. Conferring forms of suspect criminality on political activists thus gave officials control over the narrative of who was a subversive and legitimized their use of state terror.

One of the most effective ways to shore up the category of subversive was to create laws that individuals broke. If a person could be charged with a crime, the government could take cover in the notion they were protecting citizens when punishing them. This was the case with the creation of the "social dissolution" law. From 1941 until it was repealed in 1970, the majority of political prisoners faced charges of violating Article 145 of the Federal Penal Code, which targeted anyone deemed a threat to public order for acts of "social dissolution."[38] The law came to symbolize the arbitrary and repressive side of the Mexican government because its vagueness allowed for virtually anyone to be charged. Activists and their family members lobbied for the article's revocation, calling it "unconstitutional," a detriment to "free speech," and a "hindrance to democratic values."[39] They succeeded in revoking Article 145 in 1970, but this did not dissuade the government from manipulating legal means to legitimate the imprisonment of activists. Aside from continuing to use existing laws against rebellion and sedition, such as Article 144, officials retooled other national security laws to target activists, including Article 139, which defined terrorism as "acts against persons, objects, or public services that produce alarm, fear or terror."[40] The social dissolution law then set the precedent for other, similar laws to be created and used in the future. It did not matter that it was revoked: Article 145 normalized that national security was under threat and that the legal system was vested in protecting it with the help of law enforcement.

The veneer of legality meant that the government accused those presumed of being subversives of crimes but did not necessarily have to follow through on proving such crimes in a court of law. In 1972, for example, the Topo Chico prison in Nuevo León housed twenty-three "subversive elements" charged with "carrying illegal weapons, criminal association, disobeying and resisting public functionaries, threats, assault, murder, false imprisonment, robbery, and property damage."[41] There Mexican authorities detained activists on charges with no legal foundations, such as for being a "subversive," "professional agitator," "guerrilla," or "communist" or having contact with any person with the aforementioned labels. One DFS file from the Oblatos prison in Guadalajara in May 1978 cites the names of six political prisoners detained without any formal charges for "security measures."[42] As Carlos said in his interview, the government's actions were "illegal within its own laws, as though to show us that it owned illegality." The government could easily—and without fear of retribution—manipulate legal channels to imprison those suspected of guerrilla activity in the name of national security. The pretense that an individual was breaking the law was enough to justify their detention and torture without having to proceed through the judicial system to prove it.

As government agents created an enemy among the public at large, they anchored this imagined foe in images of real people. They disseminated these images in leaflets distributed from the air by helicopter and posted in marketplaces, transportation centers, hospitals, and other public venues.[43] One example found in the DFS archive included photographs of LC23S members alongside the promise of a generous reward and anonymity for whoever gave information on their whereabouts. The anonymity offered to informants also meant that their identities would not be divulged to the police, suggesting that the DFS knew that people might not trust law enforcement. To nurture a culture of reporting suspicious individuals, the DFS developed an advertising campaign via newspapers, radio, and television claiming that such reporting demonstrated a "patriotic and virile attitude against delinquents threatening the country's peace, who assassinate and kidnap innocent people."[44] The campaign tied the protection of family values to the need to report suspicious individuals; failure to do so was an "irresponsible" act that threatened the future of children.[45]

The population responded immediately when the campaign went live in mid-1976. Calls came in reporting all sorts of suspicious individuals, the majority of whom turned out to be innocent.[46] A review of DFS files on the LC23S's activities during this period show the depths individuals went to to report on suspicious activities. Municipal leaders from the community of Ecatepec in the state of Morelos, for example, sent detailed reports on what they deemed the suspicious activities of one of their local teachers.[47] Newspapers reported on operations to track down LC23S members throughout the country. "They detained ten activists! Including

2 leaders of the Liga 23 de Septiembre," reads the headline from a newspaper in Monterrey in April 1978.[48] Another newspaper details how a bullet-proof vest saved an officer in an armed battle with these same militants in Monterrey.[49] The fact that this call for information was so effective and that newspapers covered such arrests demonstrates that many people believed in the veracity of the government's narrative of threatening subversives living in their midst.

In addition, employers gave DFS agents information on employees they suspected of being leftists or labor organizers; some even went so far as to allow DFS agents to infiltrate the ranks of their employees to surveil suspects.[50] One report discusses a worker being brought in for questioning because his boss reported that he had accepted a copy of *Madera*, the LC23S newspaper, from one of his coworkers.[51] Such collaboration suggests employers believed that the DFS was an arbiter of legality and had to be supported to ensure the enemy was not among the ranks of workers. It also shows that individuals suspected those around them and were willing to inform on their own communities. The possibility that a subversive was hiding in their midst helped individuals perform mental gymnastics that set aside questions in the name of national security. Individuals did not demand evidence of a crime or due process to confer guilt. The fact that the government was willing to protect citizens from this "subversive" was to be commended, and standing in its way was unpatriotic. Opposition of any kind was then criminalized, and any person could be suspected of being a criminal.

While before the 1968 massacre of Tlatelolco the ranks of so-called subversives were filled with labor, intellectual, and rural leaders, they subsequently grew to include women and the children of an emerging urban and educated middle class. As activism grew, the state further restricted moderate spaces where young people congregated, increasing surveillance of university campuses and closing half of the rural escuelas normales in 1969.[52] Concomitantly, assuming "jipiteca" cultural trappings—listening to rock music, growing beards, and wearing miniskirts—brought young people to the attention of military and police officers.[53] Heightened surveillance of young people thus normalized the ever-watchful eye of law enforcement in their midst, at the same time reinforcing the suspicion that Mexico's youth could be harboring a foreign enemy or susceptible to dangerous, contagious influences. To be young was to be suspect. To be young on a university campus or an escuela normal—let alone to be a woman—immediately conferred suspected guilt on an individual. This meant that criminality could be spatially configured and fold into other transgressive identities, including being labeled a homosexual.[54] In his State of the Union address in September 1974, President Echeverría Álvarez stressed that these "terrorists" tended to be sexually promiscuous and "with a high degree of masculine and feminine homosexuality."[55] To be young made you suspect. To be young and gay made you even more suspect in the eyes of the government.

The countryside had its own region-specific criminal identities that melded into making the subversive. While police agencies tended to take the lead on criminalizing and targeting activists in urban centers such as Mexico City, the military traditionally occupied this role in rural areas, where the police tended to have less of a presence.[56] In the state of Guerrero, most tellingly, the military lumped guerrilla members with community activists and criminal groups.[57] As scholars have recently explored, the military's campaigns to hunt down members of Lucio Cabañas's Partido de los Pobres in the mountains of Guerrero in the early 1970s indiscriminately and sloppily destroyed entire communities.[58] Between April 1971 and the end of 1972, the military implemented the Plan Telaraña (Plan Spiderweb) in Guerrero that used "scorched earth" tactics to punish and dissuade communities from providing any support to guerrilla groups.[59]

Across six pages, the Plan Telaraña lists orders for the army and air force units stationed in Guerrero with support from military bases in surrounding states. It identified Chilpancingo in the highlands and Acapulco on the coast as bases for launching operations. The first part of the plan laid out detailed instructions for promoting social welfare projects that would set the bases for enhanced intelligence gathering by tapping telephones, infiltrating groups, and recruiting informants. The second part of the plan—termed "military action"—involved the "search, localization, siege, and neutralization or capture of *maleantes* [thugs], with the aim of reestablishing peace in critical areas of the state of Guerrero."[60] Here the plan specifies the need for the military to adopt covert tactics, such as the use of vague "irregular operations" and carrying out missions at night so as not to alert the guerrillas to their actions. The document makes ample use of the terms "maleantes" and "facinerosos" (outlaws) when referring to their intended targets. This reveals the conflation of guerrillas with unspecified criminals—people who broke unnamed laws—as being one and the same. While the military launched other campaigns later on, such as Plan Luciérnaga (Plan Firefly), Plan Atoyac, and Plan Técpan between 1973 and 1975, the Plan Telaraña stands out because it was one of the first documents that systematized the use of counterinsurgency forms of state terror at the hands of the military.[61] In it, the military overtly recognizes the dangers posed by guerrilla groups, highlights their alleged "criminality," and lays out instructions for the more forceful detention, torture, and disappearance of activists.

The language criminalizing anyone affiliated with guerrilla activity was often used to link them to the illicit drug economy. Guerrero had a long history of marijuana and poppy production that dovetailed with the growing crackdown on drug production and trafficking, much of which emanated from the United States and the Nixon administration's declaration of a war on drugs in 1971. As the 1970s progressed, the Mexican military targeted both guerrillas and marijuana growers through a "social cleansing" strategy that gave soldiers permission to kill any community member suspected of providing support to either group.[62] A follow-up report on the Plan Telaraña's actions, for example, contains a day-by-day breakdown of operations.[63] In June 1971, the report lists several run-ins with individuals involved in marijuana and poppy production. In one case, officers had a shoot-out with three men, resulting in two killed and one seriously injured. As Alexander Aviña shows, the Mexican government excused the military's large presence in Guerrero "as an anti-crime and counternarcotics campaign that targeted 'cattle-thieves,' 'bandits,' and narco-traffickers."[64] It was a covert counterinsurgency campaign masked as an antinarcotics operation to ensure the public at large did not know the true size of the guerrilla threat in the region. Aviña explains that this "criminalizing discourse provided ready-made justification for the sort of atrocities committed by the military and police in their pursuit of the guerrillas and their supporters beginning in 1969."[65] It also ensured that the military would continue to occupy the region for decades to come and that both military and police officials would take over drug-trafficking operations later in the 1970s.

In urban and rural areas, the military and the police could act with impunity as they hunted down guerrillas, insurgents, gang members, and drug traffickers. To the military and police, they were all the same. Though the euphemisms played out differently on the ground, in the eyes of the Mexican government, they were all enemies of the state. Members of rural communities might not be insurgents or criminals, but they might provide aid or shelter to help them avoid persecution by authorities. The presumption was that the rural poor would side with criminal or insurgent elements. For law enforcement, the hypotheticals rang true in the siege mentality. If we consider what Ávila Coronel and Aviña argue, we can summarize that being a member of a poor rural community in the mountains of Guerrero made an individual suspect in the eyes of the military and the police.[66]

The fact that this subversive identity could be attached to so many Mexicans demonstrates that the government's effort transcended propaganda. Seeing it as merely propaganda assigns a passive role to the Mexican population at large and devalues the complexity of the process of making this enemy so threatening. Said another way, as the DFS tapped into surveillance networks among neighborhood groups, it both gathered information and reinforced the idea that there was somebody worth surveilling. Why would law enforcement be following certain people if there was not a good reason to suspect them of wrongdoing? As the military laid bare rural communities through brutal massacres in the highlands of Guerrero, the implication was that these individuals deserved what happened because they must have been aiding criminals. The logical leaps required to justify making the subversive were thus a collaborative venture between the government and civil society that set in motion unthinking and unquestioning patterns that would continue for decades to come. The individuals whom the government implied were enemies of the state posed a threat so dire that they had to be eliminated at all costs.

The narrative of an internal enemy that threatened national security and therefore required extraordinary government measures required the complicity of many in Mexican society who chose to unquestioningly believe and justify the narrative. Whatever their personal calculus, most Mexican citizens decided to stay quiet because it *could* prove too costly to speak up. I deliberately place emphasis on "could" because it ties to the culture of fear so prevalent during the 1970s. On the one hand, the source of that fear arose from the shame of possibly being labeled unpatriotic by neighbors for criticizing the government during a time of upheaval or having one's professional reputation tarnished in the eyes of one's peers by appearing to support Communist principles antithetical to *lo mexicano*. On the other hand, that fear could cause a person to lose their job and access to government safety-net services, including schooling, housing, healthcare, and retirement benefits.[67] Behind this calculus was the dearth of successful opposition to challenge the political order.[68] Setting aside the large-scale mobilizations of students in 1968 and again in 1971, both of which resulted in brutal massacres, Mexicans of this period remembered what happened when other groups, such as doctors, nurses, and health-care workers who attempted to strike in 1964–65, spoke out and failed.[69]

Even for those who could have spoken up, especially journalists and intellectuals who had come of age during and after the 1968 student mobilizations, challenging the administrations of Echeverría Álvarez and López Portillo could mean risking their livelihoods. The government had direct control of the funding of news outlets and academia writ large, including managing promotions and access to better employment opportunities, meaning that the fear of retaliation for criticizing political leaders was a real factor in the calculus to stay quiet and toe the government's line of justification.[70]

Yet it bears emphasizing that there were individuals who risked their lives to make known what was being done in the name of national security. These included—as later chapters describe—family members clamoring for the release of their loved ones. The Comité Eureka is perhaps the best known of these organizations established by family members to demand justice for what was done to their sons and daughters.[71] Other voices included human rights activists, lawyers, progressive Catholics, and journalists denouncing abuses of power and acts of state terror. Often at great personal cost, these individuals resisted the social pressure to be silent and continued to demand a stop to the abuses.

Members of the Catholic Church who spoke out against state repression stand out because Mexico was after all a deeply Catholic nation. Perhaps the best known progressive Catholic leader was Bishop Sergio Méndez Arceo from the diocese of Cuernavaca, Morelos. While he was originally conservative, the "Red Bishop"—as he came to be called— changed his views with the rise of liberation theology, a religious current calling for Catholics to take up social justice and humanitarian causes. For his critics, liberation theology was akin to communism and a noxious foreign influence seeking to undermine a key institution for Mexicans, the church. The Red Bishop was not alone. Jaime Pensado recently wrote about lay Catholic organizations that condemned state repression at the time. He discusses what happened to rebellious priests who spoke out, including Rodolfo Escamilla García, who was killed by security forces for his outspokenness.[72] Pensado also describes the cases of two other priests who were detained and brutally tortured at CM-1 in late 1972 for their activism around liberation theology and human rights. Over the course of two days, they endured submersions in water and electrical prods and were then released, with officials accusing them of a range of unfounded crimes. Soon after, an anonymous author in the weekly news magazine, *La Nación*, decried what happened to the two priests and asked whether Mexico had "institutionalized torture."[73] That the magazine asked that question in 1972 is noteworthy, because it was one of the few journalistic voices condemning state repression.

Although the overwhelming majority of Mexican citizens chose to stay quiet about state repression, that did not mean that there were no challenges. The resistance may not have been as effective as that of the Mothers of the Plaza de Mayo in Argentina or the Vicariate of Solidarity in Chile during the dirty wars in those countries. Nevertheless, efforts of Mexicans warrant recognition both because of the sacrifices many endured and because of the courage it took to speak out during a time of tremendous censure and grave repercussions.

THE CURE FOR BEING A SUBVERSIVE: THOSE WHO TALKED

In recalling his detention, El Guaymas talked about how his comrade pointed him out to the police on the streets of Guadalajara: "They gave him a hard beating, and he gave me up." He was careful not to name the man at this point in the interview and was mindful not to assign blame. El

Guaymas had been shot in the leg and the arm when he was detained and, after spending fifteen days in the hospital recovering from his injuries, was transferred to the Oblatos prison. Once there, officers beat him until he started talking.[74] As reflected in the statements from torture victims in chapter 1, many former detainees believed that everybody talked under torture. While the primary purpose of torture was to destroy the individual and to bolster the role of law enforcement, we cannot lose sight of its secondary purpose as an interrogation tool. Inside the walls of a clandestine prison, victims understood the stakes of disclosing information: disclosure could make the pain stop, even if momentarily, though others would pay the price. Precisely because the information was gathered under extreme duress, it was unreliable and contained falsehoods. Nevertheless, accuracy did not matter in this setting because information gathering was not the only motive. To understand how government officials created the category of subversive through the act of torture, we need to place its alleged cure—divulging information—on the analytical table. This cure was short-lived for the victims because disclosing information could generate another form of deep psychological pain, namely, guilt. It could also, as discussed below, destroy individuals to the point that they renounced their activism and assisted law enforcement. The cure then could be the death of the subversive and the birth of the collaborator.

During the 1970s, the government refined its list of targeted subversives with the help of informants—nicknamed *madrinas* (godmothers)—and information extracted under torture.[75] Madrinas could, as Roberto González Villareal discusses, "be voluntary or not; they could be paid informants or not; oftentimes they were deserters from Lucio's group or were being threatened."[76] The simple fact that a tortured detainee or a madrina pointed someone out was enough justification for that person to be picked up, as happened to El Guaymas in Guadalajara. The relationship between an informant and the DFS could go further, depending on the former's usefulness. Adolfo Godoy Cabañas describes how Alfonso Vázquez, the man in the adjacent cell in CM-1, started talking. Alfonso was Genaro Vázquez's father, one of the key guerrilla leaders in Guerrero. This relationship convinced officials that Alfonso must have critical information to share on guerrilla activities. Adolfo remembered Alfonso Vázquez as "a filthy pig, a crybaby. I think it was the second month that he started crying that he was dying and he confessed to a lot of things. I don't know if it was military or federal agents who interrogated him, but after a while he started talking without having to be forced to." According to Adolfo, Alfonso gave information on his wife, his son, and other family members and received privileges in return. "He got all the services," Adolfo said. "They even gave him cigarettes and the good kind of food." Doctors would come to his cell to give him medical treatment as a privilege for being an informant. This was in stark contrast to the way that doctors otherwise were present just to keep victims alive while they underwent torture. Prisoners who collaborated with the government—like Alfonso— could show others the tangible rewards they received for disclosing information. In the context of a clandestine prison, such individuals were a testament to what could happen if one stopped being a "subversive."

David López Valenzuela, who became an informant inside Oblatos after he was picked up in 1974, went further than Alfonso Vázquez. López Valenzuela helped the DFS confirm that a bomb that failed to detonate belonged to his guerrilla group and established the veracity of a list of high-level individuals targeted for kidnappings and assassinations. For some informants, naming names was just the beginning; it could extend to feeding interrogators questions. A former political prisoner told Elena Poniatowska that López Valenzuela was the one who turned him in to the DFS, after which he was picked up, brutally tortured, and sent to Oblatos in Guadalajara.[77] Although he was blindfolded during the torture sessions, he knew that López Valenzuela was in the room guiding the interrogators' questions. If we think of this "cure" for being a subversive as a continuum, the case of Alfonso Vázquez is early in the process and that of David López Valenzuela illustrates what happens as it advances.

What about the long-term effects of engaged collaboration? What about those who embraced the "cure" to the point that they became agents of the state? For that, we turn to what happened to Gustavo Hirales, one of the original founders of LC23S, and to Manuel Mondragón y Kalb, a physician activist. If we place these two cases side by side, we can appreciate the complexities of what would drive an individual to go from opposing to wholeheartedly siding with the political order. Both men, from the perspective of the military and police forces, stood as examples of the power of rehabilitation encoded in making the subversive identity.

Within just a few short months of helping found the LC23S in 1973, Gustavo Hirales was detained by the DFS and subjected to brutal torture under Nazar Haro's supervision.[78] He was subsequently imprisoned for seven years in Topo Chico for his political activities. Sometime after his release in 1980, he joined the ranks of the PRI and became an influential figure in the Secretaría de Gobernación (Ministry of Interior). In the 1990s, he played a key role in leading the counterinsurgency efforts against the Ejército Zapatista de Liberación Nacional (EZLN; Zapatista Army of National Liberation) and other revolutionary groups.[79] To understand the dramatic shift in his political trajectory, we turn to his recollections on his time as a political prisoner.[80] Like other detainees, Hirales was beaten by regular police officers before meeting Nazar Haro for the first time. Nazar Haro oversaw the torture, which began with quoting Mao Ze-Dong, indicating that Hirales should know it was "time to lose."[81] The torturers began by immersing Hirales's head in a sink to simulate drowning until he passed out. They then strung him up by his legs to two parallel metal poles and took turns hitting him until he again passed out. The waterboarding continued during the second day, and agents forced him to drink liquor to revive him enough to continue with the torture session.[82] After five days of this routine, they took him to the DFS building in the Colonia Roma, where he met the DFS director. At the end of the meeting, Nazar Haro transported Hirales to Monterrey and deposited him at the Topo Chico prison. Along the way, Nazar Haro kept up a running political conversation with Hirales while referring to him as "Mister Nobody."[83]

Calling him "Mister Nobody" evokes the erasure of subversives: they are not fit to participate in society, so they must be separated to avoid contagion. Yet that erasure also involved knowledge of others' pain. Gustavo was aware of the fate of two comrades and leading members of the LC23S, Olivares Torres and Salvador Corral, in retaliation for the kidnapping of two businessmen.[84] Both Torres and Corral were apprehended in February 1974 and savagely tortured to death. Torres's body had multiple fractures, and his torturers had driven hot nails into his kneecaps.[85] Torres's and Corral's bodies were then thrown in front of their families' homes. For Gustavo, his own torture as well as that of others around him convinced him to take the "cure" for subversion. Not only did he go on to denounce both his comrades and the LC23S, but he also used his political formation in the guerrilla movement to help the government attack similar movements later on. He was no longer Mr. Nobody.

Let us turn now to Manuel Mondragón y Kalb to understand the long-term effects of complicity. He first came to the DFS's attention in 1965, when the agency began monitoring medical personnel who held dissident views. As a doctor at the Twentieth of November Hospital in Mexico City, Mondragón y Kalb expressed solidarity with the personnel who had taken to the streets to demand better working conditions and political democratization. In May 1965, a DFS report identified Mondragón y Kalb as "one of the most radical elements because of his point of view."[86] Just four months later, in September, a follow-up DFS report stated that the attorney general was going to bring a slew of charges—dereliction of duty, inciting crimes, abuse of authority—against forty doctors and nurses, including Mondragón y Kalb. The doctor's DFS file stops there, with no record of what came of the charges, and picks up over a decade later. We can infer that in the interim the doctor became a collaborator. In July 1977, Mondragón y Kalb, who at the time was the president of the Mexican Karate Federation, contacted the head of the DFS to reiterate his commitment to continue collaborating with the secret police. The doctor assured the DFS that the Karate Federation would provide its officers with "technical training in karate, taekwondo, kung-fu, and other martial arts" that met professional standards. In other words, Mondragón y Kalb oversaw the training of DFS agents in martial arts, which they then used to carry out their duties, including interrogations.[87] The doctor went on to serve in various public health leadership posts in subsequent administrations and headed Mexico City's Ministry of Public Safety. Most recently, he was head of the National Commission Against Addiction, which led to President López Obrador naming him special adviser on drug policy in 2018.[88]

We can infer that the protest activities Mondrágon y Kalb engaged in during the 1960s would have caused him to be flagged as a subversive actor and subject to the same interrogation techniques he taught DFS agents several years later. He has never publicly acknowledged, let alone apologized for, his complicity with the DFS. Nor have those around him— working alongside him, advancing his career—held him to account for what he did in the 1970s. The dissonance between these two realities of first being an activist and later a collaborator begs the question: How does an individual like Mondrágon y Kalb rationalize his participation in training torturers? Maybe he would argue that he did not know the full extent of human rights abuses his training contributed to; that he is excused because he was doing his patriotic duty during a time of war; that the training he provided DFS officers professionalized interrogation techniques; that it was so long ago, and he has more than made up for past mistakes. Regardless, Mondragón y Kalb has been silent about this chapter in his life, even after the DFS files released in the early 2000s proved his complicity. Had an individual of his professional stature publicly recognized his actions as mistakes, he could have opened the path for others to hold themselves accountable for how they contributed directly to such crimes. By choosing to stay quiet, he denies the public an answer for what he did. Silence equals impunity. What is detrimental about silence from people who collaborated and then went on to live public lives is that it showcases impunity for those who chose not to collaborate.

Complicity and collaboration go hand in hand. Each of the four cases studied—Alfonso Vázquez, David Lopéz Valenzuela, Gustavo Hirales, and Manuel Mondragón y Kalb—illustrates different reasons for individuals choosing the path of complicity. Aside from stopping the torture and receiving immediate perks, other events may have led them to collaborate. In the case of Hirales and Mondragón y Kalb, the reason may be found in the seven years Hirales spent at the Topo Chico prison or the ten-year gap in Mondragón y Kalb's DFS file. Regardless, the cure for political dissidence for each of these men meant becoming collaborators and then, in two of the cases, agents of the state. For others, including Hirales's two comrades from LC23S, there was no cure. They suffered death. The end point to making the subversive offered up two paths: one led to creating a new individual, no longer posing a threat to the political order; the other, to destroying the person physically and psychologically, forever marking them as broken.

CONCLUSION

In the working-class neighborhood of San Andrés in Guadalajara, there is a beautiful mural honoring what the community endured for their politi-

Figure 1. Mural of Los Vikingos in the San Andrés neighborhood of Guadalajara. The mural stretches over several blocks and depicts former guerrillas and activists and important scenes in the militant history of the area. Created several years ago, it has recently been repainted to ensure it continues to stand for the community. Photo Credit: Edgar Hermosillo Meza

cal activism across the 1970s. This area had been the epicenter for militant groups, such as Los Vikingos, the FER, and, later, part of the LC23S.[89] The mural depicts the faces of young people—several who perished at the hands of law enforcement—who belonged to these movements as well as their family members seeking justice for what they endured. In the words of Richard, a former guerrilla, "the hunting got heavy" across these years. He went on to explain, "We were just a gang of young people, a bunch of young radicals, and we didn't have the capacity to take on anybody militarily." I urged him to talk about why he and other young people—including those who are depicted in the mural just blocks from where we were seated—took such risks, knowing what was at stake. He responded, "The willingness of young people to answer the call of history to oppose the Mexican state's oppression. I valued the willingness of young people to give themselves completely to an ideal and to change things before a state we considered criminal."

Beyond victims of torture, the individuals whose stories populate this chapter sought to have a voice in the political process and represented a generational call to arms, figuratively and, in some cases, literally. Their voices, their identities, and their histories—before, during, and after they were tortured—are key to explaining the marriage of state formation and government-sanctioned terrorism. They were products of the governing regime: their parents were born near the start of PRI rule, they went to schools overseen by PRI officials, and they were expected to grow up to be obedient citizens. They also collectively expressed disillusionment with a political system premised on the promises of an institutionalized revolution and instead opted for other forms of revolution that challenged the status quo. This was the same political system that labeled them subversives and then subjected them to a cold and calculating violence that forever changed them. This labeling was much more than propaganda because it blurred the line between words and unspeakable brutality at the hands of government agents. After the emergence of widespread guerrilla activity in post-1968 Mexico, officials created the torturable subject—the subversive—as the enemy of the state. The ambiguity of who precisely fit this category made everyone suspect. It was not reserved solely for guerrilla members, student activists, those listening to counterculture music, or women wearing miniskirts on university campuses. It was not just a trope used to indiscriminately attack poor rural communities. It was an imagined enemy that confounded law enforcement and could be hiding in plain sight. So supposedly dangerous was this internal enemy of the state that it required officials to set aside due process and resort to extreme forms of violence to protect the nation and against the antinational threat. Such thinking upended thousands of Mexican lives.

3 The Torturers

When I first started this project, I assumed that torturers belonged to a closed secret brotherhood that I would not be able to gain access to. I figured these men knew one another and talked of events not to be divulged outside their ranks for the sake of national security and out of concern that one day, perhaps, Mexico would have an effective truth commission. I assumed that the brotherhood's anonymity fit the logic of counterinsurgency: a shadow war against a shadow enemy concealed among the civilian population. I thought that anonymity deferred any sense of blame and guilt from the individual to the group. It turns out that this assumption required reworking. While many torturers remain nameless, some of them are known to the public. The DFS's Miguel Nazar Haro—perhaps Mexico's most infamous torturer—looms large in victim accounts because he was present at or led so many interrogation sessions. Other officers from the DFS and the military, such as Mario Arturo Acosta Chaparro and Francisco Quiroz Hermosillo, figure in these accounts as well. While one document lists the names of 332 officers active in the state of Guerrero's dirty war, as yet there is no comprehensive list of torturers in Mexico as a whole during the 1970s.[1]

Richard, the former guerrilla member from Guadalajara who showed me that clandestine torture centers were an open secret, challenged the anonymity of torturers when he named two from the 1970s. The first was Moi Torres, a known boxer whose younger brother, Efren "El Alacrán" (the Scorpion) Torres, had won international boxing titles. The second was a *lucha libre* (Mexican wrestling) fighter known in the area for his stage presence. Both men moonlighted as torturers for the military, the DFS, and the judicial police in Guadalajara. They trained officers in how to inflict maximum pain on their victims during interrogation and carried "charolas" (badges) identifying them as DFS agents. The wrestler and the boxer went to local gyms such as the Club Gimnasio Hercules and the Club Deportivo Mutualista that were frequented by police and military officers. When I asked Richard what had become of these two torturers, he said they had died a few years ago. Unfortunately, I never learned the name of the lucha libre fighter.

Richard went on to explain that there was never any accountability for what these torturers had done in the 1970s, and they were frequently seen walking in the city with their families. He clarified that it was typical for government leaders to use men like these two to do their dirty work. As an example, he explained that the then-president of the University of Guadalajara had a group of about seven or eight boxers on his payroll whom he sent out to intimidate student or labor activists on his behalf. Richard referred to them as a "grupo de matones" (a group of thugs) who also hired out their services to the DFS and the military and, as a result, carried "charolas" of their own that they could display at will. This type of torturer fit the model of the abusive policeman in the political cartoons and social satire of Eduardo del Río, better known as Rius. Rius brought this character to life first in *Los supermachos* and later in *Los agachados*, which he published from 1968 to 1977. This policeman followed orders, partook of the spoils of a corrupt political system, and constructed his masculine identity according to the motto, "machos, borrachos y compachos" (studs, drunks, and good old boys).[2] The fact that all of these individuals—from the sophisticated Nazar Haro to the unsophisticated boxer and *luchador* in Guadalajara—did not feel the need to hide shows the depth of impunity and the ubiquity of torturers in Mexican society. In the same way that "clandestine" torture centers were known to the public, the identity of torturers was an open secret.

To a degree, impunity depended on the collaboration of civil society. As suspected enemies of the state were pulled off the street into unmarked cars, tortured in clandestine prisons, and disappeared—never to be heard from again—the overwhelming majority of Mexicans went about their business. Some Mexicans were simply too scared to protest, but others developed what Steve Stern refers to as "the habit of denial or looking the other way on matters of state violence."[3] Perhaps only partly aware of the supposed national emergency, periodically catching glimpses that something was awry in the social order or digesting censored news pieces about guerrilla threats, people turned a blind eye. Many Mexicans benefited from the PRI's authoritarian political system and its paternalism: it gave them an education, helped them reach middle-class if not higher status through secure employment, and allowed them to thrive in urban environments. So numerous were the benefits of PRI rule that many people made a kind of Faustian bargain with the PRI-led state.[4] If prodded too deeply, the veneer of normalcy would fall away, destabilizing the narrative of a "soft" authoritarianism that so many Mexicans believed in—that what took place in Mexico was not at all as extreme as what happened in the Southern Cone dictatorships. There were exceptions to this habit of denial, namely, in the increasing activism of church groups and family members demanding to know the whereabouts of their sons or daughters.

With few exceptions, individuals are not born with a predisposition to inflict extreme pain on another. As this chapter shows, torturers in Mexico learned this skill through word-of-mouth lessons and hands-on practice, much like an apprentice learns a trade. They were professionalized into an environment that nurtured their ability to shrug off moral qualms about inflicting extreme pain on others. This environment tended to be a formal space designated for the activity, where a person was supervised in hands-on training, followed orders and procedures, and understood the chain of command. They learned that these techniques were only to be used in times of emergency, that only select individuals were officially allowed to know about them, and that there would be no retribution. Torturers were confident in the knowledge they belonged to a secretive brotherhood of men—often as part of a special forces group such as the DFS's White Brigade of elite officers—with the mental stamina to do what most individuals could not fathom in their quest to defend Mexico from an insidious enemy hiding in plain sight.

Considering how to answer the question of what motivates a person to torture adds further layers to why the torture employed in Mexico across the long 1970s worked. It worked because it both destroyed the victim and emboldened the victimizer. As the previous chapter argued, the Mexican government created the category "subversive" to legitimize its counterinsurgency approach for both external and internal audiences. The public at large understood there was an internal enemy threatening their way of life; highly trained military and police officers—organized as counterinsurgency units of special forces—believed it was their prerogative to annihilate this enemy. How the military and the police understood this fact and used that prerogative is at the center of this chapter. The following pages analyze key points that help us grasp what went into creating an environment so permissive of torture that it continued well after the time of exigency passed. Placing the stories of Miguel Nazar Haro and the DFS's White Brigade side by side shows the larger framework the Mexican government employed to protect itself from threats to its authority.

This does not mean Nazar Haro was the only law enforcement leader or the White Brigade was the only special forces group that engaged in torture and other kinds of covert warfare. There were many other individuals and special forces groups across different branches of law enforcement that could have served as examples. Nevertheless, available sources—interviews, periodicals, archival documents—emphasize Nazar Haro and the White Brigade, thereby making it possible to use them as emblematic of how security forces approached the practice of torture during the era of counterinsurgency. Using Nazar Haro and the White Brigade as case studies, this chapter builds a framework of how torture was employed in Mexico and shows that the practice melded novel torture techniques developed abroad with those long employed by domestic law enforcement. The latter included the selective and strategic deployment of violence, the periodic adjustment of tactics in response to new presidential administrations, the ramping up of efforts to fend off challenges from so-called subversives, and the use of propaganda to galvanize support under the aegis of patriotism and national security. The evolution of these practices allowed for incorporating new ways of wielding state repression, such as the advent of counterinsurgency tactics adjusted for the realities of Mexican law enforcement. Moreover, placing the torturers alongside the political system that empowered them establishes that there was a shared understanding of the usefulness of employing state-sanctioned terror at a moment when the state was vulnerable to threats.

The two main institutions comprising Mexico's security apparatus during the 1970s were the military and the DFS. These two bodies were closely allied. While many DFS officers came from the police ranks, every director of the DFS—with the exception of Nazar Haro—was an active duty or retired military officer holding the rank of colonel.[5] Such close ties between the military and the DFS allowed the military to tap into the agency's surveillance powers and the DFS to use military bases for clandestine activity. Over time, joint operations between the military and the DFS became more sophisticated and had lower public profiles. The most notable secret police unit was the DFS's White Brigade, also referred to as the Special Brigade, created in 1976. As this chapter shows, there had been previous examples of special forces in Mexico, including paramilitary groups such as those used during the 1971 Corpus Christi massacre. However, under Nazar Haro's guidance, the White Brigade became the most professional of all the special forces groups. Its activities were driven by the singular goal of eradicating the LC23S. The case of Miguel Nazar Haro and his role inside the DFS gives us a window into the torture techniques employed by other groups. Nazar Haro's fair skin and blue eyes and his role in guiding the torture sessions and oscillating between the one who could ease pain or magnify it, along with his unapologetic public proclamations afterward, made him a recognizable actor for many victims. Not only does he exemplify torturers at the time, his case also enables us to understand why the government so readily resorted to the type of counterinsurgency torture techniques Nazar Haro championed.

STUDYING PAIN

Analyzing the mentality of the torturer sheds light on what drove these men—and they were primarily men—to inflict pain on others. It also sheds light on a government's rationale for endorsing torture. Christopher Browning's work on Nazi Germany helps us understand the decision tree behind an individual's choice to torture in the name of the government.[6] He proposes that soldiers drew on five factors in making the choice to hurt others. First, they used distancing to draw a clear "us versus them" divide between themselves and the people they tortured. The use of euphemisms, such as "subversive," is one way to construct the divide. Second, they detached themselves from their actions and set aside ethical thinking in the name of a counterinsurgency war. Third, they obeyed orders and normalized their behavior in the face of violent acts they would not have otherwise taken. The state of emergency, in this case against the insurgent threat posed by guerrilla groups, left no time for questions or qualms. Fourth, they saw opportunities to advance in their career by demonstrating to superiors the lengths they would go to in the name of national security. The torturer could then be promoted in rank or stand out from others of a similar rank. Fifth, they conformed to existing gender codes that valued masculine prowess and decisive action and vilified cowardice. In this gender ideology, the cowardice of the victim was on display because of the threat they represented outside of the torture chamber and their submissive position in the act of torture. I would add a sixth factor to nuance the decision tree in the Mexican case: The presence of so many individuals helped diffuse responsibility and allowed those ordering the torture and those inflicting it to deflect moral qualms. Keeping these factors in mind helps us understand *why* these men chose to torture and appreciate that they were more than passive instruments of the state who simply followed orders.[7]

Torturers employed highly specialized skills in their quest to protect the nation. They were often intellectually sophisticated enough to converse with insurgents and understand their specific language. Many showed an adept knowledge of the human mind under extreme pressure and an ability to determine what could push it beyond its limits. Many showed no remorse or qualms about following orders, up to and including inflicting pain on seemingly innocent victims, even civilians and children. An appreciation for these specialized skills normalized the use of torture in law enforcement organizations. The organization to which they belonged, whether a branch of the military or the police, institutionalized torture as standard operating procedure—departing from traditional norms of conflict against nontraditional enemies. Since the war against guerrillas and political dissidents is not a traditional conflict, the torturer fears no consequences because he is assured of the necessity of his actions and can thus carry out his orders with impunity. It was not a question of legality since the Mexican government had not actually legalized torture. Instead, legality did not matter in this state of emergency. In this context, government officials bent the rule of law in order to protect national interests.

In overt forms of war, soldiers tend to follow set character conventions, such as the hero, the savior, or the protector.[8] In Mexico's covert war, those conventions persisted and, if anything, were amplified because it was perceived as an unconventional war. Officers selected to take part in the counterinsurgency program possessed a specific skill set that made them ideal to take on unconventional enemies. The fear of censure, of reprimand from superiors, or of being subject to similar treatments as the victims drove these officials to torture. Opting out was not an option because torture was a social act. If officers dared to refuse to engage in torture, their defiance would be severely punished by others in the brotherhood. In other words, gender expectations specific to the armed forces and police units worked to censure officers who expressed repulsion or refused to participate in torture. The expectation of brutality—as a hypermasculine practice—was a specific gender convention for torturers that obligated them to take part. Below I argue that the motivations of the torturer parallel those of government leaders ordering the use of political violence to quell dissent. I study these motivations by considering the nature and operations of covert special force units and the kinds of interrogation techniques they used.

THE ARCHITECT OF MEXICO'S COUNTERINSURGENCY TORTURE PROGRAM

Carlos Salcedo said that he met two different types of torturers while at Campo Militar-1, the clandestine detention center inside the principal military base in Mexico City. The first type knew how to torture and clearly had ample experience doing it with what he termed "common delinquents." This type of torturer did not have the vocabulary to understand political prisoners. As an example, Carlos said that his first torturers did not know what "compartmentalization" meant. His guerrilla group had numerous cells, with six to twelve individuals in each. However, the cells did not know the other cells so as to avoid a total collapse of their organization if one of them was compromised by detention or infiltration—in other words, they were compartmentalized. The first torturers also stole his inexpensive watch and periodically rifled through his pockets to ensure they had not missed anything of even marginal value. In other words, the first kind of torturer Carlos encountered was little more than a corrupt officer with little to no political understanding of what drove a guerrilla movement. He resembled the long-held stereotype of unruly and self-serving police officers inflicting brutal beatings with no purpose or agenda.

Carlos met the second type of torturer several days into his incarceration. A DFS agent placed a chair in front of his cell. Carlos was no longer blindfolded. "The agent had a file and asked me to get closer to the bars so we could talk," Carlos explained. "He even offered to get me a chair so I could be more comfortable. He took out the first page from the file, my resume." He noted that they had studied at the same school, though the agent had been a few years ahead. The agent rattled off the names of several teachers and asked Carlos if he remembered them. "He is asking me where I had been," Carlos remembered. "But he already had everything written down." After going through Carlos's time at the university, the DFS interrogator continued reviewing his file, which evidently contained information stretching back to when he joined a leftist movement in 1967. They had been tracking him since then. The file contained photographs and information from a conversation Carlos had with his high school principal after he was brought to the principal's office to talk about whether he was involved in the bombing of the Bolivian embassy in the aftermath of Ché Guevara's assassination. In contrast to the first torturer, the DFS agent knew Marxist terms and could handle a political conversation. The agent was Miguel Nazar Haro.

Nazar Haro was born 1924 in Pánuco, Veracruz, to Lebanese immigrant parents. He was a middle child, with an older sister and younger brother, and grew up in a traditional Catholic household.[9] When he finished high school, his father gave him money to train to be a doctor at UNAM in Mexico City, but soon after, Nazar Haro changed his mind and decided to give law a try. He never received his degree, and at twenty-five he joined the Servicio Secreto because of his interest in investigations. According to his son, Nazar Haro felt he had "found his calling."[10] This special operations group was charged with observing and identifying active members of clandestine, antigovernment organizations that operated at the margins of the law. Nazar Haro left the Servicio Secreto in 1953 and moved to Houston, Texas, because, according to an interview he gave, his family disapproved of him being in law enforcement.[11] But the most likely explanation for his departure is that he went into exile to avoid prosecution after he was implicated by survivors in the killings of several supporters of the opposition presidential candidate Miguel Herníquez Guzmán. The killings took place the day after a heavily contested election, on July 6, 1952, in Mexico City, where many of Henríquez Guzmán's supporters gathered to protest alleged election fraud.[12]

In 1960, after he had returned to Mexico, according to an interview with a colleague of Nazar Haro at the time, he ran into an old colleague from the Servicio Secreto who now worked for the DFS. The colleague regaled him with stories of how much more powerful the DFS was than the Servicio Secreto. The day after the chance meeting, Nazar Haro went to the DFS offices and asked for a meeting with the director, Manuel Rangel Escamilla, to request employment.[13] He passed an aptitude test and entered the DFS as a guard at the agency's headquarters. In 1965, the Secretario de Gobernación and future president, Luis Echeverría Álvarez, sent Nazar Haro to Washington, DC, to study at the International Police Academy (IPA). The IPA was a branch of the Office of Public Safety, which trained police officers throughout Latin America from 1962 to 1974 as part of an initiative sponsored by the recently established US Agency for International Development.[14] Alongside police officers from Argentina and Nicaragua, Nazar Haro spent six months at the IPA, taking courses on counterinsurgency. The intention was that these officers would return to their home countries and train their subordinates.[15] During its existence, the IPA trained over 7,500 senior officers from over seventy countries in counterinsurgency measures.[16] Nazar Haro returned to Mexico secure in the knowledge of the DFS's role in protecting Mexico's national security and armed with the tools to teach others the new counterinsurgency methods.

In 1965, a group of Communist guerrillas battled the military in Ciudad Madera, Chihuahua, in a confrontation that left several dead. In response, DFS director, Fernando Gutiérrez Barrios, ordered Nazar Haro to establish a secret program to eliminate subversive groups such as the one that led the attack in Ciudad Madera.[17] He established the Special Investigations Group C-047 in November 1965, which tracked and infiltrated guerrilla groups.[18] Nazar Haro made Group C-047 a clearinghouse for intelligence threatening to the government and then used that information to orchestrate operations to bring down the guerrillas.[19] As he took the reins of C-047, Nazar Haro's new group had ten agents, five men and five women, dedicated to, in his words, "espionage and counterespionage" with the help of informants.[20] In 1970, newly elected president, Luis Echeverría Álvarez, named Luis de la Barreda, a longtime, experienced agent, to head the DFS, who in turn promoted Nazar Haro to supervise all special operations groups. In this capacity, Nazar Haro broadened the DFS's web of informants and ordered the infiltration of groups in virtually all social sectors. As Laura Castellanos describes in her study of guerrilla movements, Nazar Haro built a formidable surveillance web that tracked, cross-checked, and verified information, thereby giving him the authority to decide which individuals should be processed through legal channels and which should be sent to a clandestine torture center for interrogation.[21]

Nazar Haro did more than build the DFS's network of informants. He also helped professionalize the agency's interrogation techniques, including the use of torture.[22] Evidence suggests that the main way DFS agents learned physical and psychological interrogation techniques was through group apprenticeship. Often under the tutelage of Nazar Haro, agents watched and used a combination—at times haphazard and not carefully regulated—of touch and no-touch forms of torture on detainees. In such settings, Nazar Haro taught agents, in his words, to deploy "fanaticism against fanaticism."[23] A former agent recalled how Nazar Haro would tell DFS agents that "we were truly carrying out our duty[,] . . . that if we died in the battlefield, the institution would take care of our families and avenge our deaths. This gave us assurances and trust, it gave us strength and adrenaline to go into action."[24] According to the DFS agents, LC23S "was dedicated to killing police officers. . . . Guerrilla members were sick with communism."[25] Creating the idea of a sickness among guerrillas and emphasizing the threat LC23S posed to national security created more than the category of subversive; it justified DFS agents' use of torture techniques. So successful was Nazar Haro that President López Portillo named him DFS chief when Javier García Paniagua stepped down in 1978. He headed the agency from 1979 to 1982.

Carlos Salcedo, José Luis Moreno Borbolla, José Arturo Gallejos Najera, and others describe in detail the interplay between the more skilled and lesser skilled torturers.[26] Lazreg discusses the two types of torturers Nazar Haro employed in her study of "depth interrogation," a practice that combined both physical and psychological torture techniques. As the French officers discovered, these techniques proved especially useful in breaking down educated victims of French repression in Algiers.[27] In depth interrogation, the more physical and less psychologically oriented officers used prolonged and sustained bodily pain to weaken individuals, making them more open and vulnerable to the tactics of the more psychologically oriented interrogator. The interplay between the two types of torturers allows for depth interrogation because it "disrupts the organization of thoughts and shocks the mind out of its secrets."[28] The idea was that the choreography between physical and psychological torture made it all the easier to get even the most resistant detainee into a state of heightened vulnerability. In Mexico during the dirty war, the second, more specialized torturer who understood the choreography of depth interrogation tended to be a DFS agent.

The DFS agents that employed depth interrogation techniques included Francisco Quirós Hermosillo, Luis de la Barreda Moreno, Fernando Gutiérrez Barrios, Jesús Miyazahua Álvarez, Miguel Nazar Haro, Manuel Rangel Escamilla, and José Antonio Zorrilla Pérez.[29] Of these, Nazar Haro represents the second type of torturer.[30] He is also one of the few to publicly declare he played such a role.[31] Carlos said that Nazar Haro was both a policeman and a public official. He knew how to behave according to his rank and approached the torture session with a certain "coldness, serenity, and calculation." As Carlos's words show, Nazar Haro was sophisticated enough to devise his own interrogation style. Carlos's description of these sessions, as well as the descriptions of many other interviewees, shows how Nazar Haro approached interrogation as a group activity, where spectacle and designated roles played an important part. Nazar Haro was the protagonist, directing others to inflict harm, either physical or psychological, to break down the individual.

Nazar Haro was a distinctive individual. A former colleague described him as follows: "His physical appearance allowed him to come off as respectable, different from the police, because he was white, had blue eyes, and looked good, spoke well, a well-educated person."[32] As his victims said over and over again, Nazar Haro developed this persona inside and outside the torture chamber. Perhaps the most revealing example of how he deployed this character comes from an account by Lourdes Rodríguez, in which she describes being taken to his office inside the DFS in 1971.

> They took the blindfold off, and it was hard to get my eyes accustomed to seeing again. I see a man's back. A blond man, well dressed, and I think to myself that I'm before the judge. . . . It was a clean space, impeccable, with a decent and well-organized desk and the man is wearing not just any suit but a fine suit. He turns around, and he's not bad-looking, with blue, Mediterranean-type eyes. I ask him, "Are you the judge?," and he doesn't answer. . . . He says, "What do you want?," and I responded with a glass of water. He brings it, and I see that I'm surrounded by a bunch of murder-happy bastards.

Nazar Haro started asking Lourdes questions, and when she did not answer, one of the men came over and started beating her on the head. Lourdes's account is similar to the stories told by other detainees, which suggests that Nazar Haro used this intimidation technique on several occasions. Jesús Vicente Vásquez recalled being taken to Nazar Haro's office and recognizing there was a hierarchy among the men: "One would ask me questions, I would deny it, and those who were standing behind and at my side would hit me. I realized that the well-dressed one sitting behind the desk would give the others orders to hit me."[33] As these and many other accounts show, Nazar Haro looms large in the memories of victims.

Yolanda Isabel Casas Quiroz recalled that she couldn't stand the way Nazar Haro looked at her: "He had a blue-gray stare, very cold, and you'd have to look away." During her session, Yolanda was seated in an office chair with wheels. At first, "they'd use a soft hand, and when they didn't get answers that way, they'd slap and hit you. I flew off the chair. That first punch came from Nazar Haro. The others threatened me and took out their guns, but they wouldn't touch me. The only one who touched me was Nazar Haro." His authority rested on instilling fear in those around him, both his victims and the officers following his orders.

The training that took place in these brutal interrogations shows the interplay between the physical and psychological infliction of pain. Essentially, Nazar Haro developed his own form of "depth interrogation" that he then taught other officers to follow. We see this form of interrogation in many cases. Pablo Cabañas Barrientos, Lucio Cabañas's younger brother, spent time with Nazar Haro after his detention in early 1972. "I just saw him the first night that I was tortured," Pablo remembered. "Nazar Haro was the one who kicked me because there was always a good cop and a bad cop in interrogations." He went on to explain that he had never found a genuinely good one: "They were 'good' because they go lighter on you." Pablo understood that the interrogators agreed beforehand "who was going to be bad and the other is going to say 'leave him alone.'" The "good" interrogator, Pablo went on to explain, would "come to see me and to chat, 'How are you feeling, brother? How's the other one? These bastards are treating you badly, right?'"

Nazar Haro's particular form of depth interrogation drew heavily on humiliation. Near the end of his ten-day ordeal of repeated torture sessions, Carlos was tortured in a new way in his session with Nazar Haro. Instead of immersing him in water and threatening him with drowning, agents shoved his head in a toilet filled with feces to produce total degradation. "You are shit, and you are in the shit." Afterward, they sat him on a chair and told him, "The worst is yet to come, and you are the only one that can save you from it. Give us the names of your contacts in the north." Then they ushered a young woman into the room; she was dressed in a traditional nurse's outfit. They asked her if she was ready, and she responded affirmatively. Nazar Haro asked Carlos if he knew that one of his heroes, Fidel Castro, did not have one of his testicles and that Carlos better give him the names of the contacts in the north. Despite the evident threat, Carlos replied that he did not know any contacts. Carlos remembered Nazar Haro yelling, "Lift him up. Tie him down. Open his legs." As the nurse came toward him with her surgical kit, he said, "*Oralé*. Now we get to immortalize him. We are going to give these assholes some heroes. Fuck him [*Chíngatelo*]!" Carlos felt a cold sensation on his skin, and they removed his testicle. This was his first and last meeting with Nazar Haro. Even though men and women experienced sexual forms of torture differently, they were bound by the fact that they were being violated.[34] Castration, as part of Nazar Haro's sexualized torture techniques, is such an extreme act that it says as much about the torturer as it does about the government condoning it. In this gendered ideology, the subversive is punished by irreparably being stripped of his masculinity, an act that not only inflicts horrific pain but also ensures that he is not able to reproduce.

Inside the torture chamber, as Vicente Ovalle recently wrote, was a state of exception where the victim was "no longer a subject with rights, rather they became a subject lacking all legality to the point where they were made socially unrecognizable."[35] This anonymity further made the torture chamber a space of exception because inside its four walls the rules were different: to destroy an unconventional enemy, the government and its agents could draw on unconventional tactics. What remained after such destruction, through the infliction of physical and psychological pain, was a docile and subservient citizen. This submissive being reminded those present, regardless of their rank or level of experience, that they collectively had the power to punish and remake transgressive citizens in the name of Mexico's national security. In other words, the state of exception meant that officers could participate in extralegal activities—such as torture—without fear of retribution and with the surety that they were entrusted with the nation's security. As a group, then, those who directly or indirectly carried out torture existed in a liminal place, where flexibility characterized the rule of law and allowed them to partake in acts that they would never have done outside this space and state of exception. Legalities could be bent to conform to the needs of those protecting the nation.

A specific form of gender ideology cuts through this form of socialization. With the exception of women victims and women medical personnel who attended to them, those who were present in the torture chamber were men. Taking part in the transgressive act of inflicting pain on others in a clandestine setting gave the illusion that those who were present shared a secret that the public at large was incapable of understanding. At the same time, torturers were assured by their superior officers that such forms of interrogation were for their own protection. This performance was thus predicated on the power and superiority of patriotic men, organized and protected by the immutable hierarchy of their respective government institutions. Torturers were also shielded by their anonymity: they were called by their institutional rank, not their names. Participating in a torture session thus initiated torturers into, and reinforced their membership in, this selective brotherhood of saviors of the nation. The gender ideology at work conferred a form of hypermasculinity born out of inflicting pain on a perceived enemy in secretive spaces.

Socialization by means of torture had a theatrical component: torturers performed their assigned tasks in front of an audience. Officers followed orders, but they also gave orders and ensured that others did as instructed. Torture served a variety of purposes, including extracting information and punishing the victim; but for those who were present, it also made real the dangers posed by faceless insurgents, epitomized by the victim before them, who could be redeemed only by breaking them. The logic of counterinsurgency dictated that the torturer was an exceptional man because only a select few understood the importance of their task and possessed the necessary skills and mental strength to follow through on what was required. This logic dovetailed with the patriarchal inclinations of the brotherhood of torturers. If we think of patriarchy as the ranking of masculinities by a range of criteria that included generation, education, class, ethnicity, and physical prowess, among other factors, the performance of torture brought alive this patriarchal bond in those who participated and helped calm any apprehensions new arrivals might have had. They could not appear squeamish about following orders, nor could they raise questions about their actions before their superiors.

On-the-job training in counterinsurgency interrogation techniques was critical to ensuring obedience to the secrecy required to sustain such practices outside legal frameworks. This group dynamic that was so central to the practice of torture laid the foundations for the counterinsurgency program at large. Torturing bound torturers together, hence the idea of a brotherhood. A policeman who joined the White Brigade discussed how his group's objective was to "locate and capture subversives. . . . We would put the guerrilla member in the car and we'd give him the first warming up [*primera calentada*] to loosen them up. We then had instructions to take them to the DFS by the Monument to the Revolution. Here they did the more formal interrogations, following the orders of a commander and depending on the hierarchy of the detainee; there were times when one of the big chiefs would interrogate, above all Nazar who was a specialist."[36]

The dynamic among officers inside the torture chamber acted as a microcosm of sorts for how these institutions existed in society as a whole. They followed orders, ensuring compliance among those in lower ranks and preserving the sanctity of their respective institutions. Certainly, there may have been tensions between and among individuals, but the DFS— and by extension, the military—was nevertheless sturdy enough to weather internal conflicts. The sturdiness came in part from the rejuvenation every six years with the arrival of a new president and a new administration that adapted to changes, promoted or demoted officials, and corrected for their predecessors' mistakes. It also came from the fact that officials understood the unwritten rules governing the rules and procedures for how to secure promotions and maintain one's place in power. These rules included ensuring tensions and disagreements were kept hidden from the public. For this reason, there is scant evidence of internal conflicts between Nazar Haro and others inside the DFS and the military and between the DFS, the military, and the executive branch. Scholars have documented the everyday practices and internal tensions in the military in earlier periods that may have carried over to the 1970s.[37] Yet the sources for this period give us only fleeting glimpses of discord inside the ranks of the security forces, such as with the removal of a DFS leader and the promotion of another. We are unable to dig further because much of the evidence for this period continues to be heavily redacted or restricted. It is also likely that such conflicts were never documented in written records and that surviving individuals remain steadfast in their silence five decades later. The matter of how the executive branch, not to mention leaders of the various agencies entrusted with state repression, negotiated their differences remains an open question.

THE WHITE BRIGADE VERSUS LC23S

While Nazar Haro's C-047 was the precursor to the White Brigade, the origins of this DFS group can be found in earlier experiments with using special forces to deal with perceived enemies of the government. Mexico has a long history of regional strongmen, including state governors, using *guardias blancas* (white guards) to do their dirty work. These hired henchmen, among whom were moonlighting police officers, retired military, or members of criminal groups, would provide protection, mete out unofficial forms of punishment against political enemies, such as labor organizers, or ensure that constituents followed orders.[38] The guardias blancas operated primarily at the local or regional level; if needed, the federal government turned to its police or military branches of law enforcement to rein in dissent that went beyond their ability or spilled across regions.[39] The role of guardias blancas evolved in the 1960s as state and federal officials confronted growing political threats from insurgent groups, which required the institutionalization of paramilitary and parapolice groups as clandestine special forces. Such groups, often employing a grab bag of counterinsurgency techniques, became increasingly indispensable for political control because of their ability to quickly and discreetly eliminate threats to the status quo without troublesome legal impingements.

To understand what these clandestine special forces looked like on the ground, the following section focuses on three of them: the Batallón Olimpia (Olympic Battalion), the Halcones (Hawks), and the military's Grupo Sangre (Blood Group). By comparing the three groups, we can appreciate what Nazar Haro and the rest of the DFS leadership had in mind when establishing the White Brigade in the mid-1970s to deal with the biggest guerrilla threat the government faced to date. The government created the first of these groups, the Batallón Olimpia, by bringing together specially trained members of the military and police to covertly tackle the emerging threat of student mobilizations in the lead-up to the Olympics in 1968.[40] Members of the battalion infiltrated the leadership circles of the student movement and were present on the ground in the Tlatelolco plaza on the fateful October 2 massacre. In a move that became emblematic of the day, as the massacre began, the infiltrators each put on a single white glove to identify themselves as government agents before helping round up activists and identify the movement's leaders.

When the Batallón Olimpia disbanded in the aftermath of 1968, the Halcones rose up in its place. The Halcones were composed of former members of the military and police forces, as well as thugs for hire, who, in contrast to the Batallón Olimpia, existed outside the bounds of the law. The Halcones were effectively an institutionalized paramilitary gang, whose distance from the government allowed officials to carry out extrajudicial forms of repression with plausible deniability.[41] Officials in Mexico City's government organized the group, which had up to a thousand members, to infiltrate student groups in the city's main universities and act as informants and, when necessary, agitators to justify police action. The Halcones were likewise known for creating chaos and inciting mob violence to justify attacks by government forces on social movements.[42] The Halcones were paid from a variety of city funds and received training in martial arts and firearms at their base at the San Juan de Aragón zoo.

On June 10, 1971, after attempts to provoke the student activists to violence, the Halcones lashed out at student marchers with clubs, bats, guns, and other weapons.[43] No official death toll has been released, but oral histories indicate that the Halcones incited violence first by caning protesters, then shooting them, and then hunting them down as they received medical care in hospitals and beat them in front of terrified medical personnel.[44] It is likely that the massacre left fifty students dead and an unknown number missing. As news of the massacre filtered out, President Echeverría Álvarez ordered the disbanding of the Halcones and fired the mayor and police chief of Mexico City. These acts may have appeared like concessions to surviving student activists, but the depth of the violence was such that large-scale and peaceful student mobilizations would not erupt again until the mid-1980s.

The paramilitary nature of the Halcones reflects the fact that the Mexican government drew on a range of extralegal repressive tools to preserve a veneer of political stability.[45] Some of these extralegal tools of repression fell within the realm of mob violence in the form of public lynchings of alleged criminals.[46] As Gema Kloppe-Santamaría explains, "The endemic corruption that characterized the judicial system, the systemic abuse of force by police, and the high levels of impunity that persisted across this period all contributed to citizens' understanding of lynching as a legitimate form of justice."[47] Given that these practices were normalized at the local level, it stands to reason that such normalization would filter up into the ranks of regional and national institutions of law enforcement. The sanctioning of corruption, abuses of force, and selective enforcement of the law became standard operating procedures for all of these institutions across the mid- to late twentieth century, setting the stage for the rampant impunity and security crisis we see today.

Kloppe-Santamaría, Pablo Piccatto, and Paul Gillingham have shown that violence perpetrated by non-state actors across the mid-twentieth century, such as self-defense groups or mobs, happened parallel to and in combination with violence carried out by state actors. These interconnected forms of violence shored up and gradually centralized coercive control in the government.[48] By the time the government faced the twin threat posed by guerrilla groups and dissatisfied popular groups challenging authoritarian rule in the 1970s, it had managed to accrue enough control over a range of extralegal violent practices to provide some semblance of coordination. The fact that officials could exercise control over these extralegal practices covertly and without clear links to the government made such control more appealing because it allowed deniability. Blame for possible excesses could be placed at the feet of a rowdy mob or a corrupt police officer instead of the institutions behind them. In effect, the state's reliance on covert activity normalized the presence of extralegal violence and the selective application of the rule of law. In the same way that lynchings became a tacitly accepted and, to an extent, expected form of justice by the Mexican public, so did torture and its use at the hands of security forces. Because the extralegal forms of state-sanctioned violence happened covertly, they could easily fold in similar practices emanating from other Cold War theaters, such as Guatemala and Vietnam, where clandestine counterinsurgency tactics were employed. If anything, they appeared eerily similar. Just because this violence was extralegal did not mean that it always remained in the realm of the informal porro (government-paid infiltrator) model. It could also emerge from official institutions that tacitly sanctioned—and benefited from—extralegal forms of violence.

Counterinsurgency warfare by special forces tied directly, like Batallón Olimpia, or indirectly, like the Halcones, to the government thus became part of its de facto playbook for dealing with threats to its political control. In contrast to the Batallón, whose members acted with official sanction and legal protections, the Halcones had no similar shielding. In the aftermath of the Corpus Christi massacre in 1971, journalists published photos of Halcones members who were then recognized by neighbors and family members. At the same time, the fluidity of the Halcones' membership and organizational structure—the mixture of law enforcement and gang-affiliated members; the ambiguity of who gave the orders—allowed government officials to distance themselves from the group's actions, making the Halcones even more useful for tackling perceived threats from popular sectors across time. The Batallón was hampered by legal strictures, but its agents had the protection of the state; the Halcones operated extralegally with ease, but its members were unprotected. These differences allowed government officials to fine-tune their use of special forces depending on the types of political threat they faced.

The Batallón Olimpia and the Halcones give us a sense of the government's evolving approach to subdue popular threats to its power. The third organization, Grupo Sangre, resorted to especially extreme forms of violence.[49] Active in the state of Guerrero, Grupo Sangre emerged after Lucio Cabañas's Party of the Poor kidnapped a PRI gubernatorial candidate in 1974.[50] While the military hunted Cabañas's supporters in the mountains of Guerrero, Grupo Sangre focused its efforts on the city of Acapulco. The group was composed of retired police and military under the command of General Salvador Rangel Medina from the 27/a Military Zone.[51] Grupo Sangre used exceptionally violent torture tactics, including forcing detainees to drink gasoline, setting them on fire, and leaving their charred remains in cemeteries to instill terror in the population. Even after the group was allegedly disbanded in 1976, some of its members continued to work clandestinely at the behest of the state governor and the military commander stationed in Acapulco.[52] At the time, the DFS reported that the majority of individuals detained by Grupo Sangre were subsequently "disappeared."[53] Though it only operated in the state of Guerrero, Grupo Sangre's much more violent and extreme techniques, including disappearances, informed those of the White Brigade.

All three special forces—Batallón Olimpia, the Halcones, and Grupo Sangre—provided Nazar Haro and the DFS leadership with effective techniques as they organized the White Brigade. In the first place, these groups set the precedent for special forces acting as a covert arm of the state when it confronted threats to national security. The Batallón Olimpia proved the efficacy of joint operations and the value of cross-agency collaboration. The Halcones' operations demonstrated the usefulness of employing plausible deniability for all actions and recruiting individuals accustomed to following orders. Last, Grupo Sangre's brutality illustrated that going to extremes served to create an environment of pervasive fear among the perceived enemy and within the population at large. Going into the 1970s, Nazar Haro had examples of other covert groups to draw on when devising the White Brigade. While the White Brigade was not the first group of its kind, Nazar Haro ensured it would certainly be the most professional and determined to meet its goal: the eradication of guerrilla groups in Mexico, especially the Liga 23 de Septiembre.

To make sense of the White Brigade's creation, we need to step back and understand the threat posed by LC23S to the political status quo in the mid-1970s. Doing so demonstrates that law enforcement responses and guerrilla responses were, to a certain extent, organic and mutually constitutive in their escalation. The guerrillas' activities responded to what law enforcement was doing, which drove law enforcement to respond to what the guerrillas were doing, and so on. In essence, the two sides—the government and guerrilla groups—pushed one another to ever more violent extremes. This point is not intended to cast the guerrillas as responsible for their own demise but to recognize the tit-for-tat dynamic whereby whenever one side's tactics became more violent, the other side responded in kind or worse.

LC23S was founded at a meeting of urban and rural guerrilla leaders in Guadalajara in March 1973.[54] According to Jorge Luis Sierra, fourteen groups joined together under the banner of LC23S in the interest of combining their efforts against an increasingly repressive state.[55] These groups included the Movimiento Armado Revolucionario, Los Lacandones, Los Procesos, Los Enfermos, Frente Urbano Zapatista, and the Fuerzas de Liberación Nacional (FLN).[56] The leaders agreed that the armed route was the only option for achieving large-scale social change in Mexico, especially considering that more peaceful tactics had been violently shut down—as evidenced by the 1968 Tlatelolco massacre and the 1971

Corpus Christi massacre. Under the banner of LC23S they would coordi-
nate their efforts across Mexico to motivate class warfare to overthrow the
government from a clandestine position. Originally, the group divided the
country into four regions and established guerrilla groups in both urban
and rural areas. As membership shrank because of attrition, killings, and
disappearances, LC23S adapted a more compartmentalized strategy to
protect itself, meaning the different guerrilla member cells did not know
one another's location or activities.

Due to LC23S's membership base, national reach, and ideological commitment to the destruction of the political order, the government saw it as
a serious threat to national security—a threat that could require the sus-
pension of the rule of law and government oversight. In his unpublished
memoir of the time, Brigadier General Mario Acosta Chaparro expressed
the government's view that LC23S was at the forefront of Mexico's guerrilla movement between 1973 and 1980.[57] As Acosta Chaparro states,
LC23S's activities included producing and distributing propaganda literature, maintaining safe houses for members, and buying weapons and
vehicles. To fund these activities, LC23S turned to "revolutionary expropriations": bank heists, robberies, and kidnappings of wealthy individuals.
As one rationalized, "We don't kill, we deliver justice . . . we don't steal, we
expropriate from the rich what they took from the poor."[58]

The movement paid a hefty price for its tactics. As government officials
made clear, "We do not negotiate with criminals."[59] In late 1973, LC23S
members attempted to kidnap Eugenio Garza Sada, a wealthy Monterrey
businessman and generous contributor to anti-Communist causes.[60] The
ensuing shoot-out left two guerrillas and two of Garza Sada's bodyguards
dead. The DFS retaliated. After two LC23S members were detained in
Mazatlán, Sinaloa, the DFS transported them to CM-1 in Mexico City,
where they died either during interrogation by DFS agents or from injuries sustained during interrogation. This event fueled fractures within the
movement, as members questioned if the organization was capable of
effectively launching an armed revolution. As a result, by the end of 1976,
the group had lost some of its most experienced members, but it had also
gained new, younger ones convinced of the need for direct action. LC23S
then formed an organizing committee called the Brigada Roja (Red
Brigade) to oversee its military strategy against members of the police and

military.[61] The shift in the movement, along with losses in its ranks, meant that LC23S was a more agile organization with members committed to an armed approach to resisting the government.

Adela Cedillo justifiably cautions scholars to be mindful of sensationalizing the violent side of LC23S because of the risk of reifying official propaganda.[62] Nevertheless, violence happened. Between April 1973 and August 1976, LC23S killed members of law enforcement.[63] On May 6, 1976, four members of LC23S killed four police officers and three civilians in the Lindavista neighborhood in Mexico City. Five minutes later, they shot to death two guards in front of the Secretaría de Hacienda (Ministry of Finance).[64] On May 25, LC23S kidnapped the daughter of the Belgian ambassador and demanded ten million pesos. In response, President Echeverría Álvarez issued a statement condemning such actions as those of a group of "fascists intent on destabilizing the government."[65] On June 4, a group from LC23S killed five police officers and injured several more in a weapons raid on a police station in Ecatepec, outside of Mexico City.[66] The DFS report on the incident highlights that the attack was by four men and three women belonging to LC23S. The media's attention to these events spurred fear and paranoia among the population and left law enforcement feeling like they were under siege.[67] The DFS magnified this anxiety by issuing warnings to all law enforcement agencies with instructions not to directly engage with LC23S because it was "dangerous to bother an armed person with an emotional burden that could cause them to explode at any moment."[68] Inside the DFS, agents compiled a list of especially radical LC23S members for fear that "they are determined to commit suicidal acts."[69] The DFS wanted law enforcement to be alarmed by LC23S, nurturing a culture of fear that allowed its agents unfettered access to any and all resources and tactics to take on such a formidable enemy.

The government's experiments with covert special forces happened in an environment riddled with anxiety about subversives hiding in plain sight, and that fear required its agents to resort to even more extreme forms of violence in the name of national security. At the start of the 1970s, there were approximately seven special forces groups from different branches of law enforcement entrusted with tracking down and torturing guerrilla members in Mexico City alone.[70] Groups active in the capital included the DFS's C-047, the second battalion of the military police, and the 6/a Brigade of Special Services of the Division of Investigations for the Prevention of Delinquency, to name just three. Beyond the capital, the number of active special forces groups varied from state to state, because each governor also commanded a local special forces group to hunt, torture, and at times kill guerrillas. Each special forces group had its own leadership structure, its own procedures, and its own need to justify its existence in relation to the other six special forces groups. They did not share information with one another or actively collaborate in operations. The haphazard organizational structure bred a variety of inefficiencies. For instance, the Federal Judicial Police wasted time hunting down guerrilla members who had died while in the military's custody. And instead of handing detainees over to the DFS for interrogation, the military would question them first, compromising follow-up interrogations. The lack of central coordination and clear oversight of the activities of so many groups thus injected chaos into the government's mission to tackle the guerrilla threat. LC23S's direct attacks on members of law enforcement, however, catalyzed a change because none of the existing special forces groups had the ability to take on the perceived threat it posed.

On June 6, 1976, the DFS called a meeting of chiefs of police from all the states and members of the military. Nazar Haro gave them an overview of guerrilla activities and followed it up with a proposal to create a special group of agents to tackle the threat—a group that would gather agents from all over the country under the command of the DFS. This was the beginning of what was originally called the Special Brigade and later the White Brigade: law enforcement's answer to LC23S.[71] The White Brigade brought together specially trained members of law enforcement and the military under the command of the DFS's Nazar Haro and Colonel Francisco Quiróz Hermosillo from the Second Battalion of the Military Police. Prior to his appointment with the Military Police, Quiróz Hermosillo was stationed in the 27/a Military Zone in the state of Guerrero; he had ample experience engaging with guerrilla groups.[72] Harmonizing law enforcement efforts meant harmonizing resources. Nazar Haro and Quiróz Hermosillo also demanded enough political autonomy to ensure that the White Brigade would not be encumbered by any oversight restricting its activities. The Brigade had its own budget and facilities for interrogating detainees and training its members in paramilitary tactics. It had its own fleet of helicopters as well as expert marksmen, both of which played key roles in the disappearance of activists. They had a barracks inside CM-1 that could house eighty members, from which they launched their operations and where they stored their equipment and organized office staff.[73] In addition, the White Brigade used the DFS's headquarters in Roma Norte at Circular Morelia in its operations and employed the building's basement as a clandestine detention center.

The Brigade was originally composed of 240 members drawn primarily from the DFS and judicial police forces from all over Mexico.[74] The majority of the original members had experience in counterinsurgency tactics, including employing torture in interrogations, and came recommended from the various agencies affiliated with the Brigade. Later on, the military recruited new members by sending out calls to law enforcement agencies for additional antiterrorist training. Trainers identified promising recruits and forwarded them to CM-1 for screening. The Brigade had close ties to the military, even using CM-1 for their training in torture techniques of detained prisoners.[75] Its founding documents stipulate a clear ordering of the ranks divided into several sections: interrogation, information and analysis, logistics, and administration. It had eight operative groups of ten specially trained individuals, divided between two vehicles and a motorbike, to carry out the orders of their commanding officer. Its founding documents inventory the weapons at the Brigade's disposal as well as the training its agents received, including how to carry out detentions given the "tactics, aggressiveness, and fanaticism of LC-23S members."[76] The Brigade also had a section called the Specialized Group.[77] It focused on "explosives, communications, and special actions [and had] ... expert marksmen, personnel with psychological training, capable of evicting a hidden terrorist group and with the criteria for protecting civil population."[78] In a mutually constitutive dynamic, the government gathered resources against LC23S and other groups at the same time that LC23S gathered disparate organizations under one umbrella.

The White Brigade represented a modern approach to counterinsurgency forms of detention and torture that took into consideration lessons learned from earlier incarnations of special forces. The group also bore the strong imprint of its leader, Miguel Nazar Haro. A DFS agent described the Brigade as epitomizing Nazar Haro's style: "Everything had to be quick, exact, perfect, without fingerprints. . . . [He formed the Brigade] to get the DFS out of the public's eye and attacks on the agency's anti-subversive struggle . . . to separate this from other DFS activities."[79] In other words, this was intended to be the most elite of elite covert special forces with only the oversight of a small, select group of individuals. Its mission was clear from the start. On June 7, 1976—the day after the White Brigade's creation—Nazar Haro presented a document to DFS leaders titled "Operation Plan Number One Tracking."[80] The plan explained that the guerrilla organization had been ramping up its armed actions and posed a real security threat to the government. In response, the new Brigade would track down and "neutralize" members of LC23S.[81] The plan contained detailed information on the inner workings of LC23S, including its organization in independent command centers throughout the valley of Mexico and its use of clandestine safe houses to avoid detection by the authorities. It also included details on a propaganda campaign designed to turn public opinion against LC23S, such as distributing pamphlets with information on wanted insurgents.[82]

The propaganda campaign even swayed White Brigade members themselves. They saw LC23S as irredeemable terrorists. A former Brigade agent described their mentality as follows:

> We were fighting some bastards willing to do anything. They wanted to take down the government. It was a war and they knew just as we did that in war you have to draw on all available resources. We certainly brought our schooling, each one from our respective organization. The truth is that I don't know a single policeman from anywhere in the world who uses silk gloves when dealing with delinquents. Bottom line: the last thing the detainees inspired was compassion. They told us that we had to be tough, that these were the orders from on high, and we were.[83]

And tough they were. While on patrol on August 7, 1976, in Mexico City, Brigade members came upon a "suspicious individual" who pulled a gun on them when asked for identification. After shooting him six times, they took him to the military hospital, where he died several hours later. It is unclear from the report whether the agents had time to interrogate him, though the attached photograph shows the victim with a number of facial bruises. They found LC23S pamphlets in his bag, corroborating their suspicions that he was a guerrilla member.[84] Brigade members effectively acted with complete impunity, including a license to kill.

The propaganda also filtered into the ranks of guerrilla groups, where the White Brigade held a particular mystique. LC23S members, for example, were acutely aware of the single-mindedness among Brigade members to hunt them down. As part of his work as an LC23S member, Jaime Laguna Berber had infiltrated a metalworks organization in Mexico City in 1978. He had to be assiduously careful in his clandestine work because the factory was "like a police zone." At any moment, according to Jaime, he could be picked up by the White Brigade, tortured, and disappeared. In his mind, the White Brigade had "something like seven thousand members doing intelligence work, looking over the workers one by one, case by case. That's the price you pay if you want to grab one of the Liga. You have no idea of the rage they feel. They want to grab and kill you, no matter the cost. They're going to search you out, detain you, disappear you, that's it." For Liga members evading counterinsurgency forces, the White Brigade felt ever present and seemed ten times bigger than it actually was. This was a war, after all, and both sides had to be willing to respond in kind to both survive and achieve victory. This mutual awareness of what extremes the other side was willing to go to mirrored the fear endemic during this period.

The White Brigade and LC23S, along with other special forces and guerrilla groups, fought an unconventional war that fed off fear and uncertainty. In this dynamic, special forces groups inhabited a liminal space that placed the government's agents above the law and above reproach. The threat the guerrillas posed to Mexico was real, according to Nazar Haro in a 2003 interview: "These were organizations that put bombs in Gobernación [Ministry of Interior], in the Confederación de Trabajadores de México [Workers Confederation of Mexico], in Televisa, in the PRI, in different delegations. They wanted other countries to know that the student movement was a revolution in Mexico."[85]

CONCLUSION: THE LAST DOOR

Nazar Haro stepped down from his post in January 1982 because he had fallen out of favor with the incoming administration of President Miguel de la Madrid. Beginning in March 1982, an undercover FBI operation revealed that Nazar Haro was involved in the theft of hundreds of cars in California and their transfer to Mexico for sale. Soon after, an article in the news magazine *Proceso* accused Nazar Haro of receiving thousands of dollars from the CIA to make the DFS an ancillary of the US intelligence service.[86] According to the chief federal prosecutor in San Diego, California, William Kennedy, the CIA interceded on Nazar Haro's behalf to prevent his indictment, calling him "their most important source in Central America and Mexico."[87] In a follow-up interview with *Proceso*, Nazar Haro denied any connection to the CIA, the White Brigade, or the theft of cars. Despite evidence to the contrary, he went on to say that any action he took was "to protect my country's security. . . . I was always fighting for Mexico, the best country of all."[88]

After avoiding prosecution in the United States, Nazar Haro set up a private consulting firm to offer his services to the private sector. Not only did he investigate on behalf of his clients, but he also interceded in meetings with government officials. The world Nazar Haro knew started crumbling with the election of Vicente Fox in 2000 and the new administration's promise to shed light on what had taken place in 1968 and beyond. "After being the winner," Nazar Haro declared in 2003, "I'm defeated in the sunset of my life."[89] In February 2004, the FEMOSPP ordered his arrest for his involvement in the detention and disappearance of two LC23S leaders, Ignacio Arturo Salas Obregón and Jesús Piedra Ibarra. This was the first arrest of anyone implicated in Mexico's dirty war during the 1960s and 1970s and was met with high expectations that more arrests would follow.[90] Nazar Haro was sent to the Topo Chico prison but was subsequently transferred to a hospital because of health issues related to his age. Despite his legal troubles and failing health, he continued to defend his participation in the DFS, telling one reporter in 2005 that he took great pride in having been part of the agency: "[It is] the act in my life that I am the most proud of. . . . This country is worthy of defending it even with one's life."[91] During the Cold War, according to

Nazar Haro, the Soviets tried to "infiltrate, brainwash young people to disrupt their countries of origin."[92] Later that year, he was placed under house arrest; he was freed in May 2006. No official was ever prosecuted by the FEMOSSP before it was disbanded in 2007. Nazar Haro died in 2012 without ever having to answer for what he did.

In his interview, Carlos Salcedo used the phrase "the last door" to describe the sensation of crossing the mental threshold of intolerable pain, the type of pain that annihilates the sense of self and forever destroys a person. That metaphor of the last door can be applied to understanding why a state tortures and what happens when officials cross the threshold to inflict the type of pain Carlos described. The last door then requires us to name the torturers. And the list of torturers is long.

Among the evidence produced by the state of Guerrero's Truth Commission, there is a fifty-eight-page appendix that lists the names of 332 individuals.[93] The document contains the alphabetized names of all the military and police personnel involved in the detention, torture, killing, and disappearance of alleged subversives in Guerrero in the 1970s. Besides their name and rank, the list gives a concise description of the individual's actions during the dirty war. The descriptions are footnoted with archival documents drawn from the declassified government files of the DFS, SEDENA, and other agencies. Some descriptions are brief either because of the individual's rank or because of the lack of evidence. Juan García Nájera was an infantry lieutenant active in Ometepec, Guerrero. Alfredo Celis Gutiérrez was a DFS agent based in Guerrero in 1974, but we have no information other than the fact that he was involved, according to the DFS document, in "police-military operations."[94]

Several pages of the Guerrero Truth Commission report are devoted to Mario Arturo Acosta Chaparro, a brigadier general and head of the state's judicial police, responsible for some of the most gruesome human rights abuses at the time in the state of Guerrero, including mass killings and disappearances. This is the same Acosta Chaparro mentioned earlier in this chapter who, in 1990, wrote a long memoir for distribution to the armed forces in which he detailed his view of the "subversives."[95] His memoir lists the names of individuals who allegedly belonged to guerrilla groups, including LC23S, and he concludes that government forces virtually "exterminated" them. Ironically, Acosta Chaparro's name is featured in a list compiled in the name of those he helped destroy.

Interviewees for this book mentioned Acosta Chaparro and others like him in Guerrero. Patricio Abarca Martínez, a former activist, first got to know the voices of the torturers and could later physically identify them at the clandestine prison in Acapulco known as the Railroad.

> There were the famous brothers Bruno and Ramon, the Tarín, those were the ones who beat us up. They were tall and weighed more than 100 kilos. And then there were the ones who gave the orders. Captain Aguirre, Acosta Chaparro, Mendiola. The boss of all of them was Acosta Chaparro. There are no good ones there. All of them are bad. Even if one of them pretended to be nice, we wouldn't have believed them.

Acosta Chaparro, along with Gustavo Tarín Chávez, Francisco Quiroz Hermosillo, and others from the intelligence unit of the military police detained approximately fifteen hundred people in Guerrero.[96] These people were questioned and, more often than not, brutally tortured. When the officers decided they were done interrogating them, the officers sat these people down on what the officers called the "bench of the accused." The seated individuals thought they were going to be photographed. Instead, they were shot in the back of the head. Their bodies were put in sacks weighted with rocks, then loaded on a plane and flown out to be disposed of in the Pacific Ocean.

Some of the 332 officers in the pages of the Truth Commission report were also active in other places in Mexico or had a national presence. These include Javier García Paniagua, who led the DFS from 1977 to 1978 and oversaw Nazar Haro and the White Brigade. García Paniagua was the son of General Marcelino García Barragán, who led SEDENA from 1964 to 1970, during the defense ministry's active incursions in the state of Guerrero and its role in the 1968 massacre of students in Tlatelolco, Mexico City. After leaving the DFS, García Paniagua went on to have an illustrious career in the federal government as a member of the PRI's political elite, until his death in 1998. While it is daunting to read the 332 names and the descriptions of their actions, we are left to speculate what similar lists of military and police officers active elsewhere in Mexico would look like, how much overlap there would be, and if there was a pattern in how the military and police mobilized across the country. Chihuahua, Oaxaca, Mexico, Sinaloa, Sonora, Puebla, and other states could have similar lists if there were an effective truth commission that could name the torturers. This then is also part of closing the last door: giving names to those who tortured.

4 The Making of the Political Prisoner

Once their initial detention and torture was over, most detainees were sent to prison. After two weeks in Campo Militar-1, Elia Hernández Hernández was transferred first to Lecumberri to be sentenced in a trial and then moved to Santa Marta, the women's prison, to serve her time. She laughed when describing how crazy she and other newly arrived political prisoners looked in their oversized uniforms, their hair unkempt, and shocked that they were still alive. As time went on, Elia's family was allowed to visit her on a weekly basis. Prison was nothing, according to Elia. "We expected worse conditions or even death. Prison was the least of our worries." The transition from short-term detention to prison, Elia explained, was joyous because she was still alive. José Luis Esparza believes his life was saved when he was sent to prison. In his mind, entering the prison's doors and going through the routine of admission meant that he was allowed to live, that there was an official record that proved he had not died. Like Elia, José Luis experienced political imprisonment as a relief; it meant that he would eventually find his way back to the public sphere, where even if he was mistreated, he was alive and accounted for.

Though both Elia and José Luis expressed relief when they entered the prison's gates, it was not liberation. There was still uncertainty about what was to come; neither of them knew how long they would remain political prisoners. What they did know was that as political prisoners, they had a greater probability of making it out alive. The government had finished interrogating them, and officials had determined they no longer served an immediate purpose. Instead, detainees were being held to prolong, and to an extent officialize, their punishment because the government decreed that they had broken laws. Those who were transferred to formal prisons entered a kind of public sphere and were now visible to society. Other prisoners, prison personnel, and their families knew of their existence, even if they served as a cautionary tale of what could happen if one was suspected of posing a threat to the political status quo. This visibility conferred on them a new identity beyond that of subversive: political prisoner.

Yolanda Isabel Casas Quiroz described how, after spending four days being interrogated, the transfer to the Santa Marta women's prison felt like "having a sensation of being alive, of liberation. I felt completely free as we were being transported to prison." They crowded her into a cell with eighteen other women political prisoners; prison authorities would not let political detainees mingle with regular prisoners. Lourdes Quiñones joined Yolanda soon after, and they rekindled a friendship that began when both were members of Los Lacandones. Lourdes and Yolanda both recalled that there were women political prisoners from various guerrilla groups: LC23S, MAR, the Unión de Pueblo, and others. Lourdes remembered with fondness the community of women who nurtured her in prison. They set up a sewing collective and kept studying Marxism as part of their daily routine.

The first part of this chapter explores what it was like for detainees as they navigated the transition to political prisoner. Inherent in the process was coming to terms with the contradiction that there was a kind of freedom being out of the torture chamber, but it was illusory since they were still imprisoned. The discussion undertakes a deeper analysis of the differences between clandestine prisons and more formal institutions, including the government's penitentiaries, to argue for greater nuances in what it meant to be a political prisoner. Clandestine prisons, for example, allowed the government to covertly hold detainees for longer periods before releasing them to the public sphere of a formal prison where their existence was officially acknowledged. The individual no longer served an immediate purpose, but government agents had not yet determined what to do with them. As the next chapter shows, this was especially the case when security forces detained family members who had to remain in clandestine limbo to avoid questions of illegal imprisonment. In contrast to clandestine prisons that had limited space, formal prisons had the facilities to house many more detainees for much longer stretches of time. Formal prisons, as interviewees related, afforded government agents new sites of surveillance: undercover agents infiltrated the cell blocks or informants or guards monitored activities and visitors.

The chapter makes the case that the category of political prisoner left an indelible mark on individuals and, by extension, their loved ones. Much like the act of torture left visible or invisible scars on the body and mind of its victims, imprisonment did as well. As political prisoners, individuals lost years of their lives, away from their loved ones, communities, and careers. The conditions of the prisons themselves—inadequate food, exposure to the elements, lack of access to medical care—took a toll on their bodies. They bore the public stigma of the government announcing that they were criminals. They also shouldered the responsibility of sharing the experience of being a political prisoner with their families. Their loved ones, often as a part of or supported by civil and religious organizations, sought them out through the maze of prisons scattered across Mexico, demanding access to them, respect for their human rights, and their release. In many cases, as this and the next two chapters show, victims lingered in a nebulous prison of memories tinged with pain, regret, violation, and frustration over the lack of government accountability.

.   .   .   .   .

As Richard spoke, I jotted the names and locations of the clandestine torture centers used during the 1970s in Guadalajara on the large square of paper covering the table. He described the spaces from his own memory or from what his comrades had told him. He spoke in a low, crisp voice as he gave me the details, back erect, warming up to me as we added lines on the memory map of torture centers on the paper before us. Our conversation veered in tangents and returned to previous thoughts over the course of hours. At the end of the afternoon, my jottings looked like a large cobweb with lines connecting thoughts, rough maps, scratched-off street names as he corrected my spelling, and underlined points. The waitress jokingly referred to the table as the "office" while she refilled our cups.

When Richard first sat down, he immediately launched into what was done to him the first time he had been picked up by the *golpeadores* (thugs). He rattled off the atrocities: a wound on the back of his head, cigarette marks on his abdomen, broken bones, a word carved on his back with a knife, internal injuries. They dumped his body in a gully, more than likely thinking he would die there, but two American tourists came upon him. He recalled that one of them had a camera dangling from his neck. They helped him out of the ditch and flagged down a car to take him to the hospital. He woke up seven days later to find his father next to him. Richard had no memory of those seven days. He recalled looking up at the Americans, and the next thing he knew, his father was next to him. I wanted to ask what word they had carved on his back, but I held back, waiting for him to tell me. He never did.

As he warmed up to me, he began to pull mementos out of the plastic bag he carried. One by one, he would retrieve the item and tell me what each represented: mimeographed pamphlets he helped distribute at the schools; a photograph of his friends and their families celebrating at a dinner table after their release from prison in 1980; a photograph of one of his comrades killed by the police that he had displayed at the Day of the Dead altar that the municipality had set up the previous year. He had a stack of certificates he had made up to commemorate each one of his fallen comrades. Each contained a photo of the deceased, the date and location of their death, and a statement thanking them for their sacrifice. Richard would give them to the surviving family members to let them know that the dead had not been forgotten. The photos that remained in his plastic bag are of those whose families he had been unable to locate. He also showed me a list of about fifty names of fallen comrades, mostly men but some women, with the date and circumstances of their death. The last column showed how they had died, the majority either killed in battle or disappeared. He explained that he wanted to continue compiling the list because there were still so many that he had not yet put on it. He estimated it would be in the hundreds by the time he was done. I asked him what he thought the list would look like if he added the names of the tortured to it. He paused and said he had not thought of that. He then answered, "There would be thousands of names on that list. All of us who stayed behind were tortured. Everybody was tortured."

I wanted to know if "everybody" included him and his comrades' family members. I asked if his family knew what happened to him when he was detained and later imprisoned. His father and wife knew but no one else. His mother chose not to ask questions, and he had never told his three children, who were now adults with children of their own. One of his granddaughters had begun asking him questions about his past, and I mentioned that she might be interested to hear what he had done in his youth. He smiled and replied that maybe he would tell her one day when she was older. When I gently inquired why he was not more open about his past, he replied that he did not want to cause his family pain knowing that he had been tortured. He repeated that he did not want to hurt them. Richard's reluctance to disclose what happened to him to his loved ones signaled that he lingered in a prison of his own memory. This one might not have walls or a warden, but it still enclosed him. It became clear why: guilt and shame. I asked if anything had happened to his parents when he was a guerrilla member in the 1970s. He nodded. "They put my mother and father in Campo Militar-1 and sent word that they would only release them if I turned myself in. They tortured my father. They released them after two months." I asked if he ever considered turning himself in when this happened. He shook his head. "They did this to all our families. All our parents. I knew they would eventually be released." Memories of being a political prisoner as well as a torture victim create a tension in Richard's personal history. He wants his activism—and that of his comrades—to be remembered. Yet he is ambivalent about how to remember the price he and his loved ones paid for it.

When I asked him to tell me about the clandestine torture centers—the ones he insisted were anything but clandestine in Guadalajara during the 1970s—Richard began with what he considered the most important of these torture centers: La Mojonera. The military used this facility, located inside the Colegio del Aire, to carry out their interrogations. Only the military used La Mojonera. He then rattled off several locations used by the judicial police: a building on Avenida Unión, another on Calle Tolsá and Libertad (also used by the state prosecutor's office), the municipal police force building located near Periférico in the Colonia Santa Cecilia, and the building that today is the Centro de Prevención on the corner of La Calzada and Olímpia. Because they counted on cross-agency collaboration, DFS agents moved between the judicial police and the military but had their own building on Calle Francia in downtown Guadalajara where they tortured detainees. When I mentioned that I knew that houses in middle-class neighborhoods had also been used as clandestine torture centers, he explained that this was routinely done by the judicial police and the DFS.

Of these clandestine prisons, CM-1 in Mexico City was the most widely recognized center for torture of detainees. In September 1961, the minister of interior, Gustavo Díaz Ordaz, mandated the creation of a special prison on CM-1's grounds to exclusively house political prisoners.[1] According to its original mandate, CM-1 would be run by the military, not, the mandate noted specifically, by bureaucrats ignorant of the threat political prisoners posed.[2] The government entrusted the Second Battalion of the Military Police to administer CM-1's clandestine operations, including its cell block and torture chambers. CM-1 acted as a clearinghouse for sending prisoners to clandestine prisons, to and from other designated locales, and its own facilities. In these sites, the prisoners were interrogated according to certain procedures. Soldiers first took Pablo Cabañas Barrientos, Lucio's younger brother, to a clandestine prison in Sonora. "It was a school with many classrooms filled with desks." From Sonora, they transported him to Mexico City on a plane, tied up and hooded, with other prisoners. Once they landed, he was taken to CM-1, where he spent ten days. He was put in a small dark room. He had no blanket, and it was January, so Pablo remembered being very cold. "You could hear the screams ... that was a place of torture." Thus prisoners—and it bears repeating that these were individuals the government labeled subversive and imprisoned without due process—usually spent short stints at CM-1, weeks to months, before they were released, disappeared, or relocated to a traditional prison.

There were other clandestine detention centers in addition to CM-1. The basement of the DFS building had cells exclusively for political prisoners. The barracks of Mexico City's mounted police squad in the Tlatelolco public housing project was also at the disposal of the DFS and the city's secret service. Both José Luis Moreno Borbolla and Carlos Salcedo spent time there after they were picked up—Carlos in 1972 and José Luis in 1975. Carlos remembered that the prison in the barracks had an office, a yard, and two hallways with cells facing each other, for a total of twenty cells. José Luis recalled that it was nicknamed the "train" because the cells were small and lined up one after the other. Clandestine prisons sometimes doubled as torture centers. At the mounted police squad's Tlatelolco barracks, officers would dunk prisoners in the horses' drinking troughs, simulating drowning. They would put blindfolded prisoners into stalls with the horses while they were eating and threaten that the animals would bite them. Detentions at the horse barracks or the DFS basement tended to be short—a matter of days at most—because they did not have the capacity for longer stays, unlike CM-1 or a formal penitentiary.

Vicente Ovalle has compiled perhaps the most comprehensive list of clandestine detention centers for five of the thirty-two states in Mexico based on his work with the SEDENA, DFS, and DGIPS document collections.[3] He identified, for example, five centers in Mexico City and six in the state of Guerrero. While he goes on to list those for Oaxaca, Sinaloa, and Nuevo León, lists for other states that saw dirty war activity, including Jalisco, Chihuahua, and Veracruz, do not yet exist. He also cites which branches of law enforcement were responsible for a given center. The DFS appears in virtually every instance and is paired with the military or police forces, illustrating the cross-agency collaboration at work. Fully identifying all clandestine detention centers is still in progress.

From the clandestine center, officials took political prisoners to formal prison installations throughout the country. DFS files from the 1970s contain lists of names of "subversives" incarcerated for their political activities.[4] The numbers varied across the decade, as arrests increased and as officials relocated prisoners from one facility to another to prevent them from organizing.[5] Although most prisoners were housed in the Lecumberri penitentiary in Mexico City, groups of them were scattered in other state penitentiaries.[6] Of the sixteen political prisoners in the Sonora penitentiary, several—including four women—belonged to LC23S and were serving terms ranging from nine to thirty years for their guerrilla activities.[7] In addition to Lecumberri, Oblatos, and Topo Chico, political prisoners were incarcerated in the Reclusorio Oriente in Mexico City, Islas Marias Federal

Penal Colony off the coast of Nayarit, and Santa Martha Acatitla in the state of Mexico. Though there was some crossover, according to José Luis, officials tended to segregate political prisoners from what they referred to as "presos comunes" (common prisoners) by keeping them in separate cell blocks. José Luis remembered that in Lecumberri, political prisoners occupied the M, J, and O blocks. A DFS report from 1969 gave a more precise breakdown: of more than 3,000 inmates at Lecumberri, 334 were political prisoners, most of whom were housed in the C and M blocks.[8] The wings reserved for political prisoners were further divided depending on the kind of activity the person had been involved in. For example, activists belonging to the 1968 student movement were housed exclusively in the M block. Each cell contained at least two prisoners, though some housed up to five or six.

Álvaro Mario Cartagena López, "El Guaymas," described the layout of the Oblatos penitentiary in Guadalajara while drawing it on a piece of paper. "It had three streets, a football field, and the different pavilions that housed the prisoners. Here are the round stairs that connected the floors, ten cells above and ten cells below." Members of the FRAP were housed upstairs, while members from the LC23S were placed downstairs to avoid ideological conflicts. Rats periodically invaded the lower level, while the upper level was colder at night. El Guaymas pointed to a patio where the prisoners had painted a large mural with the image of Ché Guevara. We got a sense of how large the compound is as he outlined the location of the basketball court, the baseball field, the small restaurants, and the movie theater. He described the cell blocks where the political prisoners lived, how they were not allowed to mingle with other prisoners, and how they would share a meal with their families when they came to visit and go to the prison yard to watch a play the prisoners had put together for the entertainment of their visitors. He recalled that the prisoners always sang to their families and even put together a small musical group called Los Madera. He talked about the food stands and other small shops, such as shoe repair workshops, prisoners ran thanks to concessions from the warden.

El Guaymas then described El Corral, a space inside Oblatos. It was originally an open hall used to butcher cattle brought over from the slaughterhouse for the prison kitchen, but by the time he was imprisoned there, it had been retrofitted with cells and was where misbehaving prisoners were sent for punishment. "There were ten cells above and ten cells below. The conditions were really bad. The cells were disgusting because they never cleaned them as part of the punishment. It was like the jail inside the jail." After an escape attempt, the political prisoners were housed in El Corral for a few months while prison officials fixed their cell block. El Guaymas vividly remembers the fetid smell of El Corral. "Our families would visit us and complain how bad we all smelled. We'd bathe and change our clothes outside our cells because everything stank. There was so little air in there."

While housed in El Corral, the political prisoners met other prisoners who were there for misbehavior or mental illness. These were not the type of prisoners El Guaymas or others tried to recruit to their political cause. "Imagine the type of badasses that were there. They were the type of lumpen that would fuck you up if you tried to talk politics." El Guaymas went on to explain what he meant by "type of lumpen," drawing on his knowledge of Marxism's critique of the unthinking masses. "The type of guy, ignorant, no school, that likes to screw up, to do drugs. The only thing to do with them was to make sure they are your allies when we got in a fight, even if it wasn't in politics. Thanks to the lumpens, they didn't kill as many comrades." He went on to explain that several of the political prisoners were "sort of lumpens" themselves since they came from the San Andrés neighborhood. They were the ones who negotiated on behalf of the political prisoners with the "lumpens," and El Guaymas laughingly recalled how they spread the rumor that he had killed many police officers to earn their respect.

Prisons were key sites of surveillance by state agents because they allowed for the infiltration of guerrilla groups and the interception of information from comrades on the outside.[9] Sergio Aguayo told of the case of Alicia Valdez Rodríguez, wife of Pedro Cassian Olvera, a guerrilla member imprisoned in Oblatos. She acted as a go-between for messages from those inside the prison to comrades on the outside. After detaining and torturing her, DFS agents raided the guerrilla safe house where Rubén Mayoral, another guerrilla member, was hiding out. In the ensuing gunfight, Rubén shot and injured one of the DFS agents before evading capture. In retaliation, agents took his seventy-year-old father prisoner and subsequently disappeared him.[10] In another case, officials arrested an individual because he paid daily visits in 1974 to a political prisoner at the penitentiary in Monterrey, Nuevo Laredo.[11] After "interrogating" him, they concluded he had been the messenger between the political prisoners and guerrilla members orchestrating a prison escape. One especially devastating letter, intercepted by prison officials as it was being thrown over the prison wall in February 1974, reveals the dawning awareness among political prisoners that they were being disappeared. Political prisoners at the Acapulco penitentiary wrote that at 2:00 a.m. officials came into one of the cells and hauled away two of their comrades. The prisoners begged whoever retrieved the letter to take action to locate them.[12] Prisoners such as those in Guerrero expressed anxiety at the fragmented knowledge that their comrades were being disappeared, thereby undermining the sense of relief that a formal prison guaranteed they would make it out alive.

The cases of Adolfo Godoy Cabañas and Bertoldo Cabañas Ocampo are emblematic of the experiences of many political prisoners. When asked what the clandestine prison at the Pie de la Cuesta military air base was like, Adolfo explained that it had small rooms, each holding a few prisoners and with no beds. The guards stood outside, and nobody talked for fear they would be taken away and beaten. For interrogations they were taken next to the ocean, to a "type of shack, where there was a table with about thirty military members and judicial police officers. We were interrogated by the judicial police." After a week at Pie de la Cuesta, Adolfo and his brother were transferred to CM-1. Adolfo knew he had arrived at a military base because when he got off the back of the truck, the judicial officers handed him over to military men. "We each had a little room with a small slat window covered with paper. After they put me in there, I pulled the paper away and there was a wall about five meters in height. On top, about every fifteen to twenty meters, there was a post with guards carrying rifles. From there, every half hour, I could hear 'one, two' when they rotated." Through the little window, "I could see that they would regularly take out the dead, and at night I could see that they were torturing them." There was always a "lot of noise, screams, moans," but it was the "screams that kept us nervous."

The anxiety of what was happening, who could be trusted, and how to communicate hovered over all interactions in a clandestine prison. At

CM-1's cell block, as several interviewees explained, prisoners improvised a system of communication using the thread from their mattresses and pieces of newspaper used in the toilet to relay messages. Through the slit of a window, Adolfo would whisper to the other prisoners, including a doctor, a woman, and Genaro Vázquez's father. There were six cells on each side of the hallway. Adolfo was not sure who the woman was and described her as fair-skinned and slight and thought she might have been the wife of one of Genaro Vázquez's supporters. One time, a guard forgot to lock his door, so Adolfo peeked out and saw the woman talking to the other prisoners. He did not know who she was and why she was here, which heightened his overall anxiety about what was going on.

Finding ways to communicate helped break up the routine of imprisonment. Bertoldo Cabañas Ocampo remembered that the bed in his cell was made of cement. Like Adolfo, he would use the slit of a window to communicate with his brother, Luis Cabañas Ocampo, who was in a cell up the row from his. Prison guards figured out that they were using the window to talk and ordered it sealed shut with black paint, making the cell even darker than it already was. Bertoldo remembered that he and his fellow prisoners "would spend all day sleeping, thinking about our families. We would eat, take showers in cold water." He was at CM-1 for five months during his first detention and three months during his second detention, and after some time, the guards would let Bertoldo outside for an hour to play basketball with fellow detainees.

Even though political prisoners were no longer the victims of counterinsurgent forms of interrogation, they could still be the victims of violence. José Luis Moreno Borbolla alluded to everyday forms of brutal violence inside prison walls. While he was in prison, there were two escape attempts that led to a security crackdown. Beatings at the hands of prison gangs were common. While most gangs were made up of common prisoners, several included political prisoners who had crossed over to delinquency and become criminals. They would pounce on weaker prisoners to take food and other goods. But for José Luis, official violence stood out more, and political imprisonment played a role in spreading the word about the torture they endured. In other words, political prisoners disseminated information that law enforcement routinely used torture as a de facto police tactic. He said, "Police used torture to determine the truth, and they didn't only use it against political prisoners; it was a tradition of the Mexican police to use torture. It was popular knowledge that in the hands of the police you could be tortured." When pressed on how it was common knowledge, José Luis said that prisoners sent word to those on the outside about what they suffered. Archival documents support José Luis's assertion. In July 1969, Lecumberri political prisoners handed out pamphlets decrying their torture and asking for an end to their degrading treatment.[13] José Luis went on to explain: "The more you became involved, the more likely it was that you could be detained, that you could die in battle or while being tortured, which is what we thought had happened to many comrades since we still didn't know that people were being disappeared." José Luis's statement reflects the common sense surrounding torture: it had a long history as a law enforcement tactic in Mexico. The type of torture might not be akin to what Miguel Nazar Haro supervised, but it was a routine reality of being imprisoned there.

PRISON WITH SOME FORM OF FREEDOM

While the possibility of violence was an everyday reality for political prisoners, they also carved out a tolerable existence within the confines of the prison walls. They found degrees of freedom as they grew to know the routines and understand the unspoken rules of life in a given institution. Jaime Laguna Berber and his fellow political prisoners were eventually placed in the general population at the Santa Martha de Acatitla penitentiary. Jaime told me:

> You know that scene in the first *Star Wars* movie, where they go into a bar with all sorts of personalities? That's what Santa Martha's Dormitory Two was like. It was like Las Vegas. Imagine a fancy green rug with three billiard tables, three pool tables, and the counters up against the walls. The card tables were over there for seven eleven, twenty one, and other games. There were also taco stands, here are the ones for el pastor, there are the torta sandwiches. Marijuana and alcohol were allowed. The only thing not allowed was to show off in front of the guards. You're at the bar, you're in Vegas, you're there drinking your Cubana [rum and coke], you're betting, playing, and if you're a frequent customer you get a two for one.

At other prisons, Jaime's fellow inmates might have been imprisoned for a year or two, but at Santa Martha it was different. "You'd ask how many years they had been there, and they'd reply, 'Well, I've been here twenty' or 'I've been here forty.' And how many do you have left? 'I have a sentence of 120 years.' It's a different time dimension." Jaime summed up by saying that Santa Martha "had a heavy atmosphere because anybody could kill you." These were after all hardened criminals who required care when cohabiting in close quarters. The ever present latent and arbitrary violence had long-term effects on political prisoners, but they adapted to it in the short term. Interviewees repeatedly described the physical discomfort of being imprisoned and highlighted the oppressive everyday conditions. Sleeping conditions in the dormitories left a lot to be desired. According to Jaime, "You'd have fifteen to twenty guys sleeping in a cell. Elbow to elbow, ass to ass. You have to deal with it." He also remembered living with bed bugs. "You have to learn how to tolerate them because they are always there. It's not like you can fight with a bed bug." Insect infestations, overcrowding, filth, and disgusting food were all hallmarks of prison life that individuals learned to maneuver.

As they adapted, political prisoners established temporary alliances and forged communities to make their existence tolerable. The arrival of a new political prisoner was met with questions from fellow prisoners asking what books they read to determine their level of education and what group they belonged to in order to see with whom they would socialize. In doing so, political prisoners assessed one another's political commitments and trustworthiness based on a particular set of criteria. As José Luis described it, "Prison was like a micro-society; the individual didn't matter, it was the group that mattered." Each group had its own routine and rules. Those prisoners belonging to the Movimiento de Acción Revolucionaria were among the most regimented.[14] They had every day planned, from the moment they woke up until they went to bed, with activities such as study groups, workshops, and exercise sessions. José Luis discussed how being a political prisoner was like "going to school," even when the prisoners belonged to parties less strict than the MAR. He and his comrades edited a magazine, wrote poetry, ran workshops, and read vast numbers of books on a range of topics. Prison "made me more disciplined, organized. I started cooking," he said. This educational aspect of incarceration extended throughout the country's penitentiaries. In a raid of political prisoners' cells in September 1975, Acapulco penitentiary officers listed confiscated contraband that included marijuana and "ideologically leftist books and writings," such as *Who Is Lucio Cabañas* by José Natividad Rosales and *On War* by Karl Von Clausewitz.[15] In addition to the contraband, prison officials listed the titles of educational workshops offered by political prisoners, which included sessions on philosophy, political economy, and military theory and tactics.[16]

Upon arrival at Lecumberri in Mexico City, as José Luis described, prisoners also learned how officials inside the prison administered it. They would be assigned menial jobs and housed in crowded cells. These uncomfortable conditions gradually allowed prisoners to understand how bribes worked.[17] José Luis explained that "everything in prison could be bought. Whatever you wanted: a cell, bed, women, wine, drugs." In one especially revealing example, the DFS investigated the directors of the Ciudad Juárez penitentiary for taking pay-offs of 30,000 pesos a week to host "nocturnal trips to bars and brothels of the city" for prisoners, including several political prisoners who could afford the fee.[18] In Lecumberri, prison meals— *rancho* (mess)—tended to be just on the verge of rotten, but prisoners who had enough money could have their meals delivered from area restaurants. El Guaymas remembered that prison food at Oblatos was terrible. "They were cooking for three thousand people, so imagine how bad it was. No hygiene. It was bean, atole, something like chicken soup but with bones, mostly bread with beans." El Guaymas was fortunate enough to never have to eat rancho because his mother would bring him food every day. She always made sure to bring enough for him to share with several others.

In Lecumberri, some cell blocks could cook their own food and had access to kitchens. "You paid for your meals, you paid for your cell, because if you didn't pay for the cell, you lived in a barracks. They charged you to keep a television, a radio, a typewriter." One of his comrades either refused or could not pay. The guards put him in the common barracks, nicknamed *la cebollita* (the little onion), where he slept with about sixty other prisoners. They took away his shoes, and when his feet became infected with blood and pus from walking barefoot, they refused to take him to the infirmary. José Luis concluded that "Lecumberri was one big business."[19]

Prisoners could call their families once a week. Family and friends could visit on Tuesdays and Sundays. Lawyers could visit the other days. Although it was not official, guards allowed family to visit the other days as well because they brought money to the prisoners that they could then use to pay for privileges. José Luis's father, for instance, would frequently come with food to have lunch with him on weekdays. If their cellmates agreed, prisoners could have conjugal visits with their spouses. Visiting hours ended at 2:00 p.m. on weekdays and 6:00 p.m. on Sundays, meaning prisoners could spend substantial portions of their days with loved ones. Aside from the prison officials and guards pocketing the money, this flexibility conferred a sense of normalcy. It also made prisoners adhere to the rules, including following orders and paying the guards on time, for fear visits would be restricted. Political prisoners also sent messages in and out of the prison through their visitors. One individual visiting a political prisoner in Oblatos was arrested in June 1977 while attempting to sneak a message hidden in his shoe from one of his comrades.[20] Officials confiscated Trotskyist pamphlets from several visitors in March 1970 that were to be used for education and recruitment of fellow prisoners.[21] Some political prisoners then adapted forms of resistance and expressions of political commitment to their environment. Prison administrators knew what was going on and tolerated it up to a point.

Money and good behavior allowed prisoners to negotiate—within limits—with their captors and ease the burden of their confinement. Such negotiations demonstrated that the prison administration, despite being an agent of the government, acted with a certain self-interested autonomy and interpreted dictates from higher-level officials with some discretion. However, this looseness—as prisoners carved out forms of freedom inside their cell blocks—belies what could also be a brutal existence behind prison walls. Conflicts erupted between imprisoned members of different guerrilla groups and between political prisoners and common prisoners.[22] An April 1977 riot between political and common prisoners at Oblatos began when officials ordered a surprise search of the cell blocks for reported drugs.[23] Inmates blockaded their cell blocks, and battles ensued between different groups of prisoners and guards. The resulting report concluded that the source of the conflict lay in disagreements over the distribution of drugs among the two groups of prisoners: the "Subversives" and the "Jackals." Both groups distributed and used narcotics, including heroin and paint thinner. The report speculates that the Subversives used drugs to attempt to recruit common prisoners to their cause in the hope that, through indoctrination in Marxism, they would formally join the group once released.[24] This cycle of unrest at Oblatos continued until October 1977, when prison officials and the military finally regained control of the facility.[25]

Political prisoners could opt for more drastic actions to help their situation if day-to-day negotiations did not work. Hunger strikes inside prisons were one of the most common forms of civil disobedience documented in the DFS files.[26] A group of eighty-five political prisoners inside Lecumberri, including the writer José Revueltas, the 1968 student movement leader Eli de Gortari, and the longtime rural activist Ramón Danzos Palomino, went on a hunger strike in December 1969 to improve their treatment and call for their release.[27] They managed to mobilize students, political figures, and labor activists throughout the country to support their efforts.[28] Family members of political prisoners, through groups such as Comité Pro-Presos Políticos, also lent their support and joined protests inside Lecumberri. On January 1, 1970, approximately three hundred family members, including women and children, who were in Lecumberri to support the hunger strikers were beaten as guards raided the prison, attempting to intimidate the protesters.[29] Soon after, the government bowed to public pressure and agreed to release a number of political prisoners. Hunger strikes went on throughout the decade to demand better treatment and release. The length of the strikes varied. A 1973 hunger strike in the Acapulco penitentiary went on for several months and grew to include 110 prisoners who demanded political prisoners' release.[30] The DFS kept track of how many prisoners participated, their health status, and whether or not the strikers had support from their families or others outside the prison walls.[31] Unrest and protests in prisons, as well as attempts to regain control, happened within a broader environment that included forms of surveillance and tolerance for such actions. Perhaps it was inevitable that political prisoners and their families would protest by virtue of why they were there; however, officials had limits to how much they tolerated and, as the next chapter discusses, retaliated against family members for their activism.

THE MINUTIAE OF PRISON LIFE

Jaime Laguna Berber read all the time in prison. "Before I would read three or four pages and I'd leave it." Now he read anything he could get his hands on. "You have nothing else to do. I would even read the sports news, which I never did before. You'd read everything because otherwise you'd be staring at the wall." He also wrote while in prison. "I'm not Gramsci, but I also have my own prison notebooks. I'd write down my thoughts in tiny letters, you'd almost need a magnifying glass to read them because I had to save on paper." In Lecumberri, "we had a fabulous library," remembered Eduardo Fuentes de la Fuente. "We had recent books on a lot of different topics." He made a point to explain that the books weren't given to them by prison officials; rather they just showed up. In all likelihood, they had been smuggled in by visitors.

Francisco Mercado Espinoza, as El Guaymas recalled, organized reading workshops to discuss how to be a better revolutionary. "We would read a book about what a revolutionary should know about security measures or repression. We would then discuss it three days later." There were originally ten or twelve members in these reading groups, but the number went down to five or seven after the arrival of El Flaco, who peeled off members for not being ardent or serious enough in their reading. El Guaymas knew El Flaco well before Oblatos. "He was my buddy from the street. He'd been with me studying agronomy. Since I had never talked about him [under torture], he hadn't been burned, and he continued to be active. After his arrival at Oblatos, I hung out with him, and you wouldn't believe how far he got in just one year. He studied the most out of all of us, and politically he was the savviest." Reading groups and other forms of study reminded political prisoners of their commitment to a cause, which helped them tolerate their imprisonment.

But activism had limits inside prison walls. Several political prisoners, according to Jaime, tried to organize a hunger strike the first year. It quickly ended because prison administrators came down hard on them. Among the punishments, Jaime was sent to solitary confinement. Jaime recalls how, after the first year, prisoners just wanted to do their time and not risk extending it by protesting. Jaime later learned of a political prisoner who protested because he was not receiving his conjugal visits.

How can someone protest that he's not getting a conjugal visit? You protest conditions in prison or that they aren't feeding you. But to protest the lack of a conjugal visit is unworthy, not dignified. If that's what you drag yourself for, you're a worthless asshole. You have to have a little dignity. You're a political prisoner, a revolutionary. Don't tell me that because someone looked at you the wrong way, you're going to protest. You have to put up with it, bastard. This is a war. What did you expect? If you don't like it, then run away.

For Jamie, such complaints were beneath political prisoners. Yet conjugal visits happened organically for all prisoners and could be a source of grievance. El Guaymas remembered, "The mother and the girlfriend would arrive. The mother would say, 'Come on, my boy, eat up,' and then she'd say, 'OK, I'll be back soon, I'm going to go chat down there,' and she'd leave us alone in the cell." He went on to clarify that they would put up a blanket for privacy and tease one of their comrades whose wife made a racket. In recalling life in prison, complaints about rules and procedures, such as about conjugal visits or the quality of the food, stand out in the memories of many interviewees and frame their incarceration.

Prison life meant cohabiting with a range of different criminals who continued their illegal activities inside prison walls. Guillermo Bello López and others remembered the dangers posed by the narcos in prison. Political prisoners formed a general council of cell representatives, so each cell had to designate a leader to monitor the behavior, including drug use, of cellmates. This limited, at least temporarily, the authority of the more powerful prisoners who sold drugs and extorted money. As Guillermo explained, "They found other ways to get their money." Antonio also recalled the activities of narcos in prison. After the torture chambers, officers transported Antonio and his comrades to Oblatos, in Guadalajara. They were taken to the political prisoners' wing, away from the general population. The political prisoners' wing was strictly controlled.

For the first weeks and months after our arrival, we had a lot of restrictions over how long we could be out in the sun, how many hours we had to remain inside our cells, which was the majority of the time. Each cell was about two meters by four meters and housed two prisoners at a time. Later on, and as they caught more of us, a third prisoner had to sleep on the floor because there were only two cement cots.

Prison authorities told Antonio and the other political prisoners that they were not allowed to have contact with the general population for their safety. What he meant by "safety" became clearer when he discussed the conflicts with other groups of prisoners, in particular, those who were selling drugs. "The first group of narcos that arrived in Oblatos were the Pelacuas. They were the first group that controlled the massive distribution of drugs and demanded extortion fees in the city." They proceeded to do the same from inside Oblatos, and because the narcos and political prisoners were sworn enemies, officials kept them in separate wings. The ever-present possibility of violence—by fellow prisoners or guards—was a ubiquitous part of life for political prisoners.

Lucio Cabañas's brother, Pablo Cabañas Barrientos, offered an example of what happened when political prisoners did not get along. After CM-1, Pablo was transported to a prison in Hermosillo, where he was placed in a block with other political prisoners from the area, including two women. He was later moved to the nearby maximum security federal penitentiary in Ciudad Juárez in the state of Chihuahua because of threats he received from fellow inmates. While at the Centro de Readaptación Social (CERESO; Social Rehabilitation Center), he was put in solitary confinement for extended periods, ostensibly for his safety. There he struck up friendships with the guards.

Pablo joined the ranks of handymen at CERESO as his prison job. He had to pay fifty pesos to the chief handyman, and, according to Pablo, the chief made so much collecting this "entry fee" that he did not have to actually work. Pablo recalls that he had his "first lesson about being a peasant" when he started working inside CERESO and was told that "being a professor did not exist in here because we are all the same. You could be the president, but in here we are the same." He was put in cell number 13, which was designated for political prisoners and which housed thirteen prisoners. He was later transferred to a different cell because of conflicts with his cellmate who did not think he was political enough. Because of who his brother was, prison authorities designated him as dangerous and punished anyone who dared to talk to him. "Pity the person who got close to my cell. They'd punish him, and they were always watching. Since they thought I was dangerous, nobody, but nobody, would talk to me. Only the guards." Other political prisoners were angry that Pablo had friendly relationships with the guards, but he brushed them off, saying that "they were my only means of communication."

Prison authorities classified him as a political prisoner, but in recalling what that meant in practice, Pablo started laughing. "Those of the Liga [LC23S] didn't like me. Why did I have to talk politics with the guards? That I shouldn't be doing that; a good revolutionary didn't do that. I'd already learned the lesson that we were all the same." He referred to one of the Liga prisoners as a "despot" and said he "was like dealing with a dog." He remembered how fellow political prisoners would say, "'I support Genaro Vázquez. We are from the Liga. We are part of those who support Ché Guevara.' They wouldn't say they were with Lucio Cabañas because he was considered a reformist. They wanted me to go against Lucio, but I couldn't because he was my brother. This is why they didn't like me." In the minds of these political prisoners, Lucio Cabañas's movement was not hard line enough to achieve radical social change, making Pablo the recipient of their disdain.

> A group of students from Hermosillo came one time, asking to meet with the political prisoners. They were dressed in green wearing their Ché Guevara caps. The guards brought them into the cell. The students asked to meet with Professor Cabañas. [The others told the students,] 'He's worthless. We're the revolutionaries.' The guards told them, 'Those guys are crazy. Come over and meet Pablo. He's the one in the red shirt with holes.' They asked if I was Professor Cabañas. They replied, 'Ah, we thought you were someone else,' and I told them I wasn't as big as the ones in there. They came over and asked if they could take a photo with me.

The main reason for Pablo's incarceration was not his activism per se but because he was Lucio's brother, making him a flashpoint for anyone wanting to voice their opinion about Lucio.

The urge for connection and communication cuts through the recollections of many former political prisoners. Two of Pablo's closest friends in CERESO were Americans: a white man he called Morgan who had been imprisoned for transporting drugs and a black Vietnam veteran who was an activist and had converted to Islam. Morgan would help Pablo by giving him money and, one time, even gifted him a radio to use when he was in solitary confinement. Another of his friends was a bank robber with a cocaine habit. His nickname was "Killer 7" because it was said he had killed seven men. Pablo started a musical trio with Killer 7. Despite his drug habit, he had "a good voice and sort of played guitar." Pablo struggled to relate to other political prisoners, but he struck up friendships with other, nonpolitical prisoners. Establishing connections, especially with other prisoners, could be challenging. Political prisoners were usually segregated from other prisoners to avoid spreading propaganda. Depending on how many political prisoners were housed in the segregated wing at a given time, there could be two or three in a cell instead of five or six. Patricio Abarca Martínez described the urge to reach out to other human beings.

> You look for ways to be connected in prison. As soon as the surveillance would let up, we would have contact through the lumpen. Some would say, 'Take off the blindfold, there's no one here.' They taught us that we could communicate with a wire through the lattice window. They got me in touch with a comrade, Miguel Flores. They let my sister know where we were.

As Pablo's and Patricio's cases illustrate, there is no one-size-fits-all description of a political prisoner or what they did while in prison to make their existence tenable. Even when the prison administration tried to control it, prisoners found ways to connect with one another.

These connections could extend to prison personnel. While imprisoned in CM-1, Bertoldo struck up a close friendship with a military nurse, whom he called the Calavera (Skull). He got to know the nurse when he stopped by Bertoldo's cell to check on him. Eventually, the nurse would take letters to and from Bertoldo's house, alerting his family and wife to where he was and how he was doing. Once released, Bertoldo's friendship with the military nurse continued. "He invited us to his house in Toluca, and our families visited the nearby Toluca Volcano. He even came over to Atoyac with his sons to visit." While unusual, Bertoldo's friendship with the military nurse complicates the fixed line between prisoner and staff. In practice, the line could be murkier out of convenience or loneliness.

ESCAPE ATTEMPTS

The DFS files on prisons across the 1970s are rife with documentation of inmates attempting to escape. While most failed, some of these attempts were successful. Some included or were orchestrated by political prisoners.[32] Digging tunnels and bribing officials were among the more common escape tactics. Other, more dramatic plans included a guerrilla group launching a wholesale attack on the prison to liberate one of their leaders. LC23S failed in its attempt to free four of its members from a Sonora prison in 1975.[33] After a raid on an LC23S safe house in Ciudad Juárez in 1976, the DFS located plans for a mass escape attempt from the state penitentiary.[34] To discourage future escape attempts, prison officials and DFS officers punished those who tried and failed to escape. In one failed escape attempt, prisoners tried to tunnel out of their cells at the Acapulco penitentiary. When discovered, one of the political prisoners, in the words of the DFS agent, "showed a great deal of nervousness. When the people arrived to interrogate him, he started yelling that he was ready to be killed."[35]

Sometimes these attempts succeeded, such as in the dramatic escape of six LC23S members from Oblatos in January 1976, which left three police officers dead.[36] El Guaymas, who was part of the group, recalled that the idea of the escape from Oblatos came from Enrique Pérez Mora (aka El Tenebras), who arrived in prison already planning how to get out. Over the course of two months before their escape, El Guaymas's mother snuck in parts of a table they needed to reach a window, including the legs that measured 1.5 meters (almost 5 feet). Prisoners who made shawls saved enough thread to begin weaving a rope. Family members snuck in weapons by hiding them in the bottom of stew pots. El Guaymas's mother would always give the guards tacos, so they did not bother to inspect her pots too carefully. She also, he laughingly recalled, "would sneak in little containers filled with rum," which they would drink together as a group.

Throughout the interview, El Guaymas kept referring to Antonio Orozco Mitchel's book on the escape, titled *Oblatos: El vuelo que surcó la noche* (Oblatos: The Flight That Furrowed the Night), to point out inconsistencies in his recollections. Some were small details. The guns El Guaymas's mother snuck into the prison were not wrapped, and he took Mitchel to task for omitting the need for the table to reach the window. Some inconsistencies involved more critical parts of the story. According to El Guaymas, Mitchel did not have to twist prisoners' arms to escape because they were fearful of doing so. In fact, it only took some mild convincing for six of the ten Liga members to get on board with the idea. Even more tellingly, El Guaymas disputed Mitchel's claim that he had nothing to do with the planning of the escape and only joined in at the end when all the plans had been made. El Guaymas contended that he had participated in the planning two months before.

Other details of the escape emerged in the interview. Mitchel and El Guaymas organized a chess tournament as a cover to move the weapons between cells. "It was all very clandestine, and no one found out what we were doing." As for the escape itself, "Mitchel was the last one to come down the rope, and it got stuck. I lifted his legs to help him get it untangled. The doctor had come into the cell at that moment and grabbed his hands. If he had screamed, we would have all been caught." Six of them escaped that night. "When we got to the guard tower, the officer was sitting in his booth staring at a couple making out in their car. The couple belonged to our organization and were there to act as a distraction. I remember that when the comrades who were outside started shooting, the guards ran in the opposite direction instead of standing their ground."

Once on the street, Liga comrades met and drove El Flaco and El Tenebras away, leaving Mitchel and El Guaymas behind. He made no mention of why the Liga members chose to leave him and Mitchel behind. Rather than show anger or puzzlement, he nonchalantly proceeded with his story.

> We went into a store, bought some blankets, some food, and headed for the hills. We got to San Gaspar, and because it was so cold, we asked a peasant if we could stay in his house. We woke up in the morning, and the peasant was watching the news on his television, where they reported on the escape of guerrilla members from prison. He fed them breakfast and told them not to worry, that if anyone came to his door he would explain that they were his nephews visiting from Guanajuato.

They stayed in the town for four or five days while awaiting news of where to meet up with other Liga members.

It is unclear why there are different retellings of what happened in the escape from Oblatos. The discrepancies between accounts reveal more about the moment in which they are being remembered than about when the escape happened in 1976. Memory is a deliberate process of making choices of what gets remembered and what gets forgotten. The different accounts of the Oblatos escape—and other key turning points across the 1970s—reflect the struggle over who gets to be the arbiter of this story. This struggle takes place in a politically charged environment, where individuals jockey for position of authority in claiming to have the real "truth" of what took place. In staking their position, they discredit or question the recollections of others, heightening the political minefield of who claims the event. The escape from Oblatos illustrates this memory struggle and allows us to perceive the difficulties of remembering painful chapters in the lives of community members invested in not forgetting what happened.

THE RELEASE

According to Pablo, no one organized on behalf of political prisoners and he never met a human rights activist while he was imprisoned. He remembered the other political prisoners sending manifestos to be published. "They never read their manifestos, their letters." His fellow political prisoners would try to get Pablo to sign their manifestos, but he refused to put his name on them. Yet the process that led up to his release involved individuals stepping in on his behalf to condemn his ongoing incarceration. It began in January 1977, when a journalist from the *Washington Post*, Marlise Simons, interviewed his aunt, Celerina Cabañas. Celerina pointed the journalist to Pablo's case. In her article, Simons reported that seven of Lucio Cabañas's relatives, including Pablo, had been detained and tortured because of their familial relationship to the guerrilla leader.[37] She wrote that Pablo had been held for almost six years on charges of "conspiracy" without the benefit of a trial. According to Pablo, Simons met with the outgoing attorney general, Pedro Ojeda Paullada, later that year to discuss political prisoners. Paullada denied that there were any in Mexico. Simons told him about Pablo's case, and Paullada replied that he would take care of releasing him. Simons contacted Pablo's public defender to urge him to file the paperwork for his release in October 1977. When Pablo was finally released later in 1977, he went to the *Washington Post* offices on Paseo de la Reforma in Mexico City to thank Marlise Simons in person for all that she had done to get him released. "This is so good, my dear friend," she told him as they embraced.

After his release in December 1985, Jaime Laguna Berber got a job as a janitor. After several years, he worked as a journalist and studied law. Later, he started writing a blog on his political experiences, both past and present. Jaime said the decision to post his writings online came out of a personal crisis. He struggled with alcoholism and sought help for it. The blog, which he titled *Madera*, is about his life's journey, but he also "discusses candidates, the crisis, the problem with femicide, drug trafficking," and other topics. Jaime's openness stands as an example of what an individual can do to live with the type of trauma he endured.

Other political prisoners tell of challenges they suffered after their release. The government's offer of amnesty after 1978 forced released prisoners to reckon with the implications of amnesty. Elia Hernández Hernández was released from prison on September 23, 1977. She refused to accept the government's subsequent offer of amnesty, because, she said, "amnesty meant forgetting, forgetting what I had done and why I did it." Elia said that she had not had any psychological problems after what happened to her, that she was fine talking about her detention and imprisonment with her children. Yet, in passing, she mentioned that the prison doctor had tied her Fallopian tubes without her consent after she gave birth in prison. Her insistence that she was fine in light of her forced sterilization, not to mention her torture, suggested otherwise. Lourdes Quiñones was released in 1979 under the amnesty. Freedom, she said, felt "like riding in a car with my hair tousled in the air. When I left [the prison], I just walked and walked because I wanted to be on the street." Freedom meant making choices to walk with no destination in mind and with no one to tell her otherwise.

Survivors tell many different stories about their release from prison; all are tinged with trepidation and a sense that nothing would ever be the same as before. For José Luis Alonso Vargas and Lourdes Uranga, release from prison sent them out of Mexico. Government authorities put them both on a plane to Cuba to live in exile, in 1973 and 1974, respectively. José returned to Mexico after he was granted amnesty in 1979. Lourdes moved to Italy and married, eventually becoming an Italian citizen. She returned to Mexico much later after she received amnesty. After spending five years in prison, José Luis Esparza was released in 1982 after the amnesty order went into effect. As he went through the prison's doors, José Luis worried he was going to be shot by snipers because he could not believe they let him go. After spending twelve years behind bars, Saúl René Chacón López struggled to figure out how to work a pay phone to call his daughter to pick him up so he could go home.

Time had passed, their causes seemed to fall by the wayside, groups disbanded or were destroyed, and there was no public space to reckon with what had happened to them. The question of impunity looms large for many. Part of what makes their release so anticlimactic and hard to move beyond, it seems, is that it was not part of a general societal reckoning. There was not a broader set of cultural and political processes that these former political prisoners could attach their stories to or through which they could process their experiences. Their organizations did not exist anymore; the guerrilla struggle was over; their defeat stood for all to see. There was nowhere to return to that would help them make sense of the trauma so many experienced in the torture chambers and behind prison walls. That trauma—and the well of pain they carried—weighed heavily on them for years to come.

REGRETS

The term *arrepentidos* (those who repented) is loaded down with layers of meaning. At some point between being detained, tortured, and released, some political prisoners regretted their activism. That regret could manifest when prisoners willingly cooperated with the government—in other words, those who took on the role of a "madrina" and identified comrades in exchange for preferential treatment or a lighter sentence. It could happen as a result of living through torture or coming to terms with the enormous cost of staying committed to the cause. It could mean that the person outright denounced or quietly distanced themselves from their political activities once inside prison. They might have declined to participate in one of the many study groups organized by fellow political prisoners or outright declared they were no longer a member of the guerrilla group that brought them to prison. Whatever the reason, to be labeled an arrepentido carried an inflection of cowardice, especially if the designation came from someone who had not denounced their own membership. The stigma of being labeled an arrepentido followed individuals for decades, regardless of how they came to the designation: under duress, once imprisoned, or under torture.

When asked if there were any arrepentidos among the political prisoners he was with at Oblatos, El Guaymas first replied that there were "two or three." Then he paused and revised the number: of the twenty originally imprisoned with him, ten continued to be Liga members once incarcerated in Oblatos. In other words, 50 percent defected. Instead of focusing on the arrepentidos, El Guaymas discussed at length those who were cast out (*deslindados*) from the Liga while political prisoners. This type of discharge was also stigmatized but more leniently, according to El Guaymas. He continued to be friends with deslindados and shared with them the food his mother brought for him. He offered two examples to illustrate what he meant by deslindados. First, Liga leaders kicked Jesús Ramírez Mesa (aka El Caliman) out of the group because he gave up the location of a fellow comrade too soon under torture. Second, when an especially dogmatic Liga leader was imprisoned with them in Oblatos in 1975, he expected the rest of the Liga members to follow a rigid schedule of study groups to further their education. Several of the political prisoners balked at his demands, which led the leader to "purge" half the Liga members inside the prison. The remaining six, according to El Guaymas, are the same six who mounted the escape from Oblatos several months later.

After serving four years of a twelve-year sentence for kidnapping, Guillermo Bello López was released in 1976 from Penal Número Dos in Acapulco. "I went back to Chilpancingo," Guillermo said. "I felt insecure. Walking the streets, it feels like everyone knows who you are and they're going to point you out. Gossip about you. The reality is that no one knows you after you've been gone for four years. You lose contact." As for rejoining the armed movement, Guillermo explained that he "didn't see leadership that he could pursue in the struggle." He talks about the demoralization he felt when he learned that Lucio had been killed in 1974: "In a dreamy way, we believed we were invincible, but that wasn't the case. Now from the position of a spectator, there was a lack of military ability, little training, little discipline. We didn't have an ironclad position comparable to Shining Path or Uruguay's Montoneros, among others, who were groups with proper military training."

Guillermo explained that he could be accused of being politically lazy or that he was an arrepentido. Yet, he said, it is not that easy to describe what he felt on his release. His ambivalence about remembering this chapter of his life is palpable. This ambivalence is echoed in the accounts of many former political prisoners. There is a sense of loss, of what could have been, of not knowing how to process the pain—both physical and mental—of this defining period of their lives.

CONCLUSION

Bertoldo Cabañas explained how they disappeared people at CM-1: "They would take them out at night, with hoods over their heads, grabbing the hands of others there. They would take them out and disappear them. Nothing was known about them after. We could see them taken away through the slits in our cell doors."

The number of political prisoners decreased after 1976. As a result, José Luis notes, there were not enough of them to be segregated from the rest of the prison population, and he was moved to a cell block with the presos comunes. This also meant that after 1976, guerrilla members "knew that if they picked you up, you would be killed or tortured and then disappeared." When he was at the Tlatelolco horse barracks clandestine center, José Luis recalled, he saw the stereotypical "chubby" police officer along with what appeared to be a "new breed of officer: young, different from the stereotype, thin, strong. The cazadores [hunters]. They would walk by with shotguns and say, 'Let's go hunting.'"[38] As José Luis was being loaded up to be transported to Lecumberri in June 1975, Nazar Haro pulled him aside and told him to send a message to his comrades that José Luis's group would be "the last group that makes it to the prison," suggesting that from now on anyone captured would be killed. Afterward, José Luis stated, a few individuals here and there were captured and transported as political prisoners, but never a group of more than two or three, and it became more common to have their members disappeared.

5 The Family

El Guaymas remembered how his mother visited him every day to bring him food when he was imprisoned in the Oblatos penitentiary in Guadalajara. It was not just his mother who came to see him every day. "My wife was amazing [*bien cabrona*] the four years and eight months that I was imprisoned. She only missed ten days visiting me. Ten days the entire time I was in." What becomes clear in El Guaymas's account is that he was not alone in his suffering. What he endured as a political prisoner was a collective ordeal, beyond his comrades and including his most intimate relations. Prison became an extension of home, and families became objects of suspicion in the eyes of government officials. This chapter demonstrates how the Mexican state deployed violence against whole families linked to subversion. Repression, torture, disappearance, and imprisonment were not individual experiences but collective ones, targeting whole bloodlines. The attention to families was so intense that they became targets of the government's counterinsurgency efforts. Families were suspected of nurturing political beliefs, punished for not curbing perceived maladaptive behavior by their children, and ultimately for concealing subversives.

Families supported their children in a multitude of ways beyond visiting and bringing food. From the very beginning of the dirty war, families suffered and struggled alongside their imprisoned loved ones. Parents formed organizations, such as the Asociación de Padres y Familiares de los Presos Políticos (Association of Parents and Family of Political Prisoners), to raise awareness and ask for the release of their sons and daughters who were imprisoned in the Lecumberri Penitentiary in Mexico City.[1] They hand delivered petitions to government leaders, organized rallies, and camped outside the prison to demand better conditions for their children. When Lecumberri prisoners rioted in January 1973, thirty family members of political prisoners were trapped overnight inside the cells as the police stormed the facility to regain control.[2] These acts of civil disobedience called attention to the relatives' imprisonment and alerted the Mexican public to what was going on in the name of national security. In challenging the government and standing in solidarity with their loved ones, families got caught up in the ensuing violence. As the following pages show, family members of political prisoners became both targets and tools in the government's war on subversion. Fathers, mothers, sisters, brothers, sons, and daughters suffered torture and imprisonment and in some cases became political prisoners themselves. They were targeted for two reasons: to punish them for their acts of solidarity or to coerce a confession from their loved one. As family members became targets of violence, the act of torture extended more broadly and deeply through the bonds of kinship.

El Guaymas recalled that political prisoners organized rallies in 1974 and 1975 to demand better treatment and their families supported them. "Outside there was a committee of mothers of the political prisoners that the mothers, along with Luciano Rentería, had formed in 1974." Rentería's son, Armando Rentería Castillo, was a political prisoner along with El Guaymas in the Oblatos penitentiary. Interviewed together in 1996, Armando and Luciano, father and son, described how the prisoners and family members coordinated their activism for maximum effect. While prisoners held hunger strikes inside Oblatos, family members ensured that the public knew what was happening inside the prison walls to protect their sons from being disappeared.[3] Luciano and other parents of political prisoners at Oblatos were especially active between 1976 and 1978.[4] As discussed in earlier chapters, this is the period when there was growing awareness of the existence of clandestine torture centers and what it meant when an individual was "disappeared." Groups of family members wrote to government authorities, called journalists, worked with lawyers, and staged rallies complaining that their imprisoned children endured terrible living conditions, beatings, threats, and abuses at the hands of police and prison authorities. They denounced the fact that police showed up at their homes late at night, hauled their sons or daughters away to an unknown location, and tortured them as an act of intimidation.[5] Despite reprisals and intimidation by state agents, parents persisted in their defense of their imprisoned children, rallying hundreds of supporters outside the Oblatos penitentiary in June 1977.[6]

In what appears to be an exceedingly common practice in the Mexican case, the government targeted all family members solely because of their relationship with guerrillas.[7] In the politically charged environment of the dirty war of the 1970s, family members had no recourse to moderate paths to lobby the government. Every act was suspect and every visit monitored. Families were targets of surveillance because of possible complicity. As the case of Lucio Cabañas's family discussed in this chapter shows, they were also targets for severe punishment. The "Truth Commission Report on the State of Guerrero," originally published in 2014 and updated in 2021, lists the names of thirty-three individuals with the last name Cabañas who were detained, imprisoned, or disappeared.[8] The insidiousness and scope of harassing, detaining, and torturing so many individuals sharing the name Cabañas, irrespective of involvement in guerrilla activities, suggests a much wider net of punishment beyond the prisoner. As this and other cases—such as the Mendoza Salgado family, also discussed in this chapter—show, there was a continuum from what took place inside prison walls to what took place in broader society, where the family became the focus of blame. The government targeted families to shame them publicly for the actions of their detained loved ones, and government harassment also served as a warning to other parents to use corrective measures on their sons and daughters or risk state retaliation.

Lucio Cabañas's family was not alone in experiencing the wrath of the Mexican government simply because of their kinship to a guerrilla. Reading the rosters of disappeared, killed, tortured, and detained individuals reveals that many victims of the state had the same last names. Brothers and sisters, mothers and fathers, sons and daughters, aunts, uncles, cousins: it becomes apparent that family members were routinely targeted in both the urban and rural theaters of guerrilla warfare. Some had supported a loved one by providing munitions or giving cover. Others had sympathized with the political inclinations that had driven their loved one to radical political action. Yet, in many cases, family members who were tortured or imprisoned by the state simply shared a bloodline with a person deemed subversive. Blood relation became a category of guilt in the eyes of the government. The torture and imprisonment of family members—those who shared blood or were tied by marriage— demonstrates that in the eyes of the state the "subversive" family posed a unique threat to national security. The family unit gave birth to and raised their child to become a subversive and, as such, made the unit suspect. Was it something in the family that made this young man or woman prone to radicalization? Moreover, the subversive could always count on the loyalty of the family to provide safe harbor in a time of war. Punishing the family unit, then, served both an internal and external purpose: hurting their loved ones surely hurt the subversive. Showcasing the pain inflicted on seemingly innocent people further warned off those who might otherwise choose the same radical path taken by their family members or even community members.

PUNISHING THE FAMILY

In 1975, the DFS detained Margarita Andrade Vallejo's parents and three siblings for roughly twelve days—a typical length of stay for subversives detained during this period—in a clandestine torture center. At the time of their detention, members of the White Brigade were hunting her and others in LC23S in Mexico City. After learning of what happened to her family, Margarita committed suicide.[9] In another case, officers brought an unnamed man before his brother in a clandestine prison to identify him as a guerrilla member. His brother was "a foul-smelling bloody mess," his eyes "so swollen that he could barely open them to see" and his "mouth so battered he could hardly get the words out."[10] After a month of detention and torture, José Luis Moreno Borbolla knew that he was one of sixteen individuals in the clandestine prison at the mounted police barracks in

Mexico City. But when they were rounded up to be transferred to Lecumberri for formal processing, only thirteen remained, suggesting that three had been disappeared. One of them, José Luis knew, was the father of a guerrilla leader.[11] Why did they show this man his brutally beaten brother? Why did they imprison Margarita's family? Why did they disappear a guerrilla leader's father? Information gathering may have factored into the calculus for including family members in the experience of torture. However, the systematic pattern of extreme brutality that relatives were subjected to suggests a deeper rationale: the loved ones of subversives *deserved* to be punished in ways that guaranteed families suffered long-term repercussions across generations.

Intimidation, imprisonment, and torture of political prisoners' family members had been common practice since at least 1968.[12] But what was most shocking was the inclusion of children. Not only did agents routinely threaten children when torturing activists, but they went so far as to torture children in front of their imprisoned parents to get them to talk. We do not know the full extent of child torture or when it entered the arsenal of tactics. What we do know is that the torturing of children could be as brutal as it was for adults. A former political prisoner testified that officers brought her fourteen-month-old baby girl before her and proceeded to "apply electric shocks all over her little body."[13] The FEMOSPP report lists the cases of 204 children incarcerated primarily for the purpose of breaking their parents. Torturing children is such a depraved act in any setting that it stands to reason that it must have been couched in the language of exigent counterinsurgency for the officers performing it. If we knew more about the tactics employed or the full extent of the torture of children, we could summarize precisely why and how it was employed. As it stands, this is a glaring omission in the historical record of the period.

The torture and detention of children comes up in the documentary record mostly by implication: records of women who gave birth, children who were abducted from their parents and adopted to other families, a woman searching for her child from inside the prison's walls, and so on. At least eight women political prisoners were pregnant when detained, and four gave birth while in prison.[14] In other cases, we know children were in prisons with their parents. In an unknown number of cases, children were given up for adoption after their detention. The warden of the Women's

Prison in Mexico City reported to the DFS that one political prisoner agitated to know the whereabouts of her young son after she read in the newspaper that he was in the custody of the DFS.[15] Several cases of disappeared children who were later found by their families have recently garnered attention in the media.[16] If women gave birth while in prison, there were babies in prison with them. If children were adopted, there were babies born in prison or children imprisoned with their parents. If a woman was searching for her child who was in DFS custody, there was reason to believe the child had been detained. The ambiguity surrounding the extent to which children became victims of the war on subversion is astounding. Durable impunity means that the nature and extent of state violence experienced by children, as either direct or indirect victims, remains unknown.

As the inclusion of children suggests, torturers leveraged the intimacy of family relationships to augment the horrors of torture. The testimonies of the brother and sister Raúl and Xóchitl Mendoza Salgado about their time in CM-1 in 1977 are especially revealing.[17] These were just two of a total of six members of their family who were tortured. While it was too difficult for Raúl to describe, Xóchitl discussed how DFS officers tortured Raúl in front of her, including urinating on him and applying electrical prods to his genitals. DFS officers repeatedly raped her in front of Raúl and, after she tested positive for pregnancy, performed an abortion with her brother as witness.[18] As was common practice, officers tortured Raúl and Xóchitl for approximately ten days at CM-1 before relocating them to a prison. Rodolfo Reyes Crespo, an LC23S member, was detained by the DFS on December 24, 1973, in Guadalajara and subsequently disappeared. After taking Rodolfo to CM-1, DFS agents kidnapped his mother and tortured her in front of him.[19] In another testimony, a mother of a guerrilla member described how agents took her, her husband, her other children, and her grandmother to a torture center in a residential area of Guadalajara. The family was kept in a small, dark room for three days without access to food or water. The mother could tell that other family members were at the torture center as well and described the screams of the wife of another guerrilla member as they beat and raped her.[20]

Elia Hernández Hernández remembered that when she and her husband were detained at CM-1 the officers would take her to where they were interrogating her husband and threaten to rape or execute her. "They used a lot of psychological torture on him," Elia said. The officers told Elia that they were going to hurt her family. She explained that the officers surveilled her mother and brother because the two of them were looking for her after she was detained. When her mother and brother came to the safe house where Elia had been living, a DFS agent detained and questioned them about Elia and her husband. Her mother joined a group of family members looking for their disappeared children once she learned about Elia's detention. Her mother died of a heart attack later, when Elia was in Santa Martha Acatitla, the women's penitentiary. "That was the hardest thing that happened to me while I was in prison," Elia said. What happened to her family echoes the psychological torture her husband endured when they tortured her in front of him. Guilt, fear, concern, loss, and pain comingle in Elia's memory of how her family, especially her mother, got caught up in the war on subversion.

So many others share similar stories of their family unit getting caught up in the experience of detention and torture to suggest it was routine for security forces to target them. María de la Luz Aguilar and her husband, Raul, both members of an LC23S offshoot in Chihuahua, were warned not to go back to the family home because the police were there to take them away. About twenty officers descended on the house looking for them in 1972, falsely accusing Raul and María's brother of rape. They tore the house to pieces and threatened María's mother and sister, who were taking care of María's baby daughter. María's fifteen-year-old brother returned home during the raid, and the police detained him along with her father, mother, sister, and daughter. The officers kept the family hostage for four days, tied to chairs. In María's words, they took her father and "tied him to a chair while hitting him with a thick stick, saying they would kill us all if we showed up." During the imprisonment, María's mother recognized the DFS leader Miguel Nazar Haro's voice, which is described by so many others imprisoned for subversion. Though the DFS released them after four days, the agents patrolled outside the house waiting for María and Raul to return. What María's family endured during those four days went above and beyond the officers waiting for them to return. Her family was tortured despite it being clear they did not know her whereabouts, suggesting the DFS had a punitive agenda in mind. It also signaled to María the extremes the DFS was willing to go to to hurt her.

Military officers brutally tortured Josafath Hernandez Rios at their base in Atoyac, Guerrero, in 1970, and beat his father to death in front of him to both extract information and punish him for his subversion. The aftermath of the experience, according to Josafath, lingered and has been communicated across generations: "I have two sons. I've done my best but with this psychological damage. The truth though is that all this is transmitted to my sons. I don't live in peace. They say that one should learn to forgive, but it's really hard to forgive this type of act." The absence of peace that Josafath described is shared by many others caught up directly and indirectly in the dirty war. The experience of torture and imprisonment tore apart families in the immediate and the long term. The lingering trauma spilled over into the family unit and across new generations, leaving in its trail open wounds and unreconciled grief.

THE CASE OF LUCIO CABAÑAS'S FAMILY

Lucio Cabañas Barrientos was born in Atoyac, Guerrero, in 1938 and trained to be a schoolteacher at the Ayotzinapa Normal School. He went on to become the founder and leader of the Partido de los Pobres, a guerrilla movement out of the state of Guerrero. He died in a heated battle with the military on December 2, 1974, in Tecpán de Galeana, Guerrero. His story, however, is more than just that of an individual and the movement he led. There is no more extreme case of how the Mexican government targeted the family as part of its war on subversion than what happened to Lucio Cabañas's loved ones. Drawing together the many branches of their collective story demonstrates how deep into the family state violence could reach. State agents targeted some of Lucio's family members, such as his brother, because they joined his guerrilla activities. These same agents targeted others in his family for nothing more than they shared his last name. Such a capacious view of what made an individual fall under the designation "subversive" shows the true intent behind their persecution: As part of its counterinsurgent measures, the government

designated the family unit as both a threat and as deserving of punishment. Not only could the family harbor and aid the subversive, but the
government also viewed them as the source of subversion. After all, they
reared the individual who went on to become the enemy of the state.

Several members of Lucio Cabañas's family continue to live in the town
of Atoyac. The teacher-turned-guerrilla leader figures prominently in
their recollections of the period, beginning with the armed assault he
started against the Mexican government in 1967 and ending with his killing in 1972. Like many others in the region, community members were
profoundly shocked at the government's massacre of unarmed civilians in
Atoyac in 1967. Approximately three thousand protesters gathered on
May 18 to ask for Lucio's reinstatement as head of the local school. Federal
forces responded by shooting into the crowd, leaving seven dead and
twenty injured, and then taking over the town. Lucio and his supporters
went into hiding in the mountains, from where they mounted a guerrilla
movement calling for the violent overthrow of the government. For those
who stayed behind in Atoyac, including some of the people interviewed
for this book, the massacre marked the end of any illusion that the government represented them and the start of a very difficult period. Several
people from Atoyac came to believe in Lucio's call to arms and helped him,
either by joining his movement or by supporting his cause indirectly. All
paid a dear price.

Common themes run through the recollections of Lucio's family members. They talked about the value of education and how their parents supported their schooling, detailing with pride how far they had gone in their
own education and how they wanted the same for their children. Lucio's
younger brother, Pablo Cabañas Barrientos, recalled that Lucio urged him
to continue with his studies because he "didn't want a donkey for a
brother." Family members discussed the poverty in Atoyac, how local elites
had it in for Lucio, and how the government interfered in their lives. As
Adolfo Godoy Cabañas put it, "We wanted to be free, to work, but the government wouldn't let us." Members of the military would show up at their
homes at night or in the early morning to harass them, rummaging
through their belongings, taking whatever they wanted, and threatening
to kill them. This pattern of harassment and intimidation had both the
purpose and the effect of instilling a culture of fear in Lucio's family and

the people of Atoyac. This culture of fear sent an overt message of the consequences of aiding Lucio's insurgent activities. It also had subtler messaging of ongoing surveillance, steady intimidation, the absence of institutional protections, and extreme vulnerability. The following stories of Cabañas family members illustrate the depth of this culture of fear and the lengths the Mexican security forces went to to retaliate against the guerrilla leader.[21]

Adolfo Godoy Cabañas

Adolfo Godoy Cabañas's and Lucio Cabañas's grandfathers were brothers, and Adolfo spoke of Lucio as his "cousin." He shared Lucio's vision of social change and helped his cousin. For this reason, he was not entirely surprised when federal agents detained him on the morning of May 6, 1971. "They arrived in two new late model cars, one a Ford. Four in one car and four in the other," he recalled. They told Adolfo's mother that they just wanted to chat with him and asked where his other brothers and father were. Only one other brother was home. They put Adolfo in one car and his brother, Felicito, in the other and drove them to the military base in Pie de la Cuesta, just north of Acapulco on the Pacific coast and a few hours' drive from Atoyac. He saw both military and judicial police there. Adolfo recalled telling his brother "to only answer the truth because you don't want to say one thing and then another." The police beat them, but as Adolfo recalled, they were not nearly as badly beaten as the twelve or so other detainees imprisoned with them.

Adolfo uses the word *detainees* (*detenidos*) in his description. He noted that the detainees had suffered "really ugly beatings, they couldn't even move." They were so badly beaten that there was nowhere else on their bodies "that they could be hit, all full of blood." As soon as the police took them into the interrogation room, Adolfo said he and his brother started talking "with precision" because "if you stuttered they would hit you." They kept asking questions he did not know how to answer: "Where is Lucio? That they knew that Lucio came every day and we gave him food, that people said we were helping him." When Adolfo asked who those supposed people were, the police answered that members of the local government in Atoyac had talked, including a local PRI leader named Juan

Ponce. Using a typical interrogation tactic, the officials told Adolfo that his brother had confessed to everything, but Adolfo remained firm that he did not know anything. Adolfo stuck to his story about Lucio: "I would tell them that he is my cousin, I never denied Lucio, that I had met him, but he had never visited us in Atoyac precisely because he didn't want to compromise us." In reality, Adolfo states, "I had met him various times, but I couldn't tell them that." In other words, Adolfo owned the indisputable fact that Lucio was his family above all, even while lying about the rest.

After a week in Pie de la Cuesta, Adolfo, his brother, and the other twelve or so prisoners were transferred to CM-1 in Mexico City on the back of a truck. They spent four months there. Their family looked for them everywhere, selling everything they could, including their home, to fund the search. Adolfo did not clarify who precisely in the family did the searching because, in his view, the family is a singular unit that protects its own. The family visited prisons and were turned away because Adolfo and his brother "were not in the government's jails." That they were not "in the government's jails" was a euphemism for the fact that their detention had not been recorded in the normal police files and they had been placed in clandestine spaces. The family wrote letters to the authorities, including President Echeverría Álvarez, asking about Adolfo and his brother Felicito's whereabouts and for their release. Several officials replied that Adolfo and his brother were fine and would be returned in due time. By finally admitting that the government had Adolfo and his brother, officials messaged that this is what happened when people associated with guerrillas: they would be detained, interrogated, and "in due time" released. The experience of Adolfo's family trying desperately to find him for the four months he went missing is emblematic of others at the time whose family members had been disappeared—either temporarily or permanently. Many families faced the erasure of the paper trail, denial by officials, and a bureaucratic runaround.

Adolfo was finally released in September 1971, after four months of imprisonment. His wife remembered that it was September 17, right before his birthday. Officials took him to Chilpancingo, along with Genaro Vázquez's father and some others, where they escorted them through the basement of the Palacio de Gobierno to Chilpancingo's municipal jail. Genaro too was leading a guerrilla movement in the mountains of

Guerrero, but he was killed in a car accident in 1972. Adolfo remembered the sound of one of Genaro's supporters shaving the long beard he had grown while at CM-1. From the municipal jail, he and the others were finally released. His brother had been sent directly to Atoyac, so the family had worried when Adolfo had not shown up. Their release brought to an end the family's search and rendered their detention a temporary, rather than permanent, disappearance. This ordeal was far from over as the brothers and their family dealt with the repercussions of what they had endured in their clandestine detention.

During his interview, Adolfo pulled out a photograph of himself standing outside his cell at CM-1, saying, "This photo is proof of my disappearance." Near the end of his interview, Adolfo declared, "The government had done irreparable harm to my family, and it took a long time before things returned to normal." Adolfo testified before the FEMOSSP because, like the photograph of him in CM-1, his words were evidence of what had happened to him. In the eyes of security forces, Adolfo fit into a category of guilt by association primarily because he was from Lucio's family and suspected of aiding his cousin. The fact that Adolfo uses the language of "proof" and "evidence" in his testimony before government agencies sets up a foil: agents did not have similar proof or evidence of any crimes to subject him to torture. What he—and, by extension, his family—endured challenges the official impunity that excused the actions of those soldiers who took him and his brother in 1971. In testifying, then, Adolfo was looking for accountability for what was done to him and his family.

Pablo Cabañas Barrientos

Pablo Cabañas Barrientos, Lucio's younger brother by two years, went to a teacher training college in the state of Sonora, like Lucio had in Guerrero. Pablo taught mathematics to elementary school students in the small town of Colonia Unión de Huatabampo in Sonora and eventually married a young woman there. They had a young son and a second child on the way when soldiers came to Pablo's school to take him away. They asked for Professor Cabañas, and when he identified himself, one soldier put his hand on Pablo and said he was detained. On that day, January 17, 1972, "my life changed completely," Pablo said. He paused at this point in the interview to gather his thoughts before continuing because of the enormity of this day in his life story. Not only was he detained and subjected to torture, but he also lost his family as a result of what happened that day. Pablo's wife left him after his arrest. She never went to see him in prison. She wanted nothing to do with his family and refused their help. She moved back to her family, remarried soon after, and told their young sons that their father was dead. Though he survived detention, losing his family this way was a form of metaphorical death.

As with Adolfo, the justification for Pablo's detention illustrates the way in which family relationship was a key category of guilt in Mexico's dirty war. When he was arrested in 1972, Pablo had previously met with Lucio on two occasions after his brother took up arms in the late 1960s: once in 1967 in the mountains of Guerrero and once in 1971 in Mexico City. This was the last time Pablo saw Lucio alive. In other words, he had hardly any contact with Lucio that would confer guilt. He was simply targeted for being Lucio's brother. That January, soldiers took Pablo to a nearby empty school to interrogate him about his political activism. He told the soldiers that he had gone to a few meetings to organize a political group in the area that was intended to complement Lucio's work. They did not believe him when he explained that he was not a leader of the group, that the idea to form the group was not his, and that it was not intended to be an armed group. After the initial questioning, they moved him to a military camp near the city of Navojoa. There the soldiers continued asking him the same questions and refusing to believe him because he "was Lucio's brother." They just asked him over and over again, "Where was Lucio?" This line of interrogation began in Sonora and continued when he was transferred by plane to CM-1 in Mexico City. At CM-1, officers "started hitting, slapping across the face, hitting with a club, kicking, electric shocks all over the body, in underpants, almost naked, stick us in a barrel of cold water, dunk our heads, hands and feet tied up, thrown on the floor to be kicked wherever we fell." What becomes clear from his description is that Pablo was subjected to the torture reserved for the most threatening subversives. He was labeled dangerous, not because of his political activities, but because of his sibling relationship.

When he was released from CM-1 at the end of January, Pablo was transported to a prison in Hermosillo, Sonora, and later moved to the maximum-security penitentiary known as the CERESO. At the time, Pablo did not know that his wife had left him and returned to her family with their children, and he worried that she never visited or made contact. Had something happened to her? Had she been arrested too? Where were his children? "I was so worried because I didn't know what had happened to them. I was like this January, February, March, April, May, just desperate, and I get these anxiety attacks and just tears," Pablo remembered. "All of those things that happen when your life changes." In this period of anxiety and extreme stress, another political prisoner told him, "Pretend that you had died. Pretend that you don't exist, that the outside doesn't exist. We are in another world and you're not over there. This way you won't get anxious . . . because over there you are dead." Pablo said that this strategy helped. Later, he asked to see a doctor because "I felt really bad, emotionally I was bad." Pablo evokes the idea of self-erasure as a survival mechanism. In deciding that he did not exist—that they had died for the people he knew outside—made it easier to exist in prison. He could pretend as if his absence was final for others, while for himself it remained liminal and partial. When he found out his wife had told his sons that he had died, it confirmed this overwhelming sense of erasure. Pablo may have escaped the type of disappearance other so-called subversives were subjected to, including having their bodies dumped out of planes over the Isla Marías off the coast of Guerrero. Nevertheless, he endured another type of disappearance.

Pablo spent almost six years at the prison and was released in October 1977. His crime was being Lucio's brother. He learned of Lucio's death in December 1974 when he heard a guard saying, "Cabañas's older brother died." If the purpose of Pablo's detention, torture, and imprisonment was to drive Lucio from hiding, he would have been released after his brother was killed in 1974. But that was not it. Government officials subjected Pablo, and other close relatives of Lucio, to life-destroying violence and prolonged incarceration as punishment. Perhaps part of the official rationale for such brutality against innocent individuals was that it would act as a deterrent to others who might follow similar paths. If this were the case, though, officials would have ensured wider knowledge of what was done to the Cabañas family at the time. What happened to Pablo—detention, torture, and imprisonment in maximum-security facilities—is evidence that this was a wholly punitive act intended to destroy the Cabañas family, beginning with those closest to Lucio and extending outward across the branches of the family tree.

José Luis Arroyo Castro

José Luis Arroyo Castro, a cousin of Lucio Cabañas, listed members of his family who were disappeared—either temporarily or permanently—in the government's quest to bring down Lucio's guerrilla movement. He started with his father, then his grandfather, and then three of his uncles, all detained at different times. One of his uncles, Bertoldo, was eventually released, while the other two, Isaías and Marcial, were never found and are considered permanently disappeared. All are blood relatives of Lucio Cabañas, but none were members of his immediate family. They all lived in the town of San Vicente, located in the municipality of Atoyac. José Luis, who was fifteen years old at the time the military detained his family, remembers how his grandmother, Lucio's great-aunt, loved the guerrilla leader like a son and avidly supported his movement. Witnessing the detention of the men in his family deepened José Luis's commitment to Lucio's movement: "From this moment, I saw explicitly what is a repressive political system, that doesn't look out for anyone, and you see how it destroys people. When my father and grandfather returned to us the way that they did, the first thought that came to my mind was that I needed to give all of myself to the struggle for this movement."[22] José Luis's memory of how state violence impacted his family magnified his desire for political activism. His description of what happened is grounded in respect for what Lucio sought to achieve and admiration for his courage in standing up against an evil institution bent on destroying his own family. This David versus Goliath narrative undergirding José Luis's recollections of this period explains why he and other members of his family continue searching for the truth. They want to make sure their sacrifices were not in vain.

José Luis's grandmother, mother, aunt, and sister searched prisons throughout the region for traces of their disappeared relatives. José Luis remembered going with another uncle, Bertoldo Cabañas—who had also been detained, tortured, and released—to Lecumberri to ask about his father and grandfather. Bertoldo told José Luis to wait for him in the park across the street: "You can't come with me because they might detain you." Bertoldo asked for information about their relatives at Lecumberri, but the guards turned him away because they were not there. The odyssey of searching for their loved ones was fraught with uncertainty about finding answers as well as fear of possible retaliation for revealing their relationship to Lucio.

Eventually, government officials told the family that José Luis's father and grandfather had been detained for "being members of the Partido de los Pobres," despite there being no evidence to support the allegation. Their logic, according to José Luis, was that "you are a part of him, you are with him." Later they learned that José Luis's father never denied his relationship to Lucio Cabañas and explained over and over again to his torturers that this did not mean he was a member of Lucio's movement. Even while he was tortured, José Luis's father explained to his torturers that in the same way he would offer a glass of water and a tortilla to any of them if they visited his home, he did the same with Lucio, saying, "I wouldn't turn down giving food to my relative. If that's a crime, go ahead, but I would do the same for you as I would do for him." As José Luis and his relatives found out, the government viewed them as complicit in Lucio's activities solely because they belonged to the guerrilla leader's lineage.

After several months of searching, José Luis's family managed to locate his father and grandfather. They had both been brutally tortured. His father's torture included beatings and repeated kicks from military boots. His torturers had applied electric shocks all over his body, including prods applied directly to his head. "When we got him back, he was destroyed, torn to pieces," José Luis said. "When he took his shirt and pants off, he had large, round bruises and burns the size of apples." The doctors who treated him were angered at the severity of the torture he had endured and expressed surprise that he had survived it. José Luis explained that the torture was both physical and psychological. His grandfather had been tortured in front of his father under direct orders from an "American adviser [*asesor gringo*]" who was in the room.[23] The brutal torture they were subjected to placed these two men squarely in the category of subversives so threatening that they had to be destroyed. Neither belonged to guerrilla groups or had access to information that would have undermined a movement. Their guilt rested in being Lucio's family. Their torture was intended to punish them and destroy the Cabañas family.

After his release, José Luis's father suffered from mental illness. "[He] started doing things he had never done before," he explained. "He used to be a serious, respectful, and hardworking person. He started behaving like a child, an adolescent, and an adult." He went on: "His personality changed, and he would become violent." José Luis's father would play with his young niece as if he were a child himself. He would flirt with girls as if he were a teenager. He would overeat and bark orders at his family while wielding a gun. One night, José Luis tried to take the gun away from his father. His father cocked the gun and pointed it directly at him and his sister. "He went on through the night like this as though he was following someone else's orders." When the sun came up, he said that it was over, grabbed his guitar, and started playing music. José Luis took the opportunity to take the gun away and went to the neighbor's house to hide from him. The family took José Luis's father to Mexico City to be treated by a psychologist, who explained he was suffering the after-effects of severe torture. The doctor warned them "that it was going to be hard, you are going to have a hard life and you need to prepare yourselves." The extreme torture he endured forever changed him. However, its destruction spilled over to José Luis and others in the family across the coming decades, leaving the permanent imprint of trauma on all of them.

The story of two of José Luis's uncles, Marcial Godoy Cabañas and Isaías Castro Velásquez, highlights the ravages of the dirty war on the extended family. Isaías was taken at the same time as José Luis's father and grandfather but was not released with them. The family never found a trace of him. José Luis told about how his uncle Marcial and Clemente, another supporter of Lucio Cabañas, endured brutal torture during their imprisonment. After the military detained them in San Vicente in summer 1972, Marcial and Clemente were forced aboard a helicopter, beaten up, and flown out over the Pacific Ocean. Hovering above the water, José Luis recounted that the men

were tied by their feet and hung out of the helicopter, allowed to fall to the sea, grazing the water until it covered their heads. The first time they did it, he said he fainted, they pulled him back up on board, poured water on him to get him to regain consciousness. They kept asking, "Are you part of Lucio's group? Did you give him supplies and food?," and because he wouldn't give them the answers they wanted, they would tie him back up and throw him overboard again. The second time they threw him out, he didn't faint. He'd pretend to pass out after they submerged him in the water to get them to pull him back up. They repeated it a third time. He said he thought they had done the same thing to Isaías. Clemente thought they had possibly thrown him into the ocean and left him there.

Clemente was the last one to see Isaías alive. After the soldiers hung Isaías out the door, Clemente did not see Isaías get pulled back in, nor did he see Isaías when the helicopter landed in Acapulco. When the DFS files were released to the public in 2002, one of Isaías's nieces found a file with a note explaining that her uncle had died at a military hospital in Chilpancingo. When she returned to get a copy of the file, she was told it was no longer available.

As I explored the DFS files, I discovered that the report Isaías's niece located is a list of approximately one hundred individuals who were detained in twelve different operations in the mountains of Guerrero over the summer of 1972.[24] His name appears in the last column with five others under the heading, "Flit." We do not know what the heading stands for but can deduce that the "F" stands for "fallecidos" (deceased) since all six individuals were dead. Isaías's name is written in by hand at the end of the list and is followed by a written notation that he died in the hospital. No further details of his death are listed. Of the six dead, two others were cousins of Lucio: Domitilo Barrientos Blanco and Ezequiel Barrientos Dionicio. The other individual José Luis talked about was Clemente Valdez Valdovinos. According to the report, Clemente was detained alone on October 23, 1972, though no details are provided about what became of him.[25] The murkiness in the official record adds to the overwhelming sense that none of the families of these six dead—or the many others in other lists across the DFS files—will find justice.

The war against subversion irreparably changed the family. Their story is now one of pain, loss, and vague details, with no resolution or justice for what they endured. To this day, Isaías remains disappeared. They do not have a body, a death certificate, or anything that would shed light on precisely how he died or who killed him. All they have is the notation in the

DFS report that he died in a hospital in Chilpancingo. With no body or trace of his remains, it stands to reason why the family believes he was thrown into the Pacific Ocean. Soon after finding José Luis's father and grandfather, in 1972, the family fled to live in clandestinity in Mexico City, to escape military persecution in San Vicente. They later came out of hiding and continued their search. José Luis explained that the women of his family have never stopped looking. He said, "But the struggle continues, looking, looking [for him]. My grandmother died, my mother continued, and after my mother, we continue demanding to know from the government where they left him, where he is." In his story, we hear the weight women carried in both searching for their loved ones and ensuring that they are not forgotten. Stories of women shouldering such burdens are often repeated in the dirty war; the Cabañas family is no exception. Like his mother and grandmother, José Luis wants accountability for what was done to his family and for why they were targeted in such brutal ways. Families suffered the effects of state terror alongside their relatives, and, as José Luis's account shows, this suffering continued across generations.

Bertoldo Cabañas Ocampo

Like his relatives, Bertoldo Cabañas Ocampo is from the community of San Vicente in Atoyac, Guerrero. In contrast to his cousin Lucio, who wanted to be a teacher, Bertoldo was not interested in education. He dropped out of high school to join the army at sixteen and credits his time in the military for teaching him discipline. After three years in the army, Bertoldo returned to Atoyac to work in the civil registry and grow coffee on a plot of land. He was active in his local *comité ejidal* (collective landholding committee) and helped represent his fellow coffee farmers before the government authorities. To this day, he remembers growing up with the image of Emiliano Zapata—the famous agrarian leader of the 1910 Mexican Revolution—and admiring the Zapatistas' goal of giving land to peasants. Like other rural peoples inspired by the agrarian revolutionary hero, Bertoldo tells of Zapata's untimely death in a cowardly act of betrayal. Bertoldo's description of Zapata's assassination strikes a chord with Lucio's own killing in 1972. Both men stood up in defense of their communities and called for an armed revolution to bring about social change. Bertoldo saw Lucio and the many others like him who joined the guerrilla movement as a continuation of efforts to fulfill the unmet promise behind Zapata's call to arms.

For Bertoldo, the 1967 massacre in Atoyac was a moment of political awakening. Direct action—like Lucio took—was the only option for dealing with a government that killed its citizens indiscriminately. He was not close to Lucio growing up and only met the guerrilla leader once when Lucio and ten of his followers were in San Vicente in 1973. Bertoldo emphasized that Lucio had killed more people than Fidel Castro when he took power in Cuba. By connecting his account first to Zapata and now to Castro, Bertoldo is placing his cousin in the pantheon of revolutionary heroes. In this pantheon, the body count matters and reflects his cousin's commitment to the revolutionary cause.

Though they were not personally close to Lucio, Bertoldo and his brothers supported him. In doing so, they paid a high price. His other brother, Isaías, was injured in a shoot-out between guerrillas and the military in 1972 and died from his injuries. Bertoldo was detained by the military police for the first time in June 1971. He had taken his family to live in Mexico City to escape the military's persecution because of their search for Lucio and "so that my children could go to school." Officials picked up Bertoldo at the bus stop near his house. He remembered seeing Donato Contreras, who knew his family, point him out to the police. "He turned in a lot of my family, and he later died like a dog." Two of his cousins were also picked up at the same time: Celerina, who was later released, and Marcía Cabañas. Officers transported all three men to CM-1, where interrogators accused them of being guerrillas. Although they had hoods over their heads, Bertoldo could tell they were at a military base because he could hear the guards and the drums. While at CM-1, Bertoldo was not physically tortured but endured "hours and hours of questions." He recognized several people from San Vicente in other cells, including Agustín Flores Jiménez, Emilio Delgado, and an old man who he remembered as Don Petronilo Castro Hernandez and Don Petronilo's daughter. Emilio, according to Bertoldo, was only seventeen years old. Don Petronilo, who at the time was seventy-six, had been providing logistical support to Lucio Cabañas before being detained in April 1972. He and his daughter, Guadalupe, were brutally tortured and subsequently disappeared.[26]

Bertoldo was released after five months in CM-1, but in late 1974, he was detained again and sent back to CM-1, this time for three months. He had a form from the Ministry of Defense promising safe passage to and from Guerrero—meaning that he should have been protected from detention. But it did not stop the military from harassing him. As he was being detained the second time, Bertoldo showed the officials the form. They took it from him and escorted him back to prison. He was released in early 1975, following Lucio's death in December 1974. The pattern of harassment and detention Bertoldo endured in the war against subversion was different from that of other family members. He was not killed and disappeared like his brother or physically and mentally destroyed like his cousins. However, officials routinely harassed and twice detained him without any justification other than belonging to family of guerrilla members. Bertoldo lived in fear for himself and his children—a fear so real that he moved them to Mexico City to protect them. Even while telling of the toll it took on him to share the Cabañas name, Bertoldo commends Lucio for being a true revolutionary on par with Zapata and Castro.

Bartola Serafín Gervacio, Sofia Barrientos Serafín, Mariela Barrientos Serafín, and Humberto Barrientos Serafín

Lucio's half sister, Bartola Serafín Gervacio, lives with her daughters in the working-class neighborhood of Tláhuac in Mexico City. To reach her house, you have to walk ten blocks up a hill from where the bus drops you off. As each block passes, the streets get narrower and narrower until you reach the steep hill where Bartola's house is located. Though it was morning on a bright and sunny day, a group of men were gathered on the street drinking beer and blaring loud music. Bartola emerged from among them; she had been talking to one of her grandsons. Bartola's house was the humblest of the already humble houses on the street, with exposed beams and cement rebar coming out of the roof. One of her daughters was building a room on the roof of Bartola's house, which explained the construction. The interview took place in her small backyard. She explained that she was embarrassed to talk inside because her home was "too modest."

Bartola gave a genealogical account of her family that outlined assorted layers of relatives and degrees of parentage. They were a total of eight children from her mother's two partners. While Lucio and Pablo came from her mother's relationship with her first partner, Bartola and her four other siblings came from her mother's relationship with her second partner, Juan Serafín. As she narrated the intricacies of the family tree, she offhandedly mentioned that her brother, Manuel Garcia Cabañas, and her uncle, Antonio Onofre Barrientos, were detained by the military. She remembered meeting Lucio in San Martin when she was eight years old, after her father passed away. Lucio was attending classes at Ayotzinapa. She recalled that he was always kind to her and her brothers because "we were the younger siblings." After he took to the mountains in 1968 to evade capture, Lucio came to visit his family three times. He came under the cover of night, saw his family, and held secret meetings at the local school. After one of these visits, Bartola's older brother David, who was about twenty at the time, decided to follow Lucio to the mountains.

Everything changed for the family after 1968. After Lucio went to the mountains, the military set its sights on them. It seemed that no one connected to the family was safe. Marciana Serafín, the woman who raised Lucio and Bartola's aunt, was detained. Bartola remembered that the military came for Marciana at night and took her out of the house wearing only her nightgown. They took her to CM-1 in Mexico City, where she was imprisoned for several years. When they took Marciana, Bartola's mother knew she would be next, so she took her children and left for Acapulco. Bartola stayed behind in San Martin because she was already married and had two young daughters of her own. The military had set up an encampment in the town, and Bartola remembered that officials periodically detained members of the family for interrogation. This pattern of harassment included her cousins, Abelardo and Moisés Morales Gervacio. The military released the family members after interrogating and torturing them. In other cases, family members never returned, as was the case after Abelardo's second detention in 1974. In April 1974, Bartola and her family left San Martin, first for Atoyac and later for Acapulco. Eventually, every member of the family left San Martin, and most ended up in Acapulco. Even there, the harassment continued. The military picked up another cousin, Eugenio Gómez Serafín, at a checkpoint in Acapulco and never returned him. It became clear to the family that they would be

detained at checkpoints just because of their last names, so they decided
to move again to Mexico City.

The day Bartola and her family were detained started off normally. Her
mother woke up early and went to a local market to buy groceries. There
a plainclothes officer came up to her and embraced her as though he knew
her to mislead onlookers. He told her they knew she was Lucio's mother
and that she had better come with them. They forced her into a van, where
her son, Manuel, lay on the floor. He had visible signs of torture: there
were cigarette burns on his abdomen and bruises all over his body, and he
was bleeding from a head wound. Another man she knew from San
Martin, Leonardo de la Cruz, also lay on the floor of the van. The officer
told her that "Leoncito" had pointed her out to them. He threatened to
hurt Manuel further and to string her up at the entrance to the town if she
did not take them to the house where the rest of the family was staying.
About eight other plainclothes officers descended on the house in search
of Bartola's older brother David, Lucio's partner, Isabel Ayala, and their
baby girl, Micaela. When the officers arrived, David had already left for
the day, but the others were still at home. The officers started interrogating the family, demanding to know Lucio's and David's whereabouts.

Bartola's daughter, Mariela, had just turned five years old. "I remember
when those people came to the house," she said. "I was playing when they
came in, and they started throwing everything around. They scared us,
and I ran out of the house scared, only to see how the soldiers were beating
up my father with the butt of a gun." Bartola's older daughter, Sofia, who
was eight, described the screams of people getting beaten by the soldiers
and the fear she felt. "I was hugging my sister, my baby brother, and my
mother. I asked her what was going on and she answered, 'Nothing is
going on.' But I could hear people screaming, 'Let him go, don't take him,
he hasn't done anything.'" Sofia saw what was happening to her father at
this moment: "They thought my father was David. My grandmother kept
telling them that he wasn't David, that he was her son-in-law. We were
stunned at how they were throwing everything everywhere and the horrible words they used, all while laughing. They threatened to strangle my
grandmother." As she described this period in her life, Sofia remembered
how relatives she knew were taken away, tied up, beaten, and never seen
again. "A lot of people were disappeared during this time," she said. In the

state of Guerrero alone, the Truth Commission listed the cases of 236 individuals permanently disappeared in the dirty war. Nineteen of these individuals share a last name with Sofia and Bartola.[27] The day she and her family were detained, Sofia recalled, she froze in fear, feeling like she could not move: "The men came in yelling at my grandmother, my mother, my aunt Isabel, asking where Lucio was, where David was. Other men scoured the room, throwing all our things. I have that image of how they threw everything, all the papers, everything, and I didn't know what they were looking for."

The officers were so busy going through the family's belongings and shouting questions that they neglected to station an officer outside the house. When David approached the house, Sofia and Mariela ran out to warn him. David managed to get away. When the soldiers returned to the house, they brought in Manuel, who was naked from the waist up and had to be carried by two men because his injuries prevented him from standing on his own. "I saw him all beaten up, he was dirty, and that's the image that I have of him," Sofia said. "Naked and all burned up." She wanted to run to him, but they wouldn't let her get close.

While they had not caught David, the officers took Manuel, Isabel, and baby Micaela away. Later that night, the officers put the rest of the family in the back of a van: Bartola, her mother, sister, brother, husband, their daughters, Sofia and Mariela, and their baby boy, Humberto. They were first transported to the military base in Pie de la Cuesta and then to CM-1 in Mexico City. Bartola remembered hearing the planes taking off and landing at Pie de la Cuesta. She remembered the officers threatening to throw her children in the ocean if she did not give up the locations of Lucio's supporters. After the initial interrogation, the officers transported the family to Mexico City in a small plane. Bartola recalled that Isabel and baby Micaela were also on the plane. Once they arrived at CM-1, the soldiers took the mother and baby to one cell; Bartola's brother, Conrado, and her husband to another; and the others—Bartola, her mother, her sister, and her three children—to a third cell. After three months, Isabel and Micaela were moved into the same cell.

Sofia and Mariela have vivid memories of CM-1. Sofia recalled how her ears hurt from the altitude and noise aboard the plane to CM-1. Once they landed, a soldier put a blindfold over her eyes as they were escorted around a series of buildings painted white. "I got really scared, so I pulled off the blindfold and ran to my mother to grab her dress." They took them to a cell, and Sofia recalled that the soldiers kept asking her where her uncles David and Lucio were. She described arriving at their cell block: "Later they took us into an area where there were something like twenty little rooms on each side. They had a small window. You could hear a lot of noise, a lot of screaming. At that time, I didn't understand why there was so much screaming. They were being tortured."

Mariela was able to remember the rows of cells, the darkness, the names etched into the walls. She could still hear the booming voice of General Alejandro Lugos, the commanding officer, who would stop by their cell and who called her grandmother "boss" (*jefa*) while putting his hand on her back. This familiar gesture of respect must have fallen flat considering the circumstances. The guards would blindfold Sofia when walking outside the halls but not Mariela, so she could see where her father was. Sofia added that she had nightmares during their imprisonment and after their release that "soldiers were chasing me and I was so afraid. I'd wake up at night crying and my mother would have to come in to console me."

During the first three months, the soldiers would threaten the family and demand information. But then the questions stopped. "They just left us there locked up," Bartola said. "The questions were over." She believes they stopped asking questions because Lucio was killed eight days after they were detained. "They grabbed us on November 26, and he died on December 2." Nevertheless, the military did not release the family. "We were there for almost two years." During this time, the family did not know of Lucio's death because they had not had contact with the outside world and their captors did not inform them. One or two days a week, the guards would take them outside "for a half hour and then back in again." Bartola's daughters recalled that they could see their father on the other side of the prison wall but did not have permission to have contact with him. Mariela said, "We were not allowed to talk to anyone." General Lugos would bark orders in a loud voice. "The girls would hide because they were afraid of his voice," Bartola remembered.

Though they were not allowed to talk to anyone, Bartola remembered how they struck up a friendship with one of the women guards. On several

Sundays during their two-year stay at CM-1, the guard brought her daughters to play with Sofia and Mariela. She told them that "it was really awful to imprison little children." She would bring thread for Bartola's mother, which they used to sew sheets and pillows that the guard then sold to other prisoners on their behalf. She also brought them a small grill that they could keep inside the cell to heat milk for the children. From this guard they learned that there were two women in the neighboring cell, including Elsa Aguirre, who had known Lucio. It is unclear who the other woman was or what Elsa's association with Lucio was." The guard would tell us, 'When you get out, come and see me.' We went to see her, and she told us that Elsa had also stopped by to visit with her upon her release," Bartola remembered. "We never saw the guard again, but she was really nice." It may seem surprising that a prisoner and a guard could have this kind of relationship, and it is especially hard to understand a former prisoner visiting a prison guard after being released. Nevertheless, this interaction suggests the muddiness of what happens behind bars between individuals on different sides of them. Even while guards were complicit, they exhibited humanity and moral equivalencies in the dirty war.

On the back of the cell door, former prisoners had etched their names with a nail. "We found the names of Uncle Toño, Antonio Onofre, and others who we didn't know." Antonio had supported Lucio's activism, and Lucio, his nephew, would stay with him when visiting San Martin. Antonio boarded a bus in September 1972 in Zacatepec, Morelos, and no one ever saw him again.[28] Finding themselves in a cell where a disappeared relative has also been detained must have been terrifying and heart-wrenching at the same time for Bartola and her daughters. Sharing the same cell illustrates how Lucio's entire family—immediate and extended—shared in the collective experience of trauma. Bartola described seeing the name of another one of her cousins who was disappeared, Raimundo Morales Gervacio. "Their names were there." The names of Antonio and Raimundo etched into the wall illustrates how deep into the family tree state violence reached to punish them. The fact that both were permanently disappeared further drives home the sense that the punishment was intended to obliterate the family.

"We were disappeared, but the family never stopped looking for us," Bartola said. "I don't know how they did it, but they found us after almost two years of us being disappeared." An uncle, Manuel García Cabañas, managed to track them down and came with Bartola's sister to demand their release. Manuel, who had been captured and tortured but released, knew where to look for them. After admitting to Manuel that they had the family, military officials told him that "they didn't want to release" Bartola and her relatives "because they wanted to make them pay for everything Lucio had done." In May 1976, Manuel finally convinced the military to release Bartola, her family, Isabel Ayala, and Lucio and Isabel's daughter, Micaela. They all stayed in a hotel in Mexico City for two weeks while they figured out where to go. They did not want to return to Guerrero for fear something would happen again. That fear that the government would target them again for the sole reason of being members of Lucio's family never went away. None of them returned to Guerrero, apart from Bartola's mother, who returned to San Martin "to die in my land" about a decade after her release.

Political violence left a permanent imprint on the family that stretched from one generation to the next. Bartola's brother, David, became withdrawn once he was released, and she rarely saw him again. Sofia explained that after their release, her parents struggled to find work to support the family. Her father, Juan Serafín, finally got a job in construction. The girls had missed two years of school, so they were behind and had to make up time. Sofia said, "I was almost fifteen years old when I finished elementary school." The effects of state repression and persecution reverberated through Sofia's life from early in her childhood. Sofia remembered what it was like after they had to flee their house in San Martin, how much she wanted to go to school, and how much she disliked always having to hide indoors. The trauma of these early experiences lingered and marked her life.

Humberto Barrientos Serafín, the youngest of Bartola's children, was only a baby when the family was imprisoned in CM-1 and has no memory of his time there. Nevertheless, he has lived with the experience of those two years his whole life. Bartola's husband died soon after they were freed. According to all three of his children, he suffered from serious depression and took to the bottle to cover up the pain. Humberto explained that the depression stemmed from the torture his father endured as well as from being uprooted from his home in rural Guerrero. "He gave us everything he could," Humberto stated, "and the drinking was an escape." He wondered what it would have been like to grow up with a father who had not died so early in his life. "If you think about it, they also took our father." Humberto built on Sofia's comment that the education of all three of Bartola's children suffered because of what they endured. Learning was never the same for them after their release. What would have happened, he seemed to wonder, had they grown up in San Martin with enough stability to go to school and make a life for themselves? What would their present be like if their past did not include a two-year incarceration and the related trauma? "I needed my father," Humberto concluded.

The effects of their collective trauma forever marked this family. Much of their struggles in their post-detention lives traced back to what the government did to all of them across these years. Bartola and her family told of their long struggle over the course of three decades to find some justice for what was done to them. After Vicente Fox released the files in 2002 and set up the FEMOSPP, the family believed they would finally have their moment of reckoning. They did not. "They tell us to be patient, that it'll happen, but nothing happens," Bartola said. "It's been a long time, and the most affected people are starting to die." Sofia explained that all they want "is to have justice for all that was done to us during the dirty war. The crime continues. We hope that justice is finally had for all that was done to the prisoners, to all the people who lost family members. Let them have justice."

The Cabañas family wants some form of justice after so much effort to shed light on what happened to them. Bartola continued, "They send us to talk to people who we are told are psychologists who ask us questions as though we were being interrogated. Having to remember and recall everything to yet another person, another government official, is a form of torture." Sofia added, "They send us to talk to the attorney general, the ProVictim office, to Gobernación, it's always the same, and we have to say the same thing, give the same declaration over again." The family is united in the pain they feel—"like they're throwing dirty water on us, the bile rising out of our stomachs"—having to relive their story over and over for a new official with no end in sight. Bartola and Sofia described the weight of living with impunity and the likelihood that their family will never witness some form of justice. At the very least, they and other members of the Cabañas family want recognition that the government was at fault for subjecting them to such violence for merely sharing the same bloodline as Lucio Cabañas.

The weight of impunity can be heard in Bartola's description of the futile search for the remains of her disappeared family members. She recalls how they heard that General Acosta Chaparro, one of the military architects of the dirty war in Guerrero, had said that "they should look for the remains inside the sharks' stomachs, that salt disintegrates bones, and that they no longer exist." The idea that what she and her family endured might vanish like the bodies of the disappeared dumped off planes into the Pacific Ocean is devastating because it projects the government's attempt to destroy a bloodline. After Bartola and her family were released, they had to track down their identification documents because the military had taken all their paperwork, including birth certificates, when they were originally detained. "This was going to be a total disappearance," Sofia explained. "That no one was going to find trace of us anywhere." Taking their documents suggests part of the plan was to erase the Cabañas family from existence. That official erasure from the documentary record—in tandem with their torture, imprisonment, and disappearance—speaks to the perceived danger the family unit posed in the dirty war.

CONCLUSION

An official recognition of what Bartola, her children, and others like her endured in the war against subversion opens up the public discussion of how deeply state violence reached into family trees during the dirty war. What we see in this discussion is how torture and the imprisonment of so-called insurgents was a family affair and not solely experienced individually. The family, then, was a key unit of perceived threat in this war. Over and over, officials detained family members, not because they posed a security threat, but because they could be used as pawns in torture sessions or as deterrents to force the hands of guerrilla leaders. The family became a site of punishment, stripped of humanity and guilty merely for being part of a bloodline. The family—not the individual—is at the center of this particular brand of political violence endemic in Mexico's dirty war. More than just a collection of victims, the family has been at the forefront of social consciousness in their quest for justice for themselves and their loved ones. These mothers, fathers, daughters, sons, sisters, and brothers shared either directly or indirectly in what government officials inflicted on their loved ones in clandestine prisons and torture chambers. They have gone on to share their stories and demand forms of reckoning from the government.

Josafath Hernandez Rios told a common story of a family's quest for accountability. In the 1970s, he was brutally tortured at the military base in Atoyac when he was only sixteen years old. His father, Julio Hernandez Hinojosa, was tortured to death at the same time. "We sued the government since he died and have gotten nowhere." His frustration was palpable as he described all the times he has had to give an official declaration to assorted government agencies. He mentioned the promises made but never fulfilled, his voice heavy with disillusionment.

> They've been promising some resolution since 2002. It's been years and nothing so far. What they've been promising comes from justice, and they can't even fulfill that. For justice to be achieved, they have to make these damn assassins pay. They killed people and they deserve to be punished. Because many of the people who committed these atrocities are alive and enjoying a salary and retirement benefits. They are protected by the same military. In other words, they are using our taxes to cover their backs.

Demanding accountability extends to the disappeared, according to Josafath, whose remains have yet to be located. "As Acosta Chaparro said, we should look for them in the bellies of the sharks." In referencing the "death flights" off the coast of Guerrero and Oaxaca, Josafath has challenged us to remember the disappeared. Assessing the legacy of this period—especially from the main square in the San Andrés neighborhood of Guadalajara or in communities surrounding Atoyac, Guerrero—requires placing the family as the primary unit of analysis.

6 Three Prisoners

To grasp the lived experience of being a political prisoner and what it meant to be tortured in this age of counterinsurgency, this chapter moves from analysis to narrative.[1] We explore three stories of people who were tortured and imprisoned, beginning with their political involvement and radicalization and up through their release. Their stories illustrate the processes that have been explored in previous chapters: political dissent, torture, torturers, political imprisonment, and families. The experiences of these three individuals are primarily told from their perspective using in-depth interviews and supplemented with additional records. They come from different socioeconomic backgrounds and straddle the urban/rural divide. Rather than focus on the main protagonists of armed guerrilla movements, this chapter deliberately studies the cases of rank-and-file members of these groups. While compelling, guerrilla leaders like Lucio Cabañas and Genaro Vázquez do not represent the traditional cycle of detention, interrogation and torture, imprisonment, and release or disappearance that tended to be the norm for most activists in Mexico's dirty war. Lucio died in a heated battle with military forces in the mountains of Guerrero. Genaro perished after soldiers denied medical attention following a car accident.[2] Deaths on the battlefield or at the hands of security forces were not the most common experience in this war. Being a political prisoner subjected to torture was the norm.

These case studies provide a narrative explanation for what it was like to be a political prisoner. The common path saw young people being politically radicalized, often by peers or by events such as the 1968 Tlatelolco massacre or the 1971 Corpus Christi massacre. The choice to take up arms and opt for direct means to achieve social change appealed to young people as they witnessed the failure of moderate and institutional paths. They would then participate in armed or unarmed opposition activities, which government officials criminalized irrespective of whether they posed an actual threat to the political order. As part of that criminalization, officials labeled them subversive and ordered their detention, torture, imprisonment, and release. Previous chapters have provided snippets of these experiences; this chapter gives the whole picture layered in three different cases. The singular event of an individual's detention or of their torture then is read into a much longer chronology of a life cycle marked by idealism, elation, fear, pain, guilt, and disillusionment during their formative decades. This longer view thus helps us better appreciate what drove an individual to make a deliberate choice to join an armed guerrilla movement that could lead to their death or go against the desire of their loved ones.

The narrative choices individuals make—what gets included, excluded, amplified, or silenced—to talk about key moments in their story, such as their detention and torture, reveal how their personal histories are influenced by gender, generational, and class conventions. They have told their stories before, so the version before us has settled across the decades, and in every case we get glimpses of both regret and mourning for an idealized past—of what could have been had their dreams come to fruition. Especially revealing is how they reconstruct what became of their lives after their release. They may no longer be behind bars, but, as their words show, they continue to live in a metaphorical prison in their minds. We hear the guilt over the toll their choices took on their families and the melancholy of dashed dreams and questionable sacrifices. They express frustration for feeling left behind by new waves of social justice movements that do not respect or acknowledge their sacrifices in earlier moments. We hear resentment of ongoing debates over the "right" way to achieve large-scale social change: Should there be some compromise to work within existing institutional pathways, or should it involve taking up arms in defense of moral authority? In these moments, we get insights that go beyond the oft-told tale of heroic guerrillas battling an oppressive government and the rehearsed script that emerges from retelling the same story at different moments across decades. It is here that individuals weave between regret and defending their choices, rationalizing them in the language of victimhood or an ongoing social justice struggle.

In his study of life histories and the subjectivity of memory, Daniel James discusses the ways in which activists resort to an epic form of narrative storytelling. They resort to tropes such as attaining consciousness, embarking on a quest, adopting a moral proposition for social justice, embracing a community of like-minded individuals, taking up arms against a seemingly insurmountable enemy, and being felled defending their values. The story they tell has happened to many others and leaves little room for individual experiences. These tropes then give narrative coherence to a life story and relegate glimpses of regret and disappointment to the margins.[3] That tension between what James calls coherence and obscurity allows for the "coexistence of contradictory themes and ambivalent meanings in an account of a life."[4] Here we see that individuals recount how these movements did not rely on one leader, because movements need both leaders and followers. Vázquez and Cabañas would have been nothing without people who followed them, and LC23S had many leaders and not a singular voice. While women guerrilla members adamantly defend equality among their comrades, the longer and more involved telling of their experiences shows how gender factored into their evolution as activists. The gendered thread cuts across the two men as they describe how they endured torture and how pain "built character." The exigencies of the time, in their telling, allowed for two unresolved truths to coexist: holding fast to a language of equality negated the role of gender inside and outside their movements or even in the torture chamber, but that did not stop gender from cutting through every word of their account. At the end, the story individuals tell about their lives bears the weight of legacy and involves a selective weaving of meaning behind their memories.

THE CASE OF PATRICIO ABARCA MARTÍNEZ
AND THE PRISONER FROM GUERRERO

Patricio Abarca Martínez grew up in the Guerrero countryside, where his parents were teachers. They sent him to high school in a nearby city because there was not one close to their home. Patricio recalls having a political awakening here, first in student affairs, later as he learned what students were doing at normal schools throughout Guerrero. He first landed in prison for his political activism in the mid-1960s, following several months of strikes among the region's high school students in protest against the state governor. Police stormed the hall they were occupying during a strike one night and hauled the students away to a local jail. Officials released Patricio because he was underage; instead of being jailed, he was expelled from school as his punishment for his activism. He went to Mexico City to continue his studies at the Instituto Politécnico Nacional but had to drop out because he could not afford the school fees and living expenses. Soon after, he returned to Guerrero and joined the Communist youth movement. "We were part of the Sixties generation and I'm proud to say influenced by the Cuban Revolution, the fight against the Vietnam War, against the Yankees. It was a peaceful and, in our view, legal fight," Patricio said. He was picked up by the police on several occasions for his activism during the mid-1960s. "It wasn't serious torture. They would hit and threaten us, put us in jail. Our families would lobby, and they'd release us."

Patricio eventually got a job as a teacher in Acapulco at the Instituto México (Mexico Institute), where he met Humberto Espino Barros, who had recently returned from Cuba. Humberto "talked about the wonders of the revolution. 'Let's make a revolution happen in Mexico.' We got together a group of comrades willing to take to the mountains to join Lucio." Six of them went in search of Lucio Cabañas, guided by a member of their group who was from San Vicente. "We were in the mountains, isolated from the world and from life," but they could not locate the guerrilla leader. At the start of 1968, the group started fracturing under the pressure "of the stress, the isolation, getting fed up being with each other. We each had a task and it was like, 'You didn't do what you were supposed to do,' 'You're not the boss of us.' It got bad when one of the comrades said, 'It's your turn at the ax,' and he picked up a machete and the others felt threatened, so he took out his gun. He was just a kid and didn't know how to shoot. They're going to kill me. One day, I went to a nearby stream and escaped. I ran and ran so they wouldn't catch up with me because I thought they would kill me for being a deserter." Patricio arrived at a nearby town and talked some women into giving him money to take the bus back to Acapulco. As this first foray into activism came to a close, we appreciate that Patricio—and likely his comrades—seemed out of their depth and as if none of them were sure about the seriousness of the venture. Would they kill one another over desertion? Did they really know what they were fighting for? What was behind the romanticism of belonging to a movement that appeared in vogue at the time? Neither Patricio nor the others knew the answers to these questions because of the lack of discipline in the group. This first experience with activism, then, can be viewed as a formative yet unsophisticated guerrilla experiment.

Though he was back home, Patricio still felt politically committed to the ideals of the student movement. His commitment came into greater focus in August 1968 as the student movement in Mexico City went into full swing. His comrades sent a representative from Guerrero by the name of Carmelo Cortés Castro to the student leadership council in Mexico City. Carmelo went into hiding after the massacre of October 2, 1968, allegedly spending some time studying in the Soviet Union on a scholarship. He reappeared in 1970 to tell the Guerrero comrades what he learned while abroad.[5] Carmelo "had spent time with many guerrilla members from Central America. He told us about his studies, how to learn more about Marxism, how the guerrilla movement was spreading throughout Latin America. The dream of making a new continent. Very moving, but I told him that I was moving to Aguascalientes to be a teacher." As Carmelo's comments show, he and later Patricio represented the experiences of student activists radicalized in the aftermath of the Tlatelolco massacre in 1968. The government's response was so brutal that it convinced many activists that the only way to bring about social change would be by taking up arms and joining the guerrilla movement.

Four years later, in 1972, Patricio received a message from Carmelo, who was imprisoned in Chilpancingo for robbing a bank to fund the guerrilla activities of the movement he belonged to, the Brigada Campesina de

Ajusticiamiento (Peasant Brigade for Justice). "At that time, it wasn't so difficult to go see prisoners, and I didn't have any trouble getting to him," Patricio told me. Carmelo explained to Patricio that he was going to escape from prison and needed his help to get messages to his comrades. After two weeks of preparations, Patricio helped Carmelo secure a way out of prison and a place to hide out. Carmelo snuck out of prison late at night. Patricio gave him a gun and instructions on where to go, after which they parted ways and Patricio returned to his house. His mother, worried that the police would come to arrest Patricio because he had recently visited Carmelo in prison, burned his clothes. The following day the police "were waiting for me at the corner. That's where they detained me, and now it's really jail." The police beat him and started questioning him. "I just had to hold out." Patricio did not specify if he told police about Carmelo in this interrogation. Instead, he stressed giving his comrade time to make a clean getaway. The police released Patricio soon after, and he went back to being a teacher. The risk he took to help Carmelo escape as well as his brief stint in prison started crystallizing for Patricio his commitment to a more radical option to bring about social change.

He met with Carmelo again in December 1974 in Acapulco, and this time he agreed to join what would become the Fuerzas Armadas Revolucionarias. In the two years since they had last had contact, Carmelo had left Lucio Cabañas's Partido de los Pobres over disagreements. For both Carmelo and Patricio, the FAR was their opportunity to demonstrate their commitment to an armed revolution. This was no longer an amateur experiment tinged with ambivalence; the FAR coalesced their vision of a guerrilla movement and their willingness to die—and kill others—for their cause. "We had to develop a revolutionary program with the objective of building a new society." The program would have to lay out the steps by which to "achieve power, install the proletariat, battle the bourgeoisie and capitalism, and build a new socialist state. Each meeting with Carmelo was like a study session. We read about how the Mexican Revolution wasn't really a revolution. We learned the basics of Marxism, of Lenin. Carmelo insisted that a revolutionary shouldn't just be someone who knew how to handle weapons but also had to understand what weapons were for." According to Carmelo, a revolution is fought "with ideas and conviction of where we are going." Carmelo's ideological conviction represented a battle-tested and sophisticated vision of what armed guerrilla movements could achieve, and it resonated with Patricio.

Patricio lamented that they were never able to put this program into practice. The military came looking for Carmelo, who escaped to the state of Mexico and went into hiding. As he and his comrades attempted to regroup while in hiding, Carmelo was detained and, according to Patricio, assassinated in August 1975. With the death of their leader, the movement he had organized deteriorated. Patricio explained that Carmelo's death instilled fear among his comrades. Some decided to go back to their lives—Patricio returned to being a teacher in Aguascalientes—and others continued organizing for revolution with a different group. Two of his comrades who had returned to their lives were detained in 1977 in Cuernavaca, Morelos.

> These two made the rest of us all fall. On June 20, 1977, the police got me. I was getting off the train. They came up on either side. I think it was the federal police because of the way they behaved, cars without license plates, without uniform. I was taking my daughter to school. They started beating up the school principal, probably because I looked too young and they confused us. "Ah, Patricio, you thought you could escape from us." I felt pity and told them, "I'm Patricio." They put me in the car.[6]

He was blindfolded and handcuffed. "They took me to a place right there in Aguascalientes to interrogate me. I could hear a gate, like a big, open space. They left me lying there. I lost my sense of time, but I figure it must have been nighttime." They put him in the back of the car, and it felt like they were on a highway. Patricio continued, "They sat down and put their feet on top of me. We got to a different place. They took me out of the car and put me in a little room. Someone said, 'Take off his blindfold.' As they ripped it off, they took a piece of my flesh with it." The questioning started. "'Alright, asshole, you have two choices: life or death. We're going to decide what is best for you depending on what you give us. You're going to tell us this, where are the weapons? Where's the money?'" Patricio denied knowing where either was, which he laughingly says was the truth because there were neither guns nor money. "'Well, if you don't tell us, we already have your wife and children and we're going to do it in front of you.' It was a day of beatings, psychological torture, questions." They showed him

photographs and asked who he knew. Patricio recalled seeing the pictures
of all his comrades. "I was glad in some way to see their images there
because it meant that I wasn't alone."

They took him to another place for the night. "I didn't feel cold. It's sort
of like the mind atrophies. Later I realized it was the fourth day and I
hadn't eaten, but I didn't feel hungry. It's like the mind is on another channel. But it was good. I was happy because I thought I would soon be freed."
But that was not the case. They paraded him in front of the press and,
again, Patricio felt good because he did not think there was anything more
they could do to him and at least this way his family would know where he
was. They moved him again, this time back to Chilpancingo. "Two, three
days went by. Finally, on the fifth day, they said, 'Let's go,' and tied my
hands behind my back and blindfolded me. They brought me to Acapulco,
to a clandestine prison called the Railroad. They put me in there from
June 30 to December 6. They took me to another clandestine prison, but
this time it was a military one. The boot steps, the voice, and the plate
inscribed with 'military defense.'" He was there for fifteen days.

Patricio said that "the torture was permanent." They kept asking about
the weapons, the money, and the guerrillas. He might just be standing in
his cell, and a guard would come over, grab him by the neck, and slam him
up against the bars, demanding to know about the money. "The beatings
happened at the start. Later on, it was like we didn't exist. They wouldn't
see us, wouldn't hear us, and the most serious of all, wouldn't feed us.
Food came on Mondays, Wednesdays, and Fridays. We knew it was
Saturday and Sunday because we didn't get food. We'd wait until Monday.
The plate would have watery beans and three tortillas." The space itself
was also a form of torture. "The cell measured one meter [1.09 yds.] in
width and 1.60 [5.25 ft.] in length. I measure 1.60, so I couldn't fit lying
down. There's no bed, you sleep on the floor, no sheet, and the heat in
Acapulco is intense, so you'd take your clothes off. There was a small
faucet, so you could drink water."

Then, according to Patricio, there was the psychological torture.

My cell was close to the torture room. The room was four meters by four
meters with a big sink of water where they drowned them. Kick them in the
stomach. It was practically a daily form of torture to imagine what was

being done to them in there. The worst was between July and August 1977 when they caught a whole bunch of guerrilla members. I could hear the names of some of the comrades I knew from the urban guerrilla of the Fuerzas Armadas de Liberación. Oscar, Florentino, Amelia, the Gallegos brothers. These were people who had been with Lucio. They had up to thirty or forty detainees in there, so they didn't fit in the cells. Since there were no restrooms in there, people had to go right there and the stench was overwhelming. All tied up, beaten up, waiting, waiting, not knowing what you were waiting for.

At some point, the guards started calling people from a list. "'Put on your pants, put on your shirts.' I thought they must be taking them to the Public Ministry. They took a group away and came back for more. In the last group, I thought I heard my name, and I got my things and went with them." The guards told Patricio his name was not on the list and made him return to his cell. "I had the illusion that I was going to be freed. The truth was that they were being taken away to be disappeared. We don't know what came of the ones I knew were in there, but they were there."

Patricio cycled from detention, torture, and imprisonment to the final phase: release. As this phase proceeded, the role of his family comes into sharper relief. "My family lived this agony searching for me from Acapulco to Guerrero. My sister and my mother went to the doors of the courts, the jails, and nobody would help them. The uncertainty was very difficult." Once they learned where Patricio was, they waited outside for him every day for two months until his release. "They had us on a fattening regimen. They put us in a little room with a mattress, and our families could take us food. Fifteen days eating, and our families could visit us." Prison had taken a toll on Patricio's body. He remembers weighing about 60 kilos [132 lbs.] when he was first detained. At the end of his detention—a little over five months from the day he was picked up—he felt like he weighed half of that. In recounting his detention and torture, he did not disclose what he divulged during his interrogation. In DFS files on his detention, an agent wrote that Patricio told the officers he was recruited to the FAR by Virgilio de la Crúz Hernández. He made no mention of Carmelo's role in weighing his decision to join the FAR. Patricio also divulged that he was involved in the kidnapping of Thelma Guadalupe Soto and told the officers how he distributed the ransom of 600,000 pesos among his comrades.[7] None of

these details emerge in the narrative Patricio told of when he was tortured. Instead, Patricio's story is one of pain, degradation, fear, and endur-
ance. It is a story of what was done to him.

On his release, Patricio tried to resume his life and looked for a job. He
took stock of the toll his activism had had on his loved ones. "The mothers
are the ones who suffer the most. My mother would cry, 'Please don't do
this anymore, don't go, what's it worth to you.' We felt like we were heroes.
If we don't do it, who will? Mothers always try to protect their children."
As for his wife, Patricio is aware of how much this has cost her. "She is
noble. Sometimes she would tell me, 'It's your ideals, and who am I to take
them away from you.' This has been hard on her. It's been hard on her
body." She developed kidney disease that he thinks is the result of stress
from his imprisonment, and he now has to care for her. That sense of
repaying her for her abnegation echoes in his words.

Though he no longer participated in armed guerrilla movements after
his release, Patricio continued his political engagement in less radical
groups. At the end of the 1970s, he joined the Partido Socialista (Socialist
Party) and later on the Partido Socialista de Trabajadores (Workers'
Socialist Party) in Guerrero. He helped organize grassroots movements to
improve access to housing and in support of taxi drivers. As he explained
his continued activism, he rationalized that he was part of social movements that provided a necessary balance to Mexico's unstable political system. "Lucio was finished, but the armed movement wasn't. Genaro was
finished, but the urban movement wasn't." According to Patricio, "The
clandestine Communist Party and other movements brewing among doctors, railroad workers, peasants in Morelos" continued to put pressure on
the government after 1978. "This country was like a pot about to boil
over." In response, the government instituted political reforms intended to
diffuse the radical potential of all these social movements, including the
legalization of the Communist Party.

According to Patricio, these reforms led some of his comrades to argue
that they could accommodate the government under the premise of working within the system. Undergirding his belief is a tension between what
Patricio interprets as "accommodation," which he did not respect or agree
with, and "working within the system," which saw activists as leveraging a
political opening to achieve more measured gains. The tension between

"accommodation" and "working within the system" is an endemic feature of social movements, especially those with radical routes such as the ones Patricio belonged to over time. Different political moments and stages of growth within popular movements prompt shifts and disagreements about tactics, which is even more apparent in how the political reforms prompted a movement away from the armed route to political change for some activists—but not all. Patricio's skepticism of activists who accommodated has continued to today, as the presidency of Andrés Manuel López Obrador (AMLO) emboldens leftist movements in Mexico at the time of this writing. "Electoral processes aren't going to change anybody. It has to be a fundamental change that can only happen via a revolution. It can't be the type of revolution that we envisioned. It has to be different and include social networks and technology. A world that no longer belongs to us, it belongs to other generations."

Taking stock of AMLO's presidency, Patricio's skepticism has proven somewhat well placed as the president's many promises have not borne fruit. Patricio's answer to AMLO and his supporters that fundamental change can only happen via revolution rings hollow both because AMLO effectively co-opted such rhetoric and because Patricio is hard pressed to find an example of a revolution culminating in fundamental change. Instead, he reflects that such change has yet to be imagined, and the onus for creating it lies with future generations of young people. Patricio's coming-of-age story—from being a student genuinely wanting to believe that he could help bring about radical change, radicalized in the heyday of 1968, to someone carrying responsibilities for his family and the scars of his activism that never came to fruition—overlays the cycle of detention, interrogation and torture, imprisonment, and release of so many political prisoners from the 1970s. History has left him behind, and he is now a witness to others embarking on journeys similar to his in the 1960s.

THE CASE OF JAIME LAGUNA BERBER AND THE PRISONER FROM MEXICO CITY

In contrast to many other political activists interviewed for this book, Jaime Laguna Berber came of age as the armed popular movements suffered their final defeat in the era of counterinsurgency. He joined LC23S in 1976 at the age of seventeen and took up a clandestine life in 1977. He was detained, tortured, and imprisoned in 1980, making him possibly one of the last guerrilla members—certainly from LC23S if not all guerrilla groups from the 1970s—to suffer this fate. His chronology moves us beyond the typical life span of other activists because he was a young child in the late 1960s, and by the time he joined the guerrilla movement, he knew full well what fate might befall him. The timing of his detention and torture also shows a government more attuned to the fact it was already victorious against guerrilla groups and was ready to move its security apparatus on to new priorities, including counternarcotics operations. The question then remains as to why Jaime chose to join and stay in the ranks of a guerrilla group in the throes of defeat.

Jaime chalked up his political awakening to having lived in the Tlatelolco housing complex in Mexico City during the events of October 2, 1968. He had just turned eight years old and recalled seeing the tanks go by that day. As he went through school, his teachers came from the generation of 1968 and nurtured his political formation. They told him about "The Communist Manifesto," Chairman Mao's ideas, and the experiences of the earlier student movements. Jaime contemplated the groups available for political activism in the mid-1970s and found them lacking. President Echeverría Álvarez's "political opening" meant that many folks from the left had joined the regime and sold out, in his recollection. "Everyone talked about revolution, but nobody did anything about it. Revolution implies having a different vision of politics, not just studying Marx and distributing pamphlets in factories." Through his involvement in student politics, he learned about LC23S and joined one of its study groups. Jaime was impressed with the quality of its publications. "Their flyers weren't just mimeographs. They were photographs, something professional. That's when I realized this organization was for real." They disbanded their study group in late 1977. LC23S's leadership ordered Jaime to infiltrate a metalworks factory in order to organize workers from within and recruit them to their armed revolutionary cause. His family knew little of his activism and had no idea that he had left school. His mother, a single parent, was happy that he was getting a salary from his job and "was behaving well."

Soon after, Jaime became acutely aware of the repression he was risk-ing. Two of his comrades from the original study group, ordered to protect a safe house, were killed in a shoot-out with police in January 1978. "I could have been the one to raise my hand, and I would be one of the dead," he said. Another of his comrades was detained in April after killing two police officers. "A note came out that he had been emasculated. They cas-trated him by cutting off his penis. You realize they were following us right on our heels. The balance between being imprisoned and being alive is like a paradox of how one builds a life. You really feel like you have nothing to lose because at any moment it might all be gone." There is a vagueness about what drove him to hold fast to the guerrilla group's principles at this point. Did he stay out of fear, because he could not imagine other options, or because he had invested so much in being a part of LC23S? Regardless of the answer, he stayed, knowing full well what could happen to him.

Infiltrating the metalworks was exceedingly difficult due to surveil-lance. The heavy presence of police and members of the White Brigade inside and outside the factory meant that he could not just go about dis-tributing newspapers and striking up political conversations. He made contact with workers who wanted to take over the direction of the union. Like him, they had to work covertly and held secret meetings to which he was invited. The contact did not bear fruit for Jaime because the union reforms the workers wanted were at odds with the revolutionary aims of the LC23S, which sought to ultimately do away with unions because of the primacy of armed revolution. "It wasn't easy to reach the workers with our propaganda because while they're planning union democracy, you're planning the destruction of the union." Jaime recalled how later on the leadership of LC23S changed its recruiting tactics inside factories to accommodate workers' demands for higher salaries and greater benefits.

The double life of an undercover activist was not easy for Jaime. "You have to be playing a role all the time. It makes you schizoid, you have neu-rosis. Who do you tell? You can't go to a therapist to talk about how 'I have conflicts with my clandestine activities.'" His supervisor inside LC23S, known as La Chapis, "was made of steel, inflexible, really hard, and she wouldn't let up. You realize that you're in a militaristic organization. It doesn't mean that you have to carry a gun but that you have to have mili-tary discipline. You can't be late. There are no excuses. You caught a cold, oh well. A lot of discipline." This discipline conveys commitment to the group's moral imperative that they were doing what was right for their cause and that the greater good required sacrifices.

Jaime was detained on May 12, 1980, at 5:40 p.m. outside a public high school. "It was like a magic act. They take out a gun and say, 'Don't move, get in the car.' At that moment, it feels like you're on a TV screen, and I started seeing everything as though I was inside an aquarium." The experience of seeing the police officer pointing a gun at him was so surreal that Jaime started laughing uncontrollably from nerves. "Everything started moving really fast." He quickly realized that this was a big operation. "I was going to scream, 'I'm Jaime Lagunas and I'm from the Liga,' but I didn't say anything, and I regret it. The students started surrounding us to close off the path to the car, and a bunch of guys came out with machine guns to fend them off and escort me to the car."

The details of his narrative are crisp and clear, signaling the panic he must have felt at that moment knowing that his life was on the line and having an inkling of what was to come. "They said, 'Ricardo, you're done for, you're going to collaborate.' They called me Ricardo, and if they call you Ricardo, it's because they know you're done." Ricardo was Jaime's political alias, making it clear that his pursuers knew a great deal about his activities. Jaime continued, "Next to me was a comrade who had also been detained, and her face was deformed. It was swollen, swollen, swollen, green and purple." She had been detained a day earlier. The cars stopped at a bridge, and one of the plainclothes officers got out of one of the cars and came over to tell Jaime, "'You're going to tell our chief that you're going to collaborate.'" Jaime took note of the suits they wore. "They wore tailor-made suits in elegant colors." Unlike your typical policeman who showed up wearing "cowboy boots and big belts," these officers arrived with "a suit and tie, manicured hands, a ring here. They'd say, 'Ricardo, are you OK? We'd like you to help us out. Can you help us?'" All Jaime could think of at that moment was the lies that he could tell them.

The officers took Jaime to the basement of the DFS offices at Circular Morelia 8 in Colonia Roma. "This was all very serious. It was a dark room with a black light. The lamp on a table. You're on the table and you can't see anything. You can see the hands that come into the light with something like a hundred photographs, and they ask me if I recognize anyone."

Afterward, they took him to another clandestine prison with a well. Three officers interrogated him. "One would punch you and say, 'Names,' another one would punch you and say, 'Houses,' the third would punch you and say, 'Addresses.' Like a dance." He was there for a little over a month. "The main fear is that they're going to kill you at any moment. You live with the anguish that death is following you." He recalled how the officers paraded him and other detained comrades in front of the press, who called out questions: "Is it true you want to establish a Soviet republic? What does it feel like to kill?" "I told them that I didn't know because I had never killed. The reporter from Channel 13 then asked, 'Do the ends justify the means?'" Jaime felt the show for the press was, as he put it, "absurd." Jaime and the others were taken back to detention. After three and a half years in prison, they were taken before a judge, who decreed formal prison sentences for Jaime and his comrades. The charges ranged from armed robbery and aggravated robbery to physical harm, kidnapping, murder, and criminal delinquency. Jaime received an additional five and a half years in prison, for a total of eight.

At first Jaime's family could not locate him. They went to the school and heard what happened from the students. LC23S gave them money to have placards with Jaime's photograph printed demanding his release. His family and hundreds of others marched all over Mexico City with his image emblazoned on posters reading, "Liberty to Jaime Laguna." They—and here Jaime clarified it was mostly mothers—went into government offices and handed out pamphlets to businesspeople. Jaime had no idea what was going on outside. He had been one of six members of LC23S who were picked up, two of whom were killed. All their families, along with the mothers of the disappeared, made sure to let anyone and everyone who would listen to them know their children were missing.

Once relocated from the clandestine prisons and after he was convicted and sentenced, Jaime spent time in several formal prisons. "I stayed several days in a small prison in Xochimilco, before they closed it. They sent me to a segregated area. I didn't have anywhere to sleep, so they gave me some boxes, and I got a blanket or newspaper from somewhere to cover up. There's no food, so they sent some soup, and I used a tortilla to scoop it up because there were no utensils. Some shitty water and a roll of bread.

The food sucked." He and a comrade named Hilario were moved to a newly finished prison. It seemed they were the only ones there. "They sent him to one corner, and I was in the other corner. A guard on each side. You can't talk, you can't do anything." Eventually more prisoners arrived, and they were transferred to the general population.

Jaime recalled that one day an impeccably dressed police officer with an athletic build and dark sunglasses arrived at his cell. "He had on a walkie-talkie and an entourage of like fifteen police officers: 'Jaime, we want to talk with you.' They took me out of my cell, and, to be honest, I felt my balls go up to my throat and I just wanted to urinate. They told me that if I helped them out, they could help me out, and if I didn't, they'd beat the crap out of me. They wanted me to confirm information they had gotten out of other comrades." Jaime lived in a constant state of fear that they were going to kill him at any moment. As he told his story, Jaime made narrative choices. The impeccably dressed police officer may have been Miguel Nazar Haro, but he did not come out and say it. He did not clarify whether or not he gave up information or named names under torture. That fear of being killed at any moment must have been accentuated by the fact that Jaime knew the DFS was primarily resorting to disappearing—not imprisoning—guerrillas in the late 1970s. By 1981, Jamie realized that he and Hilario were the only political prisoners left.

Jamie and Hilario attempted to escape twice that first year. "I wanted to return to the Liga, I wanted to return to their ranks. I couldn't imagine being imprisoned for five years." The first time they attempted to escape, they made contact with four other prisoners also intent on breaking out. They managed to get their hands on plans for the prison drain system, as they were certain that one of the drains led to the outside. Once they got inside the pipe, "it was an adventure because they don't go straight, the ducts go in a zigzag precisely to avoid them being used for escapes." After almost drowning in one of the drain pipes, they attempted to surface only to realize they were still inside the prison. They gave up and returned to the original entry point. The second time involved digging a hole through a wall. "It took us over a month of hard work. We took out pieces of rock and metal grille, covered it back up with clay." The hole was eventually discovered by the guards, and after a severe beating, they were put in solitary confinement.

After their escape attempts, he and Hilario were taken to a police station. Jamie had squirreled away a razor blade. "If they beat me up again, I'm going to slice my veins open." At the station, the officers told him to turn around and put his hands behind his back.

> The light went out as they put hoods like the Ku Klux Klan over our heads. An elegantly dressed, fair-skinned man with silver hair arrived, good manners. "What's your name, son?" Jaime Lagunas. "What did they call you?" Ricardo. "OK, Ricardo, turn around please." He was pleasant, but he had with him these big goons, tall with short hair. They took us out through the government building, and you heard something really strange: silence. Everyone in the office got quiet. You could hear the typing, and all of a sudden it stopped, and people must have stared as they brought out three hooded men surrounded by a bunch of assholes. They took us out to the cars and I could hear them saying "brown, green, and blue." They laid us on the floor of the backseat. A man gets in and cocks a gun. "If they want to rescue you, the first one dead is you."

Jaime remembered that they were taken to a place where a military band was playing. They were taken to a room and their hoods came off.

> The walls had rifles and machine guns hanging. It was a strangely elegant place. Leather seats on the chairs, carpet everywhere. The man who interrogated us came over, and he was dressed like a civilian but with police insignias and his walkie-talkie. An asshole started hitting me, saying, "Looks like you want to die, right? With a gun or a bullet? You better start screaming." And I started screaming. I can't breathe, and he's slamming my head against the bookcase. Next thing I know I was traveling in a car. I felt at peace, relaxed, and I could smell the desert. I could see the sun and the light. I just wanted to go wherever it was that I was going. When I opened my eyes, I was on the floor and I couldn't breathe. I could feel myself going, but they were giving me air to make me come back. I got so angry they made me come back to life because it felt good to be slipping wherever it was that I was going.

After almost dying from this beating, Jaime spent six months in the prison infirmary. They told him that if he ever attempted to escape again, they would kill his family.

After his recovery, Jaime, Hilario, and two other political prisoners from Acapulco were transferred to the maximum-security penitentiary at

Santa Martha Acatitla. "There's no sunlight, everything is cold in that place." They each had their own cell. The walls were made of bricks with holes in them, and bats would get inside the cells at night.

> I was here for a year completely isolated. I think they wanted me to kill myself [*que me pusiera corbata*]. I didn't have contact with anyone. The light was on all day. I suppose this is a type of torture. At night, you could hear them beating up prisoners. You can't read. You can't do anything. You start having problems with stress, anguish, and you easily lose it.

A new director of the prison gave the prisoners more freedoms. Jaime remembered how he got his hands on sunflower seeds and started planting them wherever he could. He laughingly recalled taking care of these beautiful flowers in such a horrible place. He spent time in the psychiatric wing of the prison.

> There was a psychopath who would trap the bats in his cell and eat them. I couldn't figure out what planet I was on. You start losing your sense of reality. In this reality, two men are a couple, one fixes himself up like a woman and washes his "husband's" clothing. They live together. You can't say anything because the "husband" would come over and beat the crap out of you.

Jaime was right that this was a type of psychological torture because of the toll such a bleak and oppressive environment took on captives. His memories juxtaposing the beauty of a sunflower with the horror of the place dominated his description of this period.

Jaime's first job at Santa Martha was to mop the floors with a heavy blanket and a stick in the shape of a T.

> You'd be pushing it. It would get dirty. You'd have to wash it, squeeze the water out and again. I had to sleep in a room full of assholes and bedbugs. Here's your brick to polish the floor of the bathroom, and when your brick had worn down, they weren't interested in the polish. They just wanted to screw you over. You can't sit down, you can't stand up. You have to sit on your haunches. "If you stop, I'm going to beat the crap out of you." On the one hand, you're angry, full of rage. On the other hand, the silver lining is that it instilled character.

Perhaps framing the experience as building inner strength was a way for Jaime to rationalize this period of his captivity. He was not merely a passive victim of a brutal prison environment. In his telling, surviving and making it out alive made him a stronger man.

While at Santa Martha, Jaime met two other political prisoners from Guerrero who he remembered "had been treated really badly." Outside the confines of a prison, ideological differences would have marked Jaime's conversation with these men, even leading to disdainfully dismissing them as not having a viable strategy to bring about a true armed leftist revolution. But prison was different: "The circumstances don't just make you friends, they make you brothers." Jaime explained that it was like how surviving a shipwreck bonds survivors for life. One of the two men from Guerrero, Arturo Gallegos, had had eight family members disappeared. Jaime found out from guards that there were other political prisoners housed in the infirmary wing. "It was hard to know that we were separated by only a wall and there was nothing we could do for them. There was little information on them. On their side of the wall, there was an oven that was used for incineration." The assumption was that the oven was used to dispose of bodies. "One day, they put us inside our cells from early in the morning. They locked up all the cells and dormitories, and we couldn't go out. We heard that some ambulances came into the infirmary area, and it looked like they took out the comrades. The ones that were still alive." Jaime remembered that "it was painful and frustrating to be so close and so far at the same time."

Jaime was finally released on December 24, 1985. "It was like a Christmas present." When he got out, he tried to contact members of LC23S to find out what was going on with the movement. "I didn't find anybody." This was not entirely surprising. As Jaime explained, "La Liga dissolved in 1983." Finding out about the end of LC23S in prison was difficult. "It's a pity not to have been there to witness its end." Jaime described his feelings as "sadness, pain, disillusionment, feeling like an orphan." He pondered what would have happened had he succeeded in his escape attempts because it was clear to him the group was not going to come back. The sense of being left behind is palpable in Jaime's words. By the time he left prison, the world had moved on without him, and there was no way for him to make sense of or justify the enormous sacrifice—brutal torture and horrific imprisonment—he endured in the previous years. All that awaited him was the rubble of a defeated movement.

THE CASE OF YOLANDA ISABEL CASAS QUIROZ AND THE AFTERSHOCKS OF 1968

Yolanda Isabel Casas Quiroz had her political awakening in 1962 at the age of eighteen. She did not go to university, so her moment of revelation came when she was at work. She described how her supervisor at her secretarial job, Arturo Guerrero, introduced her to the idea of a revolutionary movement. She was especially drawn by his description of revolutionaries who were fighting for love and equality for all human beings. She reasoned that this uplifting message resonated for her because it reminded her of the happiness she had as a child. "My home was like a paradise, and I didn't know of any problems going on outside." Her world changed as she became an adult and her family fell apart as a result of her father's infidelity. The final break for Yolanda happened when her father threatened suicide and she finally understood how flawed he was as a human being. "All my hopes, projects, and dreams just fell apart." She carried that disillusionment with her as she joined reading groups on socialist thought and found an outlet for understanding how real social change could happen. She recalled how the concept of injustice—and righting wrongs—moved her to become politically active because she empathized with the pain of others, having watched her mother cry at her father's betrayal.

At the beginning, Yolanda took a firm nonviolence stance in her political activities. She joined a group from the Partido Comunista organizing rail workers in Mexico City. She learned about the struggle of the working class and honed her organizing skills. Her desire to stay true to the ethic of nonviolence changed after the 1968 student mobilizations. It is during this period that she joined armed guerrilla groups, starting with the Liga Comunista Espartaco and, later, Los Lacandones. Yolanda was on the front lines of the student mobilizations in Mexico City during the summer of 1968. In describing this period, she highlighted the internal battles among revolutionary groups, including among members of the Liga Comunista, over how to organize the movement and the tactics activists should employ. She was imprisoned in September of that year but released in time to join the marchers going to Tlatelolco Plaza on October 2. She described first hearing the bullets: "Everything gets lost because your brain enters a state of shock, and I could see the bullets going by. It was hard to run because everyone started running." She opened her eyes and saw a mass of people on top of each other and started running as fast as she could toward the steps and the grassy area. Once she got down there, she said, "I could see people falling down dead, which is something I will never forget."

In the aftermath of that brutal day, Yolanda changed her position on armed movements and joined her partner Carlos Salcedo's group, which would later become Los Lacandones. She said that the events of October 2 made her feel like she had been betrayed, similar to the betrayal she felt from her father's infidelity. At first, she lived in a safe house with four other group members (all male), then lived on her own where people did not know her association with militant groups. After police started asking her neighbors about her activities, Yolanda returned to live at the safe house. She described in vivid detail what it was like to take part in "expropriations" to fund the group's activities during this time. While her comrades were preparing to take an armored vehicle, Yolanda came up behind a police officer to detain him. "I grabbed him however I could and pointed my gun at him. I told him to take it easy and that nothing would happen to him as long as he obeyed me. I took his gun and told him not to move."

This period came to an end for Yolanda in February 1972 when security forces detained her. "All I could hear was how they were stomping upstairs. I had the door closed. I took off my gun and put it underneath the pillow. But there were boxes of weapons everywhere. I stayed sitting down on the edge of the bed until they came. They pull at the heavy metal door and yell at me that they know that I'm there. I didn't count how many there were, but it was at least fifteen police officers of all sizes. They asked me where the others were, and I replied, 'What others?' They pushed me down on the bed and asked what was in the boxes."

Yolanda proceeded to tell the officers a cover story about how she did not know anyone in Mexico and had been brought to the house by a young man she had met at a hotel who said he would help her. Once at the house, he started beating her up and told her not to touch the boxes. After finishing her story, the police officers put her in a Jeep and took her to their station. "They didn't blindfold me. They didn't tie me up. When we got there, they offered me a cigarette." She remembered being stunned when they gave her a sandwich in case she was hungry.

We do not know why the police officers treated Yolanda more kindly than other detainees. It could be that they believed her story of her abusive boyfriend, or perhaps they did not have a clear sense of the extent of her participation in Los Lacandones. For whatever reason, she was not subjected to the torture that she anticipated and that most of her comrades experienced when detained. When Yolanda was eventually taken to prison, she learned what the same DFS agents she met in the detention facility had done to her women comrades, which was much more brutal than anything she endured. "It makes you feel guilty. What did I do that made it so that I wasn't tortured the same way they were?" The guilt was such that she felt it was a type of mental rape. "They didn't torture me as much, and I don't know how I escaped the pain, cruelty, and misery that my women comrades suffered. They had done a lot less than I did, and some had barely done anything." Still, they were brutally tortured. Her choice of the word *rape* is telling because it implies the ultimate violation: physical penetration and physical defilement that other detained women endured. Guilt loomed large in Yolanda's memories of this period. She rationalized that the degree and form of torture should be commensurate with an individual's militant actions. To her, it did not make sense that she escaped the more brutal treatment other militant women endured. The weight she attached to this discrepancy is heavy even decades later.

Even though her torture was not as brutal as that endured by others, Yolanda was still tortured over the course of the four days. "They did not let me sleep. They keep you tired to make you weak. That's when they told me, 'We have others like you here. We're going to take you to them, and if they know you, you're going to regret it.' I was terrified." She said the worst moment for her was when they took her in front of her comrade, Jesús Torres Castrejón. "He was in pieces. They had brutally tortured him. Applied electric shocks to his testicles and different parts of his body." They undressed Yolanda in front of Jesús and asked him if he knew her true identity. She did not go on to say how Jesús responded, but the implication is that he did not reveal who she was. She clarified that the only officers she met during this time were from the DFS, including Miguel Nazar Haro.

After four days of interrogation by DFS agents, they transferred her to a women's prison. Yolanda described the feeling of being relocated to prison as "being alive . . . of being free and being liberated. I felt happy on my way to prison." She had survived after all. The feeling of joy she experienced at her transfer may be framed by what she learned soon after arriving in prison: her torture could have been much worse. The fact that she stayed for only four days with the DFS suggested they did not know that she was a high-value prisoner given her role in Los Lacandones or that she was the partner of one of the group's leaders, Carlos Salcedo. The joy Yolanda felt on her transfer may also have been compounded by the fact that the story she told the officer—that she just got caught up with the wrong crowd because she went with an abusive man—worked.

Once in prison, she was formally charged with a range of crimes, including theft and damage to property. She was put in a cell reserved for political prisoners along with seventeen other women. The women kept their spirits up by continuing their political engagement. "We had to try to stay united and take on the many possibilities prison gave us to continue to be active, present, and aware of what was going on." This experience of building solidarity and setting aside ideological differences while behind bars is a common feature among political prisoners. She made the point that women have always been involved in politics in Mexican history, from the independence battles to the revolution, and it was not any different from what drove her and her cellmates to join armed causes. Paternalism and machismo made it challenging for women to step up, but many still did. Even though most of her comrades in the various leftist and guerrilla groups she joined were men, she stated that there were women in them too. Yolanda spent six years behind bars and was released in November 1978 under López Portillo's amnesty for political prisoners.

Yolanda had a difficult time reintegrating into life with her three daughters after her release. Her family had been responsible for them for so long that her daughters did not welcome her back as their mother. Family members also condemned what she sacrificed to become a guerrilla member. They said "that I was an irresponsible mother, and my daughters absorbed that idea. My family and my sisters pulled my daughters' strings however they wanted" and turned them against her. She tried to restart her family with her three daughters, but they rebelled and pushed her away. "It was so hard to get to know each other once again." The regret and pain was palpable in Yolanda's voice as she explained what it was like to struggle to build a relationship with them. Conflicts continued, and all three daughters eventually turned away; they lived with her for some time but chose to return to live with her sisters. As she concluded telling her story, Yolanda paused to reflect on what she had said. "These are the consequences of our actions, and you have to learn to live with it, to try to make the best of it and heal however you can. Otherwise, it'll sweep you away."

By saying "it'll sweep you away," we know she is talking about a different kind of pain from what she experienced when she was interrogated. She may have escaped the worst forms of torture after she was detained in 1972. But what she came home to after her release in 1978—the alienation of her family, the estrangement of her daughters, and the consequences of her choices—was a form of extreme pain that stayed with her for the rest of her life. The judgment of her family, including her sisters, must have been especially hard given that two of them and her brother had also been politically active in the mobilizations of 1968. They did not follow Yolanda down the radical path she chose in the aftermath of the October 2 massacre. That year was a fork in the road for both Yolanda—who chose to take up arms—and her siblings—who chose to criticize her decision. Returning to the start of Yolanda's story and what drove her to become politically active in 1962, we remember that it was about being enthralled with the idea that she could be part of a movement fighting for love and equality for all human beings. Was this dream of an idealized world worth what she sacrificed? She does not give us an answer.

CONCLUSION

Taken together, the experiences of Patricio, Jaime, and Yolanda tell a story of coming of age, political radicalization, education, and contact with the generation of 1968. It is also a story riddled with internal disagreements, as well as cooperation within and between guerrilla groups. Each professed a firm commitment: they were fighting for an idealized vision of radical change that would bring them and their communities a better life. All three illustrate the shifts and changes in guerrilla tactics over time, including debates over ideological influences, the need for armed or unarmed routes to achieving change, and moving between the different radical groups active at the time. The attention each of them gives to these debates undergirds the moral impetus driving them to act, to join their respective groups, and to rationalize their legacies after their release. The fact that they each bring up these debates signals a reassessment of their activism and leaves on the table the question of whether their sacrifices were worth it.[8] They are not alone, and we hear the importance of peers and comrades in their respective life journeys. Each story begins with the sense of ripe possibility, and each story finishes with coming to terms with what could have been. None use the language of defeat, but there were ultimately no victories resulting from their actions.

Patricio, Jaime, and Yolanda were protagonists in the attempt to bring to life that dream of a more equal world so tangible to the generation coming of age in the late 1960s. If it could happen in Cuba, it could happen in Mexico. The way they saw it, if they risked being massacred like those students in October 1968 and again in June 1971, they should be brave enough to stand up for what they believe. As avenues to push for change shut down, each was imbued with an urgent sense that armed struggle was the only path. They felt there was no other way to to stand up for what they believed in. Yet the story is not complete if we do not also include what happened after the dust settled and the zeal for taking up the call to arms passed. A longer narrative trajectory that encompasses the aftermath moves us to better appreciate the cost exacted by their youthful exuberance.

History might view them as unnamed rank-and-file guerrilla members supporting assorted leaders or movements. More than cannon fodder, Patricio, Jaime, and Yolanda were an integral part of each movement, demonstrated by the torture they endured because of their participation. Why else would government agents inflict such punishment if it was not because of information they might have or because of the threat they represented? The price they paid and the scars they carry—both physical and emotional—stand as a testament to the ravages of a dirty war. In the case of Yolanda, the pain she experienced spilled over to the aftermath of her release and the impacts her choices had on her family. While it did not involve the conventional torture of a clandestine prison, this chapter of her life and the choices she made in her fight for social justice had a deep impact on her. In Jaime's case, there seems to be no place within existing emblematic memory frameworks of dirty war survivors for his experience.[9] He was too young and too late to fit those paradigms. In the case of Patricio, there is a yearning to take stock of his legacy and give relevance to his sacrifices. Taken together, these three experiences of political awakening, activism, detention, torture, imprisonment, and release show the resilience of this generation—to endure extreme pain, both physical and psychological; to endure the inhumanity inside prison walls; to continue their commitment to a movement even while imprisoned and even after being forgotten by their comrades. Resilience also shows in these three individuals' readiness to share their stories during the contemporary moment when violence continues unabated and frameworks for how to achieve broad social transformation remain at the level of empty promises.

Conclusion

TORTURE IN THE AGE OF IMPUNITY

As the 1970s drew to a close, there was a dawning awareness that the threat posed by subversives—real or imaginary—did not carry as much weight as it did at the start of the decade. Given that law enforcement had decimated guerrilla groups, the struggle to track down survivors and to challenge impunity ramped up. In 1977, Marlise Simons—the *Washington Post* reporter who had helped win the release of Pablo Cabañas—interviewed several lawyers working for the release of the hundreds of political prisoners incarcerated in Mexico at that time.[1] These lawyers, in conjunction with family members of the disappeared, had a list of 244 names of individuals currently detained on political charges, though they added that the list was "regrettably incomplete." Simons explained that lawyers in the state of Guerrero, home to Lucio Cabañas's movement, also had a list with an additional 257 names of individuals who had been disappeared. In defining what the newly circulating term meant, she wrote that they were "held incommunicado by police or military or have died in detention." She followed up by explaining that the attorney general had granted an amnesty to seventy-six prisoners, over two-thirds of whom had been detained without trial since 1971. In explaining the official rationale, Simons wrote, "Mexican governments routinely deny the existence of political prisoners or the use of torture. By acting as a safe haven for persecuted South American leftists and through much-repeated leftist rhetoric, recent administrations have also carved out a progressive image that has lent credibility to these denials." Though she was writing in 1977, her interpretation has withstood the test of time: the Mexican government's public-facing politics mask a darker core of political violence to shore up its authority.

As one lawyer interviewed by Simons in 1977 explained, the government made it nearly impossible for attorneys to defend their clients because of the lack of resources and information. "We cannot get defense witnesses to appear in court," said one lawyer, Carlos Fernández del Real. "On the rare occasions when police witnesses show, they refuse to answer questions. If we need ballistic experts they are always military officers whom we cannot trust. . . . Peasant leaders are just locked away for trying to defend the community against abuse by authorities or people with influence." One lawyer Simons spoke to explained that they themselves were never the subject of threats because they were part of what he referred to as "legal theater." In other words, the government needed attorneys to give the impression that justice, even if severely circumscribed, existed. For the official policy of denial to work, then, lawyers played the role of assiduous advocate in what was supposed to be a society founded on the rule of law; yet these same practices allowed the government to hamstring justice. While the government had proven adept at using covert extrajudicial tactics to rein in dissent and insisted on a policy of denial despite evidence to the contrary, lawyers did not have that freedom. They had to remain within the confines of legal strictures or risk public censure, which meant they would not be able to continue working on behalf of victims.

Work on behalf of the victims, especially those who were still imprisoned, continued across the 1980s. Jaime Laguna Berber said that he knew of two groups working for the release of political prisoners while he was incarcerated in the 1980s. One was composed of family members of the disappeared, and the other was the Comité Eureka de Desaparacidos (Eureka Committee of the Disappeared).[2] The Comité Eureka was established by Rosario Ibarra and approximately one hundred other women affected by the dirty war who fought for the release of political prisoners and attempted to locate the disappeared. Ibarra's son, Jesús Piedra Ibarra, was detained and disappeared in 1975. In their work for the Comité Eureka, Ibarra and other mothers led overt displays of protest in Mexico City, beginning with a hunger strike in 1978 in the atrium of Mexico City's cathedral.[3] Ibarra went on to join the now-defunct Partido Revolucionario de los Trabajadores (PRT; Revolutionary Workers Party) and in 1982 was the first woman to run for president. After serving as a federal deputy and running for president again in 1988, Ibarra left the PRT and joined Cuauhtémoc Cárdenas and the Partido de la Revolución Democrática (PRD; Party of the Democratic Revolution). She became a fixture in leftist politics for decades to come as a PRD representative in government. At this early stage in her political career, according to Jaime, Rosario Ibarra "would write letters, file complaints, and support us. In fact, she even signed a moral provision document the court demanded to release me from prison." Ibarra visited Jaime and three other political prisoners at Santa Martha Acatitla on two occasions in 1982 when she was running for political office. Ibarra epitomized the family as the nucleus of activism determined to hold the government accountable for what it had done to their loved ones.

Weeks after his release from prison in December 1985, Jaime went to a PRT central committee meeting in Mexico City. "There was Adolfo Gilly and Roberto Pasco. You see all the leaders of the movement. People you know about from reading the newspapers, lots of academics and front-line politicians. I introduced myself and they told me to go to a training seminar for a month. Go fuck yourselves! I had just gotten out of prison and they wanted to lock me up again. I said no." Jaime's retort epitomized the splits that emerged across the 1980s between the various camps of activists demanding justice. Some, such as Gilly and Pasco, took on the role of spokespersons, while others, such as Jaime, felt left behind by the political moment. Much like Jaime's story, Adolfo Gilly was arrested in 1966 for suspected guerrilla activity and served six years as a political prisoner in Lecumberri. While imprisoned, Gilly wrote *La revolución interrumpida* (The Interrupted Revolution), one of the best-known historical analyses of the 1910 Mexican Revolution, and became a key intellectual in Mexican leftist circles.[4] While Adolfo Gilly benefited from the initial wave of radical activism in the 1960s, Jaime Laguna Berber represented a more tarnished and controversial memory of the later generation of guerrillas who opted for taking up arms against the government in the 1970s. In this narrative, one was an aggrieved victim at the hands of an authoritarian state, while the other had engaged in questionable criminal activity against government forces protecting innocent civilians. Finding no room in this selective retelling of leftist movements across the long 1970s, Jaime opted out.

Efforts to obtain justice continued during the so-called transition to democracy in the 2000s. When the government of Vicente Fox established the Special Prosecutor's Office in 2002 to investigate state-sponsored violence, several members of Lucio Cabañas's family filed formal complaints about what the government had done to them. Pablo made a complaint for himself and another on behalf of his brother, Lucio. He noted the confusion among the family members about how to navigate the legal hurdles to find justice for what was done to them. His half brother Alejandro was opposed to any filings, while his other half brother, Conrado, filed for his entire family in one complaint. Lucio's daughter, Micaela, argued that she, rather than Pablo, should file on behalf of her father. Regardless, the cases were moving forward, and family members—either as direct or indirect victims—testified about what was done to them before the prosecutor. Since the Special Prosecutor's Office was disbanded in 2007, the cases are now overseen by the Attorney General's Office and the Executive Commission for Attention to Victims. Even today, Pablo remains hopeful that he and his family will eventually receive a response from the government. As of this writing, it has not happened.

Patricio Abarca Martínez summed up the feelings of many of the victims when stating, "We don't think that the system is going to punish itself. It has to come from the international level. The fact that there are human rights organizations that exist is a positive step." The arrival of Vicente Fox in 2000 and the "transition to democracy" gave Patricio expectations that there could be a change. "I even went to give my declaration, but I soon realized that it wasn't going to happen. Within fifteen days of giving my declaration, two agents from the federal police came to see me." They asked him questions about his involvement in politics, as well as that of fellow activists. They insisted on taking photographs of him and his house. He agreed to take them to one of the clandestine prisons in Acapulco where he spent several months. They said they had to get a special permit to enter the space and never bothered to return. "I quickly realized nothing was going to come of this, so all I did was give my declaration." That he states that "nothing was going to come of" giving his declaration suggests the realization of what could, in fact, happen by telling his story. Justice was not going to lead to imprisoning those who had tortured him and disappeared his comrades. Justice was not going to bring a genuine legal reckoning to prevent this from happening again.

Patricio's version of justice then involved visibility—an official recognition—for what he and others like him endured. He wanted this public recognition to make it clear that he was not a criminal and that he had not broken laws. When asked what would help heal the damage he suffered, Patricio answered, "That they know we weren't delinquents. We had ideals that we were going to change things. Maybe the method wasn't the right one, but it wasn't a crime. Nobody forced me to participate. I did it willingly." He discussed how he could have stayed on track with his studies and gone on to have a career. He could be a pensioner today, and his family would be in a better financial situation. This did not happen. "There should be a declaration of who we were, what we did, and why we did it." In other words, justice for Patricio entailed inserting a chapter in the official canon of Mexico's modern history about what happened to him and his comrades across the 1970s.

As Patricio shows, victims could have very different ideas of what justice would look like, which affected their ability to mobilize together against the government. A former supporter of Lucio Cabañas, Guillermo Bello López, explained, "Compensation should be given to those who lost a father or their mother, who were left orphaned, or whose parents were disappeared." He admired the work of the family members of the disappeared in the state of Guerrero who, despite the fact that they have received little recognition from the government, persist with their work to find out what happened and identify remains. "I see these people as tireless in their search to bring justice to their families." Yet an accounting of what happened is not enough for others. Antonio Orozco Michel, originally from the Vikingos guerrilla group in Guadalajara and later part of LC23S, made it clear that the government of the time "applied a strategy of total extermination against us. They violated the human and civil rights of all the guerrillas." This violation requires legal charges, a legal process, and a legal framework to ensure that justice and the rule of law proceed as intended. We have yet to see this happen.

·   ·   ·   ·   ·

Bowing to pressure from family members led by Rosario Ibarra and international human rights groups, such as Amnesty International, the Mexican government formally acknowledged the existence of political prisoners in 1978.[5] In September, President López Portillo declared an amnesty law that ordered the release of political prisoners.[6] Some remained detained because they had committed crimes beyond the scope of political activism, including robbery, kidnapping, and murder. By 1980, the DFS announced it had formally disbanded the White Brigade because it had eliminated the threat posed by guerrilla groups. These two events—amnesty and the elimination of the White Brigade—set in motion the end of Mexico's dirty war. Marking the end of counterinsurgency operations, however, did not signal an end to political violence and the start of a more peaceful post-guerrilla era. As Roberto González Villareal points out, political violence continued unabated as police at all levels confronted growing mobilizations from social sectors protesting the burden of neoliberal structural adjustment programs meant to address the economic crisis or expressing growing disaffection with the PRI-led state's corrupt authoritarianism.[7]

Despite the disbanding of the White Brigade, other groups essentially replaced it and continued to employ the same terroristic tactics.[8] Clandestine operation groups, including the Grupo Jaguar, took up extrajudicial activities in the name of national security. This group, composed of specially trained police officers, was formed mostly out of the Brigada Quince (Fifteenth Brigade) of the División de Investigaciones para la Prevención de la Delincuencia (DIPD; Investigation Division of the Prevention of Delinquency) and was implicated in the killing and dumping of over a dozen Colombian nationals in the Rio Tula in the state of Hidalgo in 1982. The remains showed signs of brutal torture and mutilation.[9] Bowing to pressure from the US government, the outgoing administration of President Echeverría Álvarez and the incoming president, López Portillo, shifted away from counterinsurgency in favor of counternarcotics operations with the more active involvement of the DEA. From 1977 to 1983, Operation Condor—a joint operation of the DEA, the DFS, the military, and other branches of the police—conducted a brutal siege on the communities in the highlands of the state of Sinaloa and surrounding areas to wrestle control of drug trafficking.[10] As with the White Brigade, the Grupo Jaguar and the Operation Condor officials carried out horrific acts under the cover of impunity and epitomized how the use of torture had become a permanent and structural feature of the police and military forces.

Across the 1990s, political violence continued in places such as the state of Chiapas in response to the uprising of the EZLN after 1994 and the 1995 Aguas Blancas massacre of mobilizing peasants in the state of Guerrero. Political repression did not cease after the PRI was voted out of office in the 2000 presidential elections, though it merged with counternarcotics operations in places like the state of Michoacán and Tamaulipas with the advent of drug-trafficking organizations. In the same way that imprisoning, torturing, and disappearing dissidents were both historical and contemporary issues at the height of the dirty war in the 1970s, they continue to be so today with the growing tally of victims at the hands of both the drug-trafficking organizations and government agencies. While the causes and forms of forced disappearances today are different from those of a generation ago, both periods have seen the use of torture and other human rights abuses by state institutions as well as resistance of the government—and even more, its branches of law enforcement—to acknowledge its responsibility and how it profits from this ongoing tolerance of political violence.

•   •   •   •   •

This book, with its focus on political prisoners and the use of torture, has analyzed an exceptionally violent period in Mexican history that paved the way to the even more violent period the country is witnessing in the present. It is only fitting to return to the words of the historical subjects themselves to see how they understood this violence. Carlos Salcedo explained that torture asks how much pain a person can withstand. Answering that question, according to Carlos, leads to the conclusion that torture is a form of "state terrorism because it is all about destroying an individual." Carlos cited the example of the fourteen- or fifteen-year-old child tortured in front of his mother to get her to talk to illustrate the depths of depravity of state terrorism. For him, torture represented going through "the last door" because it meant "finding out what are the limits of human pain." Carlos continued:

> No one can say you won't talk if tortured because you don't know your pain threshold or what are the paths that will most hurt you. Perhaps physically you are strong as an oak, a rock, but perhaps then they bring you your child, your father, your mother, and they break you. Torture is florid.

Describing violence as florid carries over to what made a dirty war so successful and helps explain why violence—and impunity—persists in Mexico today. The government learned that torture worked: its use punished those who dared to challenge its authority and reinforced who was in control. Mexico never had a transitional justice framework demarcating an institutional break ending the dirty war. There was no withdrawal of the military or other government agencies entrusted with carrying out these abuses in the name of national security. By this metric, the dirty war was a success.

By its very nature, inflicting pain—whether physical or psychological—on another human being is an intimate act. One individual is defenseless, vulnerable, stripped bare, and at the mercy of the other, who wields the authority to decide degrees of pain and moments of relief. One individual can touch the other in any and all of the most sensitive regions inside and outside the body with no regard for boundaries. It may be through the act of rape by another human being or a foreign object; it may be from the seemingly gentle officer asking about the person's well-being and offering a way to make the seemingly endless pain stop. Marnia Lazreg sums up this intimacy by stating that, at its core, torture is about sex.[11] Much like a lover, a torturer is so attuned to his victim's body that he knows their most vulnerable places and when they are going to break.[12] Joanna Bourke describes killing as an intimate act and proposes that it conjures intimate feelings, specifically, pleasure, in the person doing the killing.[13] In penetrating the body, the torturer also penetrates the mind and breaks down any and all barriers making up the individual. By its very design, there is no place to hide secrets in the torture chamber. The stark walls, the echo of the chamber, the fetid smells, the presence of medical personnel, and the foreboding tools of the trade provoke fear and anticipation of pain. Pain and the fear of pain dull the mind and make it vulnerable to breaking. It may be a matter of hours or days, but, as Carlos stated, "everyone breaks under torture."

The type of torture at the heart of this book was not the frenzied infliction of pain for its own sake. It was rather a methodical, at times clinical, and procedurally sanctioned act as part of an unconventional war. Torture formed a central part of the counterinsurgency strategy in the post-1968 period, which meant that violence became bureaucratized. The procedural aspects of the torture session, including the number of officers involved in the process, enabled those participating in it to distance themselves from their victims and any guilt they might feel for their role in inflicting pain. It made torturing a less personal practice and one sanctioned by the very institutions a soldier or officer belonged to. The torturers were also following orders: being told by superiors who to torture gave soldiers the illusion they were not making choices, just following orders. The chain of command stripped them of responsibility for committing a heinous act. The decision was already made, reinforced by an immutable chain of command, and they were merely executing it as part of their duty. The procedural nature of torture also allowed for modern and nonmodern ways of inflicting pain to coexist. Some methods of torture, such as hanging a victim for an extended period by the limbs, have a history going back centuries. However, the concomitant application of electrical shocks to the already hanging victim was a recent innovation. The melding of these forms of torture during this period meant it became routine practice for police and military officers after the 1970s.

In contrast to Argentina, Chile, South Africa, and other countries where torturers confessed in the aftermath of legal forms of reckoning, few Mexican torturers have publicly divulged their participation. As Leigh Payne found in the Southern Cone cases, perpetrator confessions tend to be contingent on finding an audience or being compelled to confess for amnesty.[14] There is nothing to compel torturers to publicly disclose their complicity in Mexico. In contrast to other cases Payne studies, torturers in Mexico have a limited vocabulary to draw on to rationalize their acts or connect their acts to a narrative beyond the individual. Even if there were confessions in Mexico today, they might not find a national audience because of the messiness of ongoing violence. Unlike the other cases, no clear transition from violence circumscribes a before and after date to delimit confessions. Political violence has ebbed and flowed since the 1970s in Mexico and is so much worse today than it was fifty years ago that it belies the importance of confessions. What good are the confessions of heinous acts from fifty years ago when they would pale in comparison to events of the past few years? Without an effective truth commission or justice framework to spur dialogue, without the confessions of torturers or survivor groups engaging in public debates over what transpired in the 1970s, impunity reigns supreme. Having a legal framework that strips torturers of their impunity gives a sense of resolution and the illusion that this brutal chapter in a country's history came to a conclusion. Justice could be punitive, restorative, and preventive in this framework. Even if not all perpetrators were punished, there would be an overall social reckoning that what was done was wrong and went against the broader social good.

To analyze how impunity and, by extension, official acquiescence function on the ground, I turn to the example of torture by law enforcement in contemporary Mexico. There are no known official or unofficial statistics on the use of torture in the drug war and today's security crisis, but there is general consensus that it has been widely practiced by both law enforcement agencies and drug-trafficking organizations from when Felipe Calderón declared the start of the Drug War to today. A March 2018 United Nations (UN) report on human rights in Mexico concluded that torture continues to be widely practiced in Mexico by a range of legal and extralegal actors.[15] The number of complaints filed at the Comisión Nacional de Derechos Humanos in Mexico has risen dramatically, with about half of them attributed to members of law enforcement.[16] All branches have been accused of torture, including police forces at the municipal, state, and federal levels and judicial police forces at the state and federal levels. The various branches of the military also appear on this list of perpetrators. Researchers from the Centro de Investigación y Docencia Económica (CIDE; Center for Economic Research and Teaching), one of the foremost social science institutions in Mexico, estimate that almost 60 percent of individuals detained by law enforcement are subjected to some form of torture to either gather information or inflict punishment. This percentage is higher among detainees from the lower socioeconomic classes because they lack the resources to challenge, condemn, or bring attention to what was done to them.

Torture plays a central role in policing and public security operations by military and police forces across contemporary Mexico. For example, in the 2014 Ayotzinapa case of the 43 students disappeared, the UN found evidence of torture in thirty-four cases of individuals detained as part of the investigation.[17] This included five detainees, whose testimonies are key to the government's official theory of the case. Agents from the attorney general's Agencia de Investigación Criminal (AIC; Criminal Investigation Agency) used electrical shocks, sexual assault, rape, threats to kill them or their families, asphyxiation with plastic bags, and waterboarding. One of the detainees died during the interrogation session as a result of the torture.

The legal framework and safeguards to prevent and punish the use of torture are routinely and willfully disregarded by members of law enforcement at all levels. There is a consensus among security experts on both sides of the border that government security agents who carry out torture do so with near-absolute impunity. For example, the General Law on Torture that came into effect in June 2017 is openly violated by the executive and judicial branches of government. Moreover, the Federal Specialized Torture Investigations Unit, created in 2015 by the attorney general, opened 8,335 investigations of torture by members of the police and the military. As of 2019, the unit has only presented charges on 17 of these cases, issued only 2 arrest warrants, and has had no convictions since the office was created.[18] This pattern continues today: in a follow-up report in 2022, the CNDH cited the fundamental lack of resources and legal wherewithal to follow through on investigations and prosecutions for acts of torture at the hands of the police and military.[19]

As the UN summarized in 2018, there are profound structural inadequacies in the law enforcement and judicial branches of Mexico's government. Only 2 to 3 percent of all reported crimes are successfully prosecuted in Mexico today.[20] Not a single complaint of the thousands filed before the National Commission on Human Rights has led to a successful prosecution, and only one has moved to the indictment stage. There are numerous examples of cases brought before public safety agencies that are either mismanaged or dropped entirely. It is general knowledge, especially among individuals without access to secure financial resources, that reporting crimes, such as torture, kidnapping, or assault, will lead to nothing or generate repercussions. A recent nationwide victimization survey in Mexico allows us to better appreciate the scale and scope of impunity.[21] Approximately 10 percent of crimes, including kidnapping, extortion, and theft, are reported to the authorities. When the respondents were asked why they did not report the crime, over half replied it was because they thought it was a waste of time and nothing would come of it. The futility of reporting crimes is real: of reported crimes, fewer than 7 percent were successfully investigated, let alone prosecuted. Likewise, individuals are concerned that reporting a crime to authorities creates a risk for the person doing so.

$$\cdot \quad \cdot \quad \cdot \quad \cdot \quad \cdot$$

Near the center of Mexico City in the popular Roma Norte neighborhood stands a nondescript modern office building that is one of the few sites to remember Mexico's dirty war. The five-story building has been retrofitted with earthquake-proof beams and is surrounded by other new and old construction as a testament to the ravages of the massive earthquakes that devastated this neighborhood in 1985 and again in 2019. Throughout the 1970s and up to when the agency was dismantled in 1985, the building at Circular de Morelia sporting the number 8 outside was the DFS headquarters. It was one of the key locations from which members of the security forces, drawn from the police and military, orchestrated the detention, torture, release, and disappearance of many so-called dissidents with alleged ties to the guerrilla groups threatening the Mexican state at the time.

Other countries that experienced similar dirty wars, such as Chile and Argentina, have enacted a range of memory sites and established museums under the adage of never forgetting their respective dark chapters when their security forces tortured and killed their own citizens in the name of public security. The Parque de la Memoria (Memory Park) situated in front of Rio de la Plata in Buenos Aires commemorates the thousands of Argentines who fell victim to state-sponsored terrorism, many of them thrown from planes into the river facing the park while still alive. Santiago has a museum dedicated to remembering the atrocities and human rights abuses perpetuated on their citizens as the twentieth century came to a close. These locales, which are accompanied by hundreds more mapping out the geographies of repression in both urban and rural areas, are prominent tourist destinations and are frequently visited by groups of schoolchildren reckoning with understanding their nations' histories. In both countries, the sites of memory—museums, parks, monuments—are accompanied by robust and detailed Truth Commission reports that enumerate, detail, and chart what happened. In Chile and Argentina, the courts intervened with their version of reckoning and indicted, tried, and imprisoned perpetrators.

This is not the case in Mexico, which is why Circular de Morelia 8 looms large as a site of memory for survivors, their loved ones, and advocates and is generally unremarkable to most people who walk by the building—that is, unless they stop to read the plaque outside the front door announcing what it used to house or the plaque on a small pedestal in the garden across the street. The plaque in the garden consists of six tiles survivors placed there in February 2019 and subsequently replaced after it was vandalized. The tiles depict images and words: "In this building, Morelia 8, existed a center for forced disappearance and torture in the years of the 1970s and 1980s. Here Miguel Nazar Haro tortured: first with the Federal Security Directorate and then with the White Brigade. As state policy, they kidnapped, tortured, and killed militants and activists. With impunity, Miguel Nazar Haro set up a family business here for private security." At the bottom, the words "Memory, Truth and Justice" are in capital letters and accompanied by two images: one of a person being dragged away by two men dressed in uniform and the other a bloodied body on the ground.[22]

The timing of installing the plaque—as well as its destruction by vandals—lines up with the current political tides in Mexico. President Andrés Manuel López Obrador has formally acknowledged this particularly dark chapter of Mexico's history in unprecedented ways and unlike any of his predecessors. As his supporters have claimed, the president "put

Figure 2. The tiles depict images and words: "In this building, Morelia 8, existed a center for forced disappearance and torture in the years of the 1970s and 1980s. Here Miguel Nazar Haro tortured: first with the Federal Security Directorate and then with the White Brigade. As state policy, they kidnapped, tortured, and killed militants and activists. With impunity, Miguel Nazar Haro set up a family business here for private security." At the bottom, the words "Truth and Memory, Justice" are in capital letters and accompanied by two images: one of a person being dragged away by two men dressed in uniform and the other a bloodied body on the ground. Photo Credit: Sitio de Memoria, Circular de Morelia 8

in evidence the aberrations of the PRIista governments and its history of aggressions, crimes, torments that will convert the ghosts of horror into an archive of documents and museums."[23] He named individuals to lead an effort to remember the dirty war through the Secretaría de Gobernación, which has set up a website called Sitios de Memoria (Sites of Memory) to educate the public on major hallmarks of this period. As of 2023, Circular de Morelia 8 was designated the headquarters of the Dirección General de Estrategías de Derechos Humanos (General Direction of Human Rights Strategies), which includes the offices of the Comisión Nacional de Derechos Humanos and signals the government's recognition that this was a building where human rights had been violated.

Circular de Morelia 8 also houses Mexico's newly created Truth Commission, known as the Comisión para Acceso a la Verdad, Esclarecimiento Histórico e Impulso a la Justicia de violaciones graves a derechos humanos de 1965–1990 (Commission for Access to the Truth, Historical Clarification, and Promotion of Justice for grave human rights violations from 1965 to 1990). In a June 2021 meeting commemorating the fiftieth anniversary of the Corpus Christi massacre of students in Mexico City, AMLO received several survivors and their families at the Presidential Palace. After leaving the closed-door meeting, family members told the press that they were "left with the hope that we can arrive at the truth and that justice will be done."[24] It was at this meeting that AMLO announced this new attempt at a truth commission to much fanfare and expectation.[25] Many observers, including me, imagined that these efforts would remain at the level of performance and fail to produce tangible results. We need only remember what happened with earlier attempts to seek an official account and redress, such as the FEMOSPP.

It is true that the president affirmed the human rights abuses that took place during the dirty war and gave the survivors and their families much-needed validation that what was done to them was wrong. Yet it is still too early to tell if this new commission will net results beyond documenting what happened or continue to exist if AMLO's successor, Claudia Sheinbaum, is not as sympathetic to this cause. As of this writing, she has only just assumed the presidency and has yet to define her stance on the atrocities committed during the 1970s dirty war. The cautionary words of Rodolfo Gamiño Muñoz, one of the key architects of the 2006 FEMOSPP report, ring true, suggesting that Mexico seems determined to forget. He describes his frustration at seeing the report he helped put together transformed into a heavily redacted "official" version that finally saw the light of day in 2007.[26] He also tells of the contentious process that went into gathering evidence for the report—in particular, from former guerrilla members demanding some accounting for what they endured and calling for justice. A clear split emerged inside the FEMOSPP between its aim to tell the history and to offer a pathway to transitional justice through the courts.[27] That split was never reconciled and is emerging in today's attempt at reinvigorating a truth commission in Mexico. The fact that the architects of Mexico's dirty war are dying of old age, including former president Echeverría Álvarez, in July 2022, makes that split even more evident: soon there will be no one left to prosecute.

Putting anything concrete in motion to act on AMLO's "defense of human rights and recovery of collective memory" will undoubtedly raise the hackles of the military, an institution staunchly invested in preserving its heroic role against insurgent guerrilla groups of the 1970s. As is becoming increasingly apparent, AMLO needed a close alliance with the Mexican military to maintain control. The president's staunch defense of the Mexican military when the US government arrested General Salvador Cienfuegos, the now-retired head of the military, in December 2020, demonstrated the close relationship between these two branches of government. We can draw from other examples to show the depth of the alliance, including the direct involvement of the military in large-scale infrastructure projects such as the building of a new multimillion-dollar airport outside of Mexico City and a rail line across the Yucatán Peninsula. AMLO had too much invested in this relationship to threaten the military with justice for atrocities it committed decades ago.

This reality has nonetheless not stopped families, victims, and activists from continuing to tell their stories with the hope it will have an effect. While it did not happen with AMLO, it is unclear if President Sheinbaum will follow up with providing financial reparations to the victims and their families or order the courts to pursue the perpetrators of the abuses. Setting aside the question of justice and indemnification, there are glimmers of hope. Two, in particular, stand out. Until recently, access to the DFS files declassified under President Vicente Fox in 2002 remained heavily restricted and when available were so redacted that they bore a resemblance to informal reclassification. Pressure from scholars and human rights activists—specifically those involved in the newly formed Truth Commission—is gradually easing access to these documents to the point that they are now accessible to the public. This same commission is compiling empirical data from these documents and countless interviews to finally settle on an official version of what precisely happened during this period. This includes the number and names of victims detained, tortured, imprisoned, and disappeared.

The second glimmer of hope comes on entering Circular de Morelia 8 today. Though I had heard the basement of Circular de Morelia 8 described

Figure 3. Circular de Morelia 8, headquarters of the DFS in the 1970s and 1980s. Today the building houses the Dirección General de Estrategías de Derechos Humanos, with the Sitio de Memoria in the basement. Photo Credit: Sitio de Memoria, Circular de Morelia 8

Figure 4. The interior of the Sitio de Memoria in the basement of Circular Morelia 8. This is the same basement where DFS agents brought detainees to be interrogated and tortured in the 1970s. Today it houses a series of exhibits detailing the history of the DFS and what took place in the main room, the three cells at the back, and the crawl space. Photo Credit: Sitio de Memoria, Circular de Morelia 8

many times, nothing prepared me for what it was like to see it for myself. There is a garage door that opens and a ramp going down into the basement. The space is narrower than I imagined, clean, though with a musty smell and with white walls and a concrete floor. The main room is about ten meters by ten meters (about 11 by 11 yds.). At the back, there are three small rooms and a staircase leading up. Near the front is a small hallway leading to a U-shaped area underneath the steps and ramp. You would have to get down on your hands and knees to fit there. Detainees would be brought down the ramp after their "calentamiento"—the beatings they received during their capture and transport to Circular de Morelia. They would be thrown into the crawl space with other detainees already there awaiting interrogation. With the door closed and in the cramped, dark crawl space, they would hear the screams of torture victims coming from the main room, knowing they were next.

Today the main space in the basement has large signs describing the history of the DFS and what took place here. Life-size images of victims hang on the walls. There is an image of Ana María Parra Ramos on one wall soon after she was first detained in 1971. Her hair is tied back, her clothes are in place, and she is holding her hands in front of her, as if this were a routine photograph. On the back of this wall and inside a small room that used to be a cell, there is a second life-size photograph of Ana María, taken after her second detention in 1979. Her hair and clothes are disheveled, her face is bruised, there is a bloody bandage on her forehead, and her hands are behind her. When she was first detained, she was a member of the Movimiento de Acción Revolucionaria, and she served seven years in prison. On her release in 1978, she joined LC23S, to which her two children, Violeta and Adolfo, also belonged. Adolfo was detained and disappeared in 1975. Ana María was never seen again after her second detention. Yet another Mexican family ravaged by political violence. One of the small rooms beyond the main space in the basement has a growing library of books, while another contains mementos of the DFS during its heyday of the 1970s, including the famous charolas (badges) and emblems with the agency's well-known tiger. The third room describes the torture inflicted on the victims in that space and contains small signs describing the different forms of torture employed. The basement and the floors above it—as a whole—are a testament to the fact that families, victims, and activists persevere and will not let this period of Mexican history be forgotten.

Archives and Archival Abbreviations

Archivo General de la Nación
Archivos de la Represión/Article 19
Centro Académico de la Memoria de Nuestra América
Centro de Estudios del Movimiento Obreros y Socialista
National Security Archive, George Washington University

Caja	(box)
EXP	Expediente (file)
VOL	Volumen (volume)
LEG	Legajo (folder)
H	Hoja (page)
Foja	Alternate word for "Hoja"
B	(back of page)
AGN	Archivo General de la Nación
DFS	Fondo Dirección Federal de Seguridad
DGIPS	Fondo Dirección General de Investigaciones Políticas y Sociales
SEDENA	Fondo de la Secretaría de la Defensa Nacional

Notes

1. Unless specified otherwise, all translations from Spanish to English are my own.

2. For a general history of guerrilla groups in Mexico, refer to Francisco Ávila Coronel, *La guerrilla del Partido de los Pobres: Historia social, género y violencia política en Atoyac de Álvarez, Guerrero (1920–1974)* (Mexico City: Plaza y Valdés, 2022); Alexander Aviña, *Specters of Revolution: Peasant Guerrillas in the Cold War Mexican Countryside* (Oxford: Oxford University Press, 2014); Marco Bellingeri, *Del agrarismo armado a la guerra de los pobres: Ensayos de guerrilla rural en el México contemporáneo, 1940–1974* (Mexico City: Ediciones Casa Juan Pablos and Secretaría de Cultura del Gobierno del Distrito Federal, 2003); Barry Carr, *Marxism and Communism in Twentieth-Century Mexico* (Lincoln: University of Nebraska Press, 1992); Laura Castellanos, *México armado, 1943–1981* (Mexico City: Era, 2007); Enrique Condés Lara, *Represión y rebelión en México (1959–1985)*, 3 vols. (Mexico City: Benemérita Universidad Autónoma de Puebla and Miguel Ángel Porrúa, 2007–9); Fernando Herrera Calderón and Adela Cedillo, *Challenging Authoritarianism in Mexico: Revolutionary Struggles and the "Dirty War," 1964–1982* (New York: Routledge, 2012); Fritz Glockner Corte, *Memoria roja: Historia de la guerrilla en México (1962–1968)* (Mexico City: Ediciones B, 2007); Donald Hodges, *Mexican Anarchism after the Revolution* (Austin: University of Texas Press, 1995); Donald Hodges and Ross

Gandy, *Mexico under Siege: Popular Resistance to Presidential Despotism* (New York: Zed Books, 2002); Carlos Montemayor, *La guerrilla recurrente* (Mexico City: Editorial Debate, 2007); Juan Fernando Reyes Peláez, "Introducción a la historia de la guerrilla en México (1943–1983)," unpublished manuscript (Mexico City, 2010); Jorge Luis Sierra Guzmán, "Fuerzas armadas y contrainsurgencia, 1965–1982," in *Movimientos armados en México siglo XX*, ed. Verónica Oikión Solano and Marta Eugenia García Ugarte (Mexico City: El Colegio de Michoacán and CIESAS, 2006), 361–404. A comprehensive overview of these groups across the twentieth century can be found in the three-volume work edited by Oikión Solano and García Ugarte, *Movimientos armados en México*.

3. My historical view of counterinsurgency torture comes largely from Alfred McCoy, *A Question of Torture: CIA Interrogation, from the Cold War to the War on Terror* (New York: Holt Paperbacks, 2006), esp. 21–107; and Alfred McCoy, *Torture and Impunity: The US Doctrine of Coercive Interrogation* (Madison: University of Wisconsin Press, 2012), 3–113.

4. Marnia Lazreg, *Torture and the Twilight of Empire: From Algiers to Baghdad* (Princeton, NJ: Princeton University Press, 2008), 6. I draw on Lazreg's definition of torture as "the deliberate and willful infliction of various degrees of pain using a number of methods and devices, psychological and physical, on a *defenseless* and *powerless* person for the purpose of obtaining information that a victim does not wish to reveal or does not have. It is the powerlessness of the victim, the inability to defend herself and her absolute vulnerability to the torturer that captures the specific character of torture" (original emphasis). In this definition, the context of torture, including its purpose and desired effects on the victims, underpin the practice.

5. For a concise chronology of domestic and international events across the period in question, refer to Jaime M. Pensado and Enrique Ochoa, eds., *México Beyond 1968: Revolutionaries, Radicals, and Repression During the Global Sixties and Subversive Seventies* (Tucson: University of Arizona Press, 2018), 297–319.

6. As Renata Keller shows, the Cuban government did not provide support to these Mexican activists to ensure it did not run afoul of the Mexican government's recognition of it. *Mexico's Cold War: Cuba, the United States, and the Legacy of the Mexican Revolution* (Cambridge: Cambridge University Press, 2015).

7. There are many descriptions of these clandestine torture centers. See, e.g., José Arturo Gallegos Nájera, *La guerrilla en Guerrero: ¡A merced del enemigo!* (Mexico City: Centro de Investigaciones Históricas de los Movimientos Sociales, 2009), for a description of a torture center at the military base at Pie de la Cuesta; and Camilo Vicente Ovalle, *[Tiempo suspendido]: Una historia de la desaparición forzada en México, 1940–1980* (Mexico City: Bonilla Artigas Editores, 2019), 110–46, for a discussion of the many clandestine prisons throughout Mexico.

8. Giorgio Agamben, *State of Exception*, trans. Kevin Attell (Chicago: University of Chicago Press, 2005), 250–51.

9. Agamben, *State of Exception*, 2, 29.

10. Lazreg, *Torture and the Twilight*, 20–33, 87–107; Maria-Monique Robin, dir., *Escadrons de la mort: L'Ecole française*, DVD (Ideal Audience, 2003). In *Escadrons de la mort* Robin draws the connection between the French military's counterrevolutionary tactics in Algeria and those employed in Latin America's military dictatorships of the 1970s. In her interviews with officers, they use the term "dirty war" to explain why these tactics both worked and appealed to other militaries. For comparison with South American cases, see James P. Brennan, *Argentina's Missing Bones: Revisiting the History of the Dirty War* (Oakland: University of California Press, 2018); Marguerite Feitlowitz, *A Lexicon of Terror: Argentina and the Legacies of Torture*, 2nd ed. (New York: Oxford University Press, 2012); Lesley Gill, *The School of the Americas: Military Training and Political Violence in the Americas* (Durham, NC: Duke University Press, 2004); Victoria Langland, *Speaking of Flowers: Student Movements and the Making and Remembering of 1968 in Military Brazil* (Durham, NC: Duke University Press, 2013); Cecilia Menjívar and Néstor Rodríguez, *When States Kill: Latin America, the U.S., and Technologies of Terror* (Austin: University of Texas Press, 2005); Steve J. Stern, *The Memory Box of Pinochet's Chile*, 3 vols. (Durham, NC: Duke University Press, 2004–10).

11. I am not alone or the first to call for a dirty war or state terror analysis of the long 1970s in Mexico. See, e.g., Sergio René de Dios Corona, *La historia que no pudieron borrar: La Guerra Sucia en Jalisco, 1970–1985* (Guadalajara: La Casa del Mago, 2004); Jorge Mendoza García, "La tortura en el marco de la Guerra Sucia," *Polis: Investigación y Análisis Sociopolítico y Psicosial* 7, no. 2 (2011): 139–79; José Sotelo Marbán, *Informe histórico a la sociedad mexicana: ¡Qué no vuelva a suceder!* (Mexico City: Fiscalía Especial para Movimientos Sociales y Políticos del Pasado, 2006). Examples of scholarship on these topics are Ávila Coronel, *La guerrilla del Partido de los Pobres*; Vicente Ovalle, *[Tiempo suspendido]*; Ariel Rodríguez Kuri, *Historia mínima de las izquierdas en México* (Mexico City: El Colegio de México, 2021).

12. Camilo Vicente Ovalle, *Instantes sin historia: La violencia política y de estado en México* (Mexico City: UNAM, 2023), 73–75.

13. Claudia E. G. Rangel Lozano and Evangelina Sánchez Serrano, "La guerra sucia en los setenta y las guerrillas de Genaro Vázquez y Lucio Cabañas en Guerrero," in *La guerrilla en la segunda mitad del siglo*, vol. 2 of Oikión Solano and García Ugarte, *Movimientos armados en México*, 495–526. Also see Claudia E. G. Rangel Lozano, "La historia oral como método interdisciplinario: La desaparición forzada de personas durante la guerra sucia en Atoyac, Guerrero," in *De la literatura a la política: Seis siglos de transformación social en México (memoria de la décima quinta semana nacional de la ciencia y la*

tecnología), ed. F. Ávila Juárez (Mexico City: Universidad Autónoma de Guerrero, 2009), 126.

14. Adela Cedillo and Fernando Herrera Calderón, "Análisis de la producción historiográfica en torno a la llamada 'Guerra Sucia' mexicana," in *El estudio de las luchas revolucionarias en América Latina (1959-1996): Estado de la cuestión,* ed. Verónica Oikión Solano, Eduardo Rey Tristán, and Martin López (Zamora: El Colegio de Michoacán, Universidad de Santiago de Compostela, 2014), 263–88.

15. Cedillo and Herrera Calderón, "Análisis de la producción historiográfica," 264. Cedillo and Calderón consequently follow the historiographical thread from one silencing talk of a dirty war in the 1970s and 1980s to the contemporary moment.

16. CNDH, "Informe especial sobre las quejas en materia de desapariciones forzadas ocurridas en la década de los 70 y principios do los 80," 2001. The original report on human rights abuses from the CNDH can be found at https://www.cndh.org.mx. The official version of the FEMOSSP report is heavily edited and excludes critical information. For access to the unredacted, draft version, see Kate Doyle, "Draft Report Documents 18 Years of 'Dirty War' in Mexico," National Security Archive, February 16, 2006, accessed January 18, 2015, http://www2.gwu.edu/~nsarchiv/NSAEBB/NSAEBB180/index.htm.

17. "Protestas familias de desaparecidos," *Animal Político,* June 22, 2022, https://www.animalpolitico.com/2022/06/protestas-familias-desaparecidos-amlo-comision-verdad-guerra-sucia/.

18. Laura Castellanos, "La Comisíon de la Verdad no puede obviar la responsabilidad del Ejército en México," *Washington Post,* July 26, 2022, https://www.washingtonpost.com/es/post-opinion/2022/07/26/comision-de-la-verdad-mexico-ejercito-guerra-sucia-amlo/. Information on the creation of this new commission as well as access to its government-sponsored website can be found at Presidency of the Republic, "Comisión de la Verdad para la Guerra sucia presentará resultados antes de que concluya sexenio: Presidente," Gobierno de México, December 10, 2021, https://www.gob.mx/presidencia/prensa/comision-de-la-verdad-para-la-guerra-sucia-presentara-resultados-antes-de-que-concluya-sexenio-presidente.

19. I discuss this process of consolidating an authoritarian regime in Gladys I. McCormick, *The Logic of Compromise in Mexico: How the Countryside Was Key to the Emergence of Authoritarianism* (Chapel Hill: University of North Carolina Press, 2016). See also Roderic Ai Camp, *Political Recruitment across Two Centuries: Mexico, 1884–1991* (Austin: University of Texas Press, 1995); Gilbert Joseph and Jürgen Buchenau, *Mexico's Once and Future Revolution: Social Upheaval and the Challenge of Rule since the Late Nineteenth Century* (Durham, NC: Duke University Press, 2013); Jonathan Schlefer, *Palace Politics: How the Ruling Party Brought Crisis to Mexico* (Austin: University of Texas Press, 2008).

20. Roderic Ai Camp, *Politics in Mexico* (New York: Oxford University Press, 1993); Kevin J. Middlebrook, *Paradox of Revolution: Labor, the State, and Authoritarianism in Mexico* (Baltimore: Johns Hopkins University Press, 1995); Jeffrey W. Rubin, *Decentering the Regime: Ethnicity, Radicalism, and Democracy in Juchitán, Mexico* (Durham, NC: Duke University Press, 1997).

21. I discuss this process in detail in *Logic of Compromise*. See also Hodges, *Mexican Anarchism after the Revolution*; Tanalís Padilla, *Rural Resistance in the Land of Zapata: The Jaramillista Movement and the Myth of the Pax Priísta, 1940-1962* (Durham, NC: Duke University Press, 2008).

22. Jorge Castañeda, *La utopía desarmada: El futuro de la izquierda en América Latina* (Mexico City: J. Mortiz and Planeta, 1993); Elisa Servín, *Ruptura y oposición: El movimiento henriquista, 1945-1954* (Mexico City: Ediciones Cal y Arena, 2001); Montemayor, *La guerrilla recurrente*.

23. Wil G. Pansters, "Zones of State-Making: Violence, Coercion, and Hegemony in Twentieth-Century Mexico," in *Violence, Coercion, and State-Making in Twentieth-Century Mexico: The Other Half of the Centaur*, ed. Wil G. Pansters (Stanford: Stanford University Press, 2012), 8; original emphasis. Pansters develops these ideas further in "Zones and Languages of State-Making: From *Pax Priísta* to Dirty War," in Pensado and Ochoa, *México Beyond 1968*, 33-52.

24. Pansters, "Zones and Languages of State-Making," 40-41. See, e.g., Gema Kloppe-Santamaría, *In the Vortex of Violence: Lynching, Extralegal Justice, and the State in Post-Revolutionary Mexico* (Oakland: University of California Press, 2020); Sandra C. Mendiola-García, *Street Democracy: Vendors, Violence, and Public Space in Late Twentieth-Century Mexico* (Lincoln: University of Nebraska Press, 2017).

25. Pansters, "Zones and Languages of State-Making," 40-41.

26. Agamben, *State of Exception*.

27. Daniel Newcomer, *Reconciling Modernity: Urban State Formation in 1940s León, Mexico* (Lincoln: University of Nebraska Press, 2007), 143-76.

28. I develop the arguments for this first stage in *The Logic of Compromise*. For a broader history of intelligence agencies in Mexico, see Aaron W. Navarro, *Political Intelligence and the Creation of Modern Mexico, 1938-1954* (University Park: Pennsylvania State University Press, 2010); Sergio Aguayo Quesada, *La charola: Una historia de los servicios de inteligencia en México* (Mexico City: Editorial Grijalbo, 2001).

29. Robert F. Alegre, *Railroad Radicals in Cold War Mexico: Gender, Class, and Memory* (Lincoln: University of Nebraska Press, 2013); Castellanos, *México armado*; Carlos Montemayor, *La violencia de estado en México: Antes y después de 1968* (Mexico City: Debate, 2010); Elisa Servín, *Ruptura y oposición: El movimiento henriquista, 1945-1954* (Mexico City: Ediciones Cal y Arena, 2001).

30. For an overview of these events, see Florencio Lugo Hernández, *El asalto al cuartel de Madera: Testimonio de un sobreviviente: 23 de septiembre de 1965* (Mexico City: Universidad Autónama Chapingo, 2006).

31. Ávila Coronel, *La guerrilla del Partido de los Pobres*; Aviña, *Specters of Revolution*; Hodges and Gandy, *Mexico under Siege.*

32. Elaine Carey, *Plaza of Sacrifices: Gender, Power, and Terror in 1968 Mexico* (Albuquerque: University of New Mexico Press, 2005); Montemayor, *La violencia de estado*; Elena Poniatowska, *Fuerte es el silencio* (Mexico City: Era, 1981); Julio Scherer and Carlos Monsiváis, *Los patriotas: De Tlatelolco a la guerra sucia* (Mexico City: Aguilar, 2004).

33. Jaime M. Pensado, *Rebel Mexico: Student Unrest and Authoritarian Political Culture during the Long Sixties* (Stanford: Stanford University Press, 2013).

34. See Javier Garciadiego and Emilio Kourí, eds., *Revolución y exilio en la historia de México: Del amor de un historiador a su patria adoptiva: Homenaje a Friedrich Katz* (Mexico City: Era, 2010), esp. Gabriela Díaz Prieto, "Un exilio venturoso: Chilenos en México (1973–1990)," 793–815. See also Daniela Morales Muñoz, "Brasileños asilados en México: Dos casos de excepción," *Historia Mexicana* 70, no. 2 (October–December 2020): 839–91; Lousie E. Walker, *Waking from the Dream: Mexico's Middle Classes after 1968* (Stanford: Stanford University Press, 2013).

35. Eric Zolov, *The Last Good Neighbor: Mexico in the Global Sixties* (Durham, NC: Duke University Press, 2020), 4–9.

36. For more on the melding of counterinsurgency with counternarcotics during the López Portillo administration, see Adela Cedillo, "Operation Condor, the War on Drugs, and Counterinsurgency in the Golden Triangle (1977–1983)," Working Paper, Kellogg Institute for International Studies, University of Notre Dame, May 2021.

37. See, e.g., Marco Bellingeri, *Del agrarismo armado a la guerra de los pobres: Ensayos de guerrilla rural en el México contemporáneo, 1940–1974* (Mexico City: Ediciones Casa Juan Pablos and Secretaría de Cultura del Gobierno del Distrito Federal, 2003); Calderón and Cedillo, *Challenging Authoritarianism*; Barry Carr, *Marxism and Communism in Twentieth-Century Mexico* (Lincoln: University of Nebraska Press, 1992); Castellanos, *México armado*; Glockner Corte, *Memoria roja*; Jaime López, *Diez años de guerrillas en México* (Mexico City: Editorial Posada, 1974); Montemayor, *La guerrilla recurrente.*

38. For an overview of this massacre, see Walker, *Waking from the Dream*, 27–29; Poniatowska, *Fuerte es el silencio*, 69–71, 155–45. Kate Doyle, "The Corpus Christi Massacre: Mexico's Attack on Its Student Movement, June 10, 1971," uses declassified intelligence files from the National Security Archive at George Washington University to tell the story of events of this day, including the brutal killings of students, as well as the role of the US in training on-the-ground para-

military operatives carrying out the massacre; https://nsarchive2.gwu.edu /NSAEBB/NSAEBB91/.

39. Several scholars have argued for this "hardening" of the government's approach to opposition after 1968. See, e.g., Adela Cedillo, "La crisis del poder, las guerrillas y endurecimiento del régimen después de 1968 en México," *Jornadas de Historia de Occidente*, no. 31 (2009): 151–70.

40. *La Jornada*, March 27, 2007.

41. These figures are in Calderón and Cedillo, *Challenging Authoritarianism*, 8. They relied on the CNDH report, which lists 532 cases of verified disappearances, as well as other human rights groups, including the Asociación de Familiares de Detenidos Desaparecidos y Víctimas de Violaciones a los Derechos Humanos en México.

42. For a history of the intelligence services in Mexico, see McCormick, "The Forgotten Tale of Antonio Jaramillo," in *Logic of Compromise*, 77–105; Aguayo Quesada, *La charola*; and Navarro, *Political Intelligence*.

43. Aguayo Quesada, *La charola*; Navarro, *Political Intelligence*.

44. For this history, see Carlos A. Pérez Ricart, "U.S. Pressure and Mexican Anti-Drugs Efforts from 1940–1980: Importing the War on Drugs?," in *Beyond the Drug War in Mexico: Human Rights, the Public Sphere, and Justice*, ed. Wil G. Pansters, Benjamin T. Smith, and Peter Watt (New York: Routledge, 2017), 33–51; Everard Meade, introduction to *The Taken: True Stories of the Sinaloa Drug War*, by Javier Valdez Cárdenas (Norman: University of Oklahoma Press, 2017), 3–52; Paul Kenny and Mónica Serrano, "Part I: The Background," in *Mexico's Security Failure: Collapse into Criminal Violence*, ed. Paul Kenny, Mónica Serrano, and Arturo C. Sotomayor (New York: Routledge, 2012), 27–86.

45. Alfred McCoy, "Covert Netherworld: An Invisible Interstice in the Modern World System," *Comparative Studies in Society and History* 58, no. 4 (October 2016): 847–79. Though McCoy focuses on Asia, many of his conclusions apply to the Mexican case, especially the slippery transition from dirty war into drug war in the closing decades of the twentieth century.

46. This is a rich line of inquiry that scholars are only just beginning to explore. For Colombia, see Lina Britto, *Marijuana Boom: The Rise and Fall of Colombia's First Drug Paradise* (Oakland: University of California Press, 2020). For Mexico, see Aileen Teague, *"Dirty War" on Drugs: The United States, Mexico, and the Origins of Militarized Policing, 1969–2000* (New York: Oxford University Press, forthcoming); Alexander Aviña, *A War against Poor People: Dirty Wars, Narcotics, and the Cold War Roots of Mexico's Contemporary Drug Violence* (forthcoming). See also the introduction and essays in part 3 of Wil G. Pansters and Benjamin T. Smith, eds., *Histories of Drug Trafficking in Twentieth-Century Mexico* (Albuquerque: University of New Mexico Press, 2022), esp. Adela Cedillo, "The War on Drugs, Counterinsurgency, and the State of Siege," 240–62.

47. For more on the imprisonment of Siqueiros, Vallejo, and others in the earlier part of the 1960s, see Condés Lara, *Represión y rebellion*, 125–90.

48. Archivo General de la Nación, Mexico City—Dirección Federal de Seguridad (hereafter AGN-DFS), Exp. 100-14-1-69 L 18 H 276 (December 19, 1969).

49. AGN-DFS, Exp 100-14-1 L 24 H 19 (October 3, 1973).

50. US Embassy in Mexico to Secretary of State in Washington, June 26, 1974, "Cabañas Issues Third Communiqué with 'Outrageous' Demands; GOM Mounts Military Operation against Him," National Security Archive, http://nsarchive.gwu.edu/NSAEBB/NSAEBB105/Doc15.pdf.

51. Ignacio Arturo Salas Obregón, *Cuestiones fundamentales del movimiento revolucionario o manifestó al proletariado: Liga Comunista 23 de Septiembre* (Mexico City: Editorial Huasipungo, 2003), https://ligacomunista23.files.wordpress.com/2015/05/cuestiones09.pdf.

52. For an earlier history of this looseness surrounding prison life, see Pablo Piccato, *City of Suspects: Crime in Mexico City, 1900-1931* (Durham, NC: Duke University Press, 2001); Carlos Aguirre, *The Criminals of Lima and Their Worlds: The Prison Experience, 1850-1935* (Durham, NC: Duke University Press, 2005).

53. US Department of State Confidential Report—Mexico A-79 (March 24, 1975), http://nsarchive.gwu.edu/NSAEBB/NSAEBB89/mexhr06.pdf.

54. Paul Gillingham and Benjamin Smith, eds., *Dictablanda: Politics, Work, and Culture in Mexico, 1938-1968* (Durham, NC: Duke University Press, 2014).

55. Hugo Velázquez, Francisco Ávila Coronel, and Eneida Martínez assisted me with interviewing these individuals.

56. My methodology for working with oral histories draws on Steve J. Stern, *Remembering Pinochet's Chile: On the Eve of London 1998* (Durham, NC: Duke University Press, 2004); Alessandro Portelli, *The Death of Luigi Trastulli and Other Stories: Form and Meaning in Oral History* (Albany: State University of New York Press, 1991); Daniel James, *Doña Maria's Story: Life History, Memory, and Political Identity* (Durham, NC: Duke University Press, 2000). The reader will note, for example, my attention to questions of collective memory (Stern); reading testimonies for what an individual says, as well as the silences, omissions, and errors (Portelli); and the tropes individuals use to make sense of traumatic events (James).

57. Carlos Borbolla, *La guerra sucia: Hechos y testimonios* (Colima: Universidad de Colima, 2007); José Luis Moreno Borbolla, "La Brigada Roja: Comité Regional de la Liga Comunista," in *La Liga Comunista 23 de Septiembre—Cuatro décadas a debate: Historia, memoria, testomonio y literatura*, ed. Rodolfo Gamiño Muñoz et al. (Mexico City: UNAM, 2014); Carlos Salcedo García, "Grupo guerrillero Lacandones: La luz que no se acaba," unpublished manuscript (Símbolo Digital, Mexico City, 2004); Carlos Salcedo Gárcia, "Grupo Lacandones," in Gamiño Muñoz et al., *La Liga Comunista 23 de Septiembre*,

183–204; Antonio Orozco Michel, "Ayer y hoy: La vida por un ideal (Testimonio)," in Gamiño Muñoz et al., *La Liga Comunista 23 de Septiembre*, 157–66; Lourdes Uranga López, *Comparezco y acuso* (Mexico City: Universidad Autónoma de Chapingo/Plaza y Valdés, 2012).

58. I have worked with these specialized historical collections since summer 2002. Others have written about the challenges surrounding these materials. See, e.g., Tanalís Padilla and Lousie E. Walker, "Dossier: Spy Reports: Content, Methodology, and Historiography," special issue, *Journal of Iberian and Latin American Research* 19, no. 1 (July 2013). Pablo Piccato, "Comments: How to Build a Perspective on the Recent Past," *Journal of Iberian and Latin American Research* 19, no. 1 (July 2013): 91–102, gives further context to working with these types of sources.

CHAPTER 1

1. AGN-DFS, Exp 100-10-16-4, L 5, H 80 (June 29, 1972).
2. Vicente Ovalle, *[Tiempo suspendido]*, 109–52.
3. McCoy, *Torture and Impunity*, 8.
4. Vicente Ovalle, *[Tiempo suspendido]*, 328.
5. Feitlowitz, *A Lexicon of Terror*, 23.
6. Feitlowitz, *A Lexicon of Terror*, 67.
7. Feitlowitz, *A Lexicon of Terror*, 66.
8. Feitlowitz, *A Lexicon of Terror*, 57–58.
9. Vicente Ovalle, *[Tiempo suspendido]*, 119–152.
10. Vicente Ovalle, *[Tiempo suspendido]*, 122.
11. Lazreg, *Torture and the Twilight*.
12. For more on this discussion, see Darius Regalis, *Torture and Democracy* (Princeton, NJ: Princeton University Press, 2009).
13. Lazreg, *Torture and the Twilight*, 3.
14. Lazreg, *Torture and the Twilight*, 237–38.
15. Lazreg, *Torture and the Twilight*, 239.
16. Roberto González Villareal, *Historia de la desaparición: Nacimiento de un tecnología represiva* (Mexico City: Editorial Terracota, 2012), 45–57. González Villareal tracks the escalation and geographic distribution of disappearances from 1970 to 1974.
17. González Villareal, *Historia de la desaparición*, 59–60.
18. Euphemism was not exclusive to torture. Officials used it in the context of, for example, covering up what took place after the 1968 massacre at Tlatelolco. See Raúl Álvarez Garín, *La estela de Tlatelolco: Una reconstrucción histórica del Movimiento estudiantil del 68* (Mexico City: Editorial Itaca, 2002).
19. Lazreg, *Torture and the Twilight*, 111.

20. Lazreg, *Torture and the Twilight*, 112.

21. Aguayo Quesada, *La charola*, 185; AGN-DFS, Exp 100–12, L 2, H 74, H 134–141 (October 12, 1977); Exp 11–235, L 36, H 76 (March 15, 1976); Exp 11–235, L 43, H 160 (April 17, 1977); Exp 11–235, L 46, H 1 (July 9, 1977).

22. María de los Ángeles Magdaleno Cárdenas, quoted in Alfonso Garcia Morales et al., "México: La fiscalía especial para movimientos sociales y políticos del pasado," in *Entre la memoria y la justicia: Experiencias latinoamericanas sobre Guerra Sucia y defensa de Derechos Humanos*, ed. Rubén Ruiz Guerra (Mexico City: UNAM, 2005), 233. As mentioned earlier, this reliance on euphemisms was by no means unique to Mexico. See, e.g., Feitlowitz, *A Lexicon of Terror*; Rita Maran, *Torture: The Role of Ideology in the French-Algerian War* (New York: Praeger, 1989).

23. This chapter relies on Carlos Salcedo's interviews for this project. He has also published his testimony: Salcedo, "La luz que no se acaba."

24. José Arturo Gallegos Nájera, *La guerrilla en Guerrero: Testimonio sobre el Partido de los Pobres y las Fuerzas Armadas Revolucionarias* (Mexico City: Editorial Lamm, 2004). See also José Arturo Gallegos Nájera, *¡A merced del enemigo! Detenciones, interrogatorios, torturas, mazmorras, y . . . algo más* (Guadalajara: Centro de Investigaciones Históricas de los Movimientos Sociales, Universidad de Guadalajara, 2009).

25. Gallegos Nájera, *La guerrilla en Guerrero*.

26. Gallegos Nájera, *¡A merced del enemigo!*, 28.

27. For further discussion on the Ayotzinapa normal school during this period, see Tanalís Padilla, *Unintended Lessons of Revolution: Student Teachers and Political Radicalism in Twentieth-Century Mexico* (Durham, NC: Duke University Press, 2021), 133–88.

28. Gallegos Nájera, *¡A merced del enemigo!*, 80.

29. Gallegos Nájera, *¡A merced del enemigo!*, 28.

30. Alberto Ulloa Bornemann, *Surviving Mexico's Dirty War: A Political Prisoner's Memoir*, ed. and trans. Arthur Schmidt and Aurora Camacho de Schmidt (Philadelphia: Temple University Press, 2007), 31.

31. Ulloa Bornemann, *Surviving Mexico's Dirty War*, 29.

32. Poniatowska, *Fuerte es el silencio*, 106.

33. Poniatowska, *Fuerte es el silencio*, 42.

34. We know about the role of medical personnel in these sessions from interviews. Later chapters discuss an especially egregious case of a doctor who went on to train torturers. The role of doctors has been documented in other cases of dirty war. For Argentina, see Feitlowitz, *Lexicon of Terror*.

35. Aguayo Quesada, *La charola*, 186.

36. Poniatowska, *Fuerte es el silencio*, 110.

37. Saúl López de la Torre, *Guerras secretas: Memoria de un exguerrillero de los setentas que ahora no puede caminar* (Mexico City: Artefacto Editor, 2001), 83.

38. CNDH, "Informe especial."

39. Verónica Oikión Solano, "Represión y tortura en México de la década de 1970: Un testimonio político," *Historia y Grafía*, no. 37 (July–December 2011): 115–48.

40. Oikión Solano, "Represión y tortura en México de la década de 1970," 126.

41. For more on Nazar Haro, see Aguayo Quesada, *La charola*, 125, 182–84.

42. Aguayo Quesada, *La charola*, 127–28.

43. Aguayo Quesada, *La charola*, 128.

44. Aguayo Quesada, *La charola*, 129–30.

45. Aguayo Quesada, *La charola*, 130.

46. Dios Corona, *La historia que no pudieron borrar*, 131–33.

47. Dios Corona, *La historia que no pudieron borrar*, 170.

48. Dios Corona, *La historia que no pudieron borrar*, 164–66.

49. Ulloa Bornemann, *Surviving Mexico's Dirty War*, 121–22.

50. McCoy, *A Question of Torture*, 83–84.

51. Gallegos Nájera, *La guerrilla en Guerrero*, 29.

52. Gallegos Nájera, *La guerrilla en Guerrero*, 29.

53. McCoy, *Torture and Impunity*, 22.

54. McCoy, *Torture and Impunity*, 22.

55. Aside from women interviewed for this project, there are rich collections of women's testimonies. See, e.g., the collection of interviews in chapters 8 and 9 of María de Jesús Méndez Alvarado, "México: Mujeres insurgentes de los años 70: Género y lucha armada" (PhD diss., Universidad Nacional Autónoma de México, 2015); and, for Guerrero specifically, "Memoría del primer encuentro estatal por los derechos humanos de las mujeres," Atoyac, Guerrero (2008).

56. AGN-DFS, Exp 11-240-78, L 11, H 168-174 (August 2, 1978).

57. Calderón and Cedillo, *Challenging Authoritarianism*, 180–81.

58. Méndez Alvarado, "México," 156–202.

59. Méndez Alvarado, "México," 163–88, details the types of torture women endured, including physical and psychological forms of sexual violence.

60. Lucía Rayas, "Subjugating the Nation: Women and the Guerrilla Experience," in Calderón and Cedillo, *Challenging Authoritarianism*, 167–81.

61. CNDH, "Informe especial."

62. Lazreg, *Torture and the Twilight*, 142–44.

63. Gallegos Nájera, *¡A merced del enemigo!*, 87–93.

64. Gallegos Nájera, *¡A merced del enemigo!*, 91.

65. For a detailed discussion of the diplomatic and economic ties between the United States and Mexico during the 1960s, see Zolov, *The Last Good Neighbor*. Note that Zolov studies the diplomatic relationship between the two countries and posits that Mexico had its own diplomatic agenda above and beyond the US. See also Keller, *Mexico's Cold War*. For a more detailed analysis of the Cold War's

impact on these relations, see Daniela Spenser, ed., *Espejos de la guerra fría: México, América Central, y el Caribe* (Mexico City: CIESAS, 2004). Vicente Ovalle discusses the influence of the US government's counterinsurgency doctrine on Mexico in *Instantes sin historia*, 65–68.

66. Many of these files are located at the National Archives at the University of Maryland, College Park, https://www.archives.gov/college-park. The work of activists, scholars, journalists, lawyers, and others making ample use of the Freedom of Information Act has transformed research with declassified materials. Many of these files can also be found online through the National Security Archive Project of George Washington University, https://nsarchive.gwu.edu. The CIA's website includes a "Freedom of Information Act Reading Room" where we can locate many of these as well, https://www.cia.gov/readingroom/.

67. Zolov, *The Last Good Neighbor*, 8.

68. Zolov, *The Last Good Neighbor*, 296.

69. Keller, *Mexico's Cold War*, 223–24.

70. Keller, *Mexico's Cold War*, 223–24.

71. McCoy, *A Question of Torture*, describes the content and dissemination of these manuals throughout Latin America. Gill, *The School of the Americas*, 49 and 137–39, also refers to the use of "Torture Manuals" in military intelligence courses taught through the School of the Americas before their ban in 1996.

72. Gill, *The School of the Americas*; Micol Seigel, "Objects of Police History," *Journal of American History* 102, no. 1 (June 2015): 152–61.

73. Gill, *The School of the Americas*, 83.

74. McCoy, *Torture and Impunity*, 21.

75. McCoy, *A Question of Torture*, 51.

76. McCoy, *A Question of Torture*, 52.

CHAPTER 2

1. Examples of such interpretations of Mexico by Hollywood filmmakers are *The Red Dance*, directed by Raoul Walsh (Fox Film Corporation, 1928); *Hot Pepper*, directed by John G. Blystone (Fox Film Corporation, 1933); *Mexican Spitfire*, directed by Leslie Goodwins (RKO Radio Pictures, 1940); and *Viva Zapata!*, directed by Elia Kaza (20th Century Fox, 1952).

2. For more information on what transpired, see FEMOSPP, "Informe Documenta sobre 18 años de 'Guerra Sucia' en México" (2006), accessed October 17, 2017, https://nsarchive2.gwu.edu/NSAEBB/NSAEBB180/index2.htm; Carey, *Plaza of Sacrifices*; or other sources previously cited on the events surrounding the 1968 massacre.

3. Scherer García and Monsiváis, *Los patriotas*, 14.

4. Others have explored how the Mexican security forces created the narrative of an internal enemy. See, e.g., Vicente Ovalle, *[Tiempo suspendido]*, 93–107; Francisco Ávila Coronel, "La visión oficial de la guerrilla y el fenómeno de la magnificación en el caso de la guerrilla del Partido de los Pobres (PDLP) (Atoyac, Guerrero)," in *Reflejos de la Guerra Sucia en el estado de Guerrero: Historia, literatura, música e imágenes*, ed. Ana María Cárabe (Mexico City: Miguel Ángel Porrúa, 2015), 75–110.

5. Lazreg writes that "subversion connotes not only the overthrow or destruction of an existing political order, but also the undermining, and corrupting of a *moral* order." That psychological dimension of the threat posed by so-called subversives—as a clash of civilizations bent on destroying a way of life—implicitly shored up the Mexican security forces, both the military and the police, as a "bulwark against an immoral and shadowy adversary." Lazreg, *Torture and the Twilight*, 21; original emphasis.

6. While I have already discussed debates over the 1968 Tlatelolco massacre, there is a rich scholarship on the 1967 massacre at Atoyac. See, e.g., Julio César Ocaña Martínez, "Atoyac, a 25 años de Lucio Cabañas: Una reflexión política," unpublished manuscript (Mexico City, 1995).

7. Penny Lernoux, *Cry of the People: The Struggle for Human Rights in Latin America—The Catholic Church in Conflict with U.S. Policy* (New York: Penguin Books, 1982).

8. Aguayo Quesada, *La charola*, 312.

9. FEMOSPP, "Informe Documenta sobre 18 años de 'Guerra Sucia' en México."

10. While this book pays attention to guerrilla movements in the states of Mexico, Guerrero, and surrounding areas, it is important to recognize how widespread they were. See, e.g., for Jalisco, Adela Cedillo, *El fuego y el silencio: Historia de las FPL* (Mexico City: Comité 68 Pro Libertades Democráticas, 2008); Dios Corona, *La historia que no pudieron borrar*; Juan Antonio Castañeda et al., *Memoria guerrillera, represión y contrainsurgencia en Jalisco* (Guadalajara: Grafisma Editores, 2012); for Aguascalientes, Daniel Carlos García, *Fulgor rebelde: La guerrilla en Aguascalientes* (Mexico City: Filo de Agua, 2006); for Sonora, Ignacio Lagarda Lagarda, *El color de las amapas: Crónica de la guerrilla en la sierra de Sonora* (Mexico City: Universidad Tecnológica del Sur de Sonora, 2007); and for San Luis Potosí, Javier Padrón, *Los bombazos de 1975: Terrorismo de estado (el rochismo y la guerra sucia)* (Mexico City: Ediciones Ruta Crítica, 2005).

11. Padilla, *Unintended Lessons of Revolution*, provides a comprehensive study of *normalista* activism.

12. For further references on both of these guerrilla leaders, see Armando Barta Verges, *Guerrero bronco: Campesinos, ciudadanos y guerrilleros en la*

Costa Grande (Mexico City: Era, 2000); Juan Miguel de Mora, *Lucio Cabañas, su vida y muerte* (Mexico City: Editores Asociados, 1975); Juan Miguel de Mora, *Las guerrillas en Mexico y Jenaro Vasquez Rojas: Su personalidad, su vida y su muerte* (Mexico City: Editora Latino Americana, 1972); Orlando Ortiz, *Genaro Vázquez* (Mexico City: Editorial Diógenes, 1972); Ángel Custodio Reyes Serrano, *¡Trinchera . . . ! Lucio Cabañas y Genaro Vázquez y su guerrilla* (Mexico City: Costa-Amic Editores, 1985); José Natividad Rosales, *¿Quién es Lucio Cabañas? ¿Qué pasa con la guerrilla en México?* (Mexico City: Editorial Posada, 1974); José Natividad Rosales, *La muerte (?) de Lucio Cabañas* (Mexico City: Editorial Posada, 1975); Luis Suárez, *Lucio Cabañas: El guerrillero sin esperanza* (Mexico City: Roca, 1976).

13. Ávila Coronel, *La guerrilla del Partido de los Pobres*; Aviña, *Specters of Revolution*.

14. Tanalís Padilla, "'Latent Sites of Agitation': *Normalistas Rurales* and Chihuahua's Agrarian Struggle in the 1960s," in Pensado and Ochoa, 66.

15. Vicente Ovalle, *[Tiempo suspendido]*, 167–76.

16. Pensado, *Rebel Mexico*, 201–34; Hugo Velázquez Villa, *El 68 como discurso de Estado* (Guadalajara: Sindicato de Trabajadores Académicos de la Universidad de Guadalajara, 2017), 189–214.

17. Fernando Herrera Cálderon, "Working-Class Heroes: Barrio Consciousness, Student Power, and the Mexican Dirty War," in Pensado and Ochoa, *México Beyond 1968*, 156.

18. There is a rich literature on the history of all these guerrilla movements, some of which has already been cited. To add to the bibliography of guerrilla groups in Mexico, see Leticia Carrasco Gutiérrez and Hugo Velázquez Villa, *Breve historia del MAR: La guerrilla imaginaria del Movimiento de Acción Revolucionaria* (Guadalajara: Universidad Autónoma de Guadalajara–CUCSH, 2010); Hugo Esteve Díaz, *Amargo lugar sin nombre: Crónica del movimiento armado socialista en México (1960–1990)* (Guadalajara: La Casa del Mago, 2013); Agustín Evangelista, *Carmelo Cortés Castro y la guerrilla urbana: Fuerzas armadas revolucionarias* (Mexico City: Centro de Investigaciones Históricas de los Movimientos Sociales, 2007); Rodolfo Gamiño Muñoz and Jesús Zamora, eds., *Los Vikingos: Una historia de lucha política social* (Guadalajara: Colectivo Rodolfo Reyes Crespo, 2011); Fernando Pineda Ochoa, *En las profundidades del MAR (el oro no llegó de Moscú)* (Mexico City: Plaza y Valdés, 2003).

19. This point is also made in Pensado, *Rebel Mexico*, 169–70. See also Patrick Barr-Melej, *Psychedelic Chile: Youth, Counterculture, and Politics on the Road to Socialism and Dictatorship* (Chapel Hill: University of North Carolina Press, 2017).

20. Though outside the scope of this chapter, young women also suffered for their guerrilla activity. See Herrera Calderón and Cedillo, *Challenging Authoritarianism*; Lucía Rayas Velasco, *Armadas: Un análisis de género desde el cuerpo*

de los mujeres combatientes (Mexico City: El Colegio de México, 2009); Luz María Aguilar Terrés, "Guerrilleras: Antología de testimonios y textos sobre la participación de las mujeres en los movimientos armados socialistas en México, segunda mitad del siglo XX," unpublished manuscript (Mexico City, 2014).

21. Walker, *Waking from the Dream*, 30–37.

22. Walker, *Waking from the Dream*, 33.

23. Walker, *Waking from the Dream*, 33. See also Eric Zolov, *Refried Elvis: The Rise of Mexican Counterculture* (Berkeley: University of California Press, 1999).

24. Roger Bartra, "Memorias de la contracultura," *Letras Libres*, September 30, 2007, https://letraslibres.com/revista-mexico/memorias-de-la-contracultura/.

25. For the case of Brazil, see Benjamin Cowan, *Securing Sex: Morality and Repression in the Making of Cold War Brazil* (Chapel Hill: University of North Carolina Press, 2016); Langland, *Speaking of Flowers*.

26. For more on clandestine life, see Fritz Glockner Corte, *Veinte de cobre: Memoria de la clandestinidad* (Mexico City: Joaquin Mortiz, 1997).

27. AGN-DGIPS [Dirección General de Investigaciones Políticas y Sociales], Caja 1913-A, Exp 1.

28. There is a rich scholarship detailing the role of women in guerrilla movements. See, e.g., Macrina Cárdenas Montaño, "La participación de las mujeres en movimientos armados," in Oikión Solano and García Ugarte, *Movimientos armados en México, siglo XX*, 2:129–43; Gabriela Lozano Rubello, "Militancia y transgresión en la guerrilla mexicana: Una mirada crítica feminista al case fe la Liga Comunista 23 de Septiembre," *Revista de la Carrera de Sociología Entramados y Perspectivas* 5, no. 5 (2015): 100–109, for a discussion of women's role in LC23S. Méndez Alvarado, "México," discusses gender discrimination inside guerrilla groups in chap. 4 and their specific activities in chap. 7

29. "Especial Nazar Haro, un tigre que murió en su propia jaula," *El Universal*, January 28, 2013.

30. Pensado, *Rebel Mexico*, 202.

31. Along with Pensado, *Rebel Mexico*; see Álvarez Garín, *La estela de Tlatelolco*; Carey, *Plaza of Sacrifices*.

32. Pensado, *Rebel Mexico*, 202.

33. Pensado, *Rebel Mexico*, 236–37.

34. Walker, *Waking from the Dream*, 45–72; Luis Herrán Avila, "The Other 'New Man': Conservative Nationalism and Right-Wing Youth in 1970s Monterrey," in Pensado and Ochoa, 195–214.

35. Herrán Avila, "The Other 'New Man,'" 200–210.

36. Keller, *Mexico's Cold War*, 227.

37. These reports, as Keller writes, were partly based in the fact that from the mid-1960s to the early 1970s several groups of Mexicans did travel to these countries for such training. Keller, *Mexico's Cold War*, 227. See also Walker, *Waking from the Dream*, 51–59.

38. Halbert Jones, "Social Dissolution: Article 145 of the Mexican Federal Penal Code in International Context, 1941–1970" (Paper presented at the Boston Area Latin American History Workshop, Cambridge, MA, April 2009).

39. Centro de Estudios del Movimiento Obreros y Socialista (CEMOS), Caja 1475 A, Exp 17, F 11, "Letter to the Mexican Congress from the wives and mothers of eighty political prisoners," November 22, 1962.

40. Secretaría de Servicios Parlamentarios, *Código Penal Federal*, June 7, 2013, 32. The use of false evidence was a long-standing practice. See, e.g., *Los Procesos de México 68: La criminalización de las víctimas* (Mexico City: Comité 68 por Libertades Democráticas, 2008).

41. AGN-DFS, Exp 100–17, L 28, H 228 (April 8, 1972).

42. AGN-DFS, Exp 11–122, L 14, H 49 (12 May 1978).

43. AGN-DFS, Exp 11–235, L 38, H 46–48 (June 1976).

44. AGN-DFS, Exp 11–235, L 38, H 46–48 (June 1976), 47.

45. AGN-DFS, Exp 11–235, L 38, H 46–48 (June 1976), 47.

46. AGN-DFS, Exp 11–235, L 37, H 215–216. AGN-DFS, Exp 11–235, L 52, contains several telegrams from individuals denouncing their neighbors for suspicious activities.

47. AGN-DFS, Exp 11–235, L 48, H 2–6 (July 8, 1977).

48. AGN-DFS, Exp 11–235, L 50, H 172. Note that this article is about the detention of Violeta Tecla Parra and other LC23S leaders on April 5, 1978.

49. AGN-DFS, Exp 11–235, L 51, H 206 (April 1977).

50. Castellanos, *México armado*, 268.

51. AGN-DFS, Exp 11–235, L 48, H 19–22 (October 17, 1977).

52. Padilla, *Unintended Lessons of Revolution*.

53. Bartra, "Memorias de la contracultura"; Pensado, *Rebel Mexico*.

54. For more, see Víctor Macías-González, "Los homosexuales como sujetos peligrosos en la Ciudad de México (1940–1960)," in *Hampones, intocables y pecatrices: Sujetos peligrosos de la Ciudad de México (1940–1960)*, ed. Susana Sosenski (Mexico City: Fondo de Cultura Económica, 2019), 84–119.

55. Luis Echeverría Álvarez, Fourth Government Report (speech, opening of Congress, Mexico City, September 1, 1974), https://es.wikisource.org/wiki /Discurso_de_Luis_Echeverría_Álvarez_en_su_Cuarto_Informe_de_Gobierno.

56. Thomas Rath discusses the role of the military in policing duties in rural Mexico, though before the 1970s, in *Myths of Demilitarization in Postrevolutionary Mexico, 1920–1960* (Durham, NC: Duke University Press, 2013), 115–43.

57. José Sotelo Marbán, "El ejército mexicano y la guerra sucia en Guerrero," unpublished manuscript (Mexico City, 2002), provides a detailed overview of the sources in the Secretaría de la Defensa Nacional (SEDENA) and DFS files tracking the military's actions in the state of Guerrero across the 1970s. Note that this document is an unpublished work and Sotelo Marbán was one of the key researchers of the FEMOSPP.

58. Ávila Coronel, *La guerrilla del Partido de los Pobres*, 156–220. See also Alexander Aviña, "A War against Poor People: Dirty Wars and Drug Wars in 1970s Mexico," in Pensado and Ochoa, 134–52.

59. For a more detailed analysis of the plan, see Verónica Oikión Solano, "El Estado mexicano frente a los levantamientos armados en Guerrero: El caso del Plan Telaraña," *Tzintzun: Revista de Estudios Históricos*, no. 45 (January–July 2007): 65–75. Sotelo Marbán also provides his overview of the Plan Telaraña, in "El ejército mexicano," 217–19.

60. AGN-SEDENA, Caja 93–94, maleantes, "Operación Plan Telaraña," 1971, 4. This document can be accessed online at Archivos de la Represión, https://biblioteca.archivosdelarepresion.org/item/75817#?c=&m=&s=&cv=&xy wh=1843%2C733%2C1286%2C1929&r=270.

61. For a concise overview of these operations, see Evangelina Sánchez Serrano, "Terrorismo de Estado y la repression en Guerrero durante la guerra sucia," in *Desaparición forzada y terrorismo de Estado en México: Memorias de la represión en Atoyac, Guerrero durante la década de los setenta*, ed. Andrea Radilla Martínez and Claudia E. G. Rangel Lozano (Mexico City: Universidad Autónoma de Guerrero, 2012), 131–74.

62. Ávila Coronel, *La guerrilla del Partido de los Pobres*, 177.

63. AGN-SEDENA, Caja 93–94, "Operación Plan Telaraña," 23.

64. Alexander Aviña, "Mexico's Long Dirty War," *NACLA Report on the Americas* 48, no. 2 (Summer 2016): 147.

65. Aviña, "Mexico's Long Dirty War," 147.

66. Ávila Coronel, *La guerrilla del Partido de los Pobres*, 156–219; Aviña, "A War against Poor People," 134–48.

67. For more on this calculus for the emerging middle-classes in the 1970s, see Walker, *Waking from the Dream*.

68. I have referred to this as "the logic of compromise" in previous scholarship.

69. Gabriela Soto Laveaga, "Protests, Peasants, and Physicians: The Role of Mexican Doctors in Urban and Rural Uprisings, 1964–1969" (paper presented at the Latin American Studies Association Congress, San Francisco, 2012); Gabriela Soto Laveaga, "Shadowing the Professional Class: Reporting Fictions in Doctors' Strikes," in "Dossier: Spy Reports: Content, Methodology, and Historiography in Mexico's Secret Police Archive," ed. Tanalís Padilla and Louise Walker, special issue, *Journal of Iberian and Latin American Research* 19, no. 1 (July 2013): 30–40.

70. Echeverría Álvarez, Fourth Government Report. In his 1974 State of the Union speech, the same one in which he implied that being a homosexual made a young person prone to becoming a terrorist, Echeverría Álvarez suggested that subversives got ideas from watching TV or reading news from sources not allied with the government. These connections extended to individuals producing content for them.

71. The Comité Eureka is discussed at length in the conclusion. For now, I want to point out that many of the organization's documents can be found at the Centro Académico de la Memória en Nuestra América at the Universidad Autónoma de la Ciudad de México, https://selser.uacm.edu.mx/expedientes.php.

72. Jaime Pensado, "Silencing Rebellious Priests: Rodolfo Escamilla García and the Repression of Progressive Catholicism in Cold-War Mexico," *The Americas* 79, no. 2 (2022): 263–89.

73. Pensado, "Silencing Rebellious Priests," 280.

74. AGN-DFS, Exp 11–235, L 50, H 150–160 (April 5, 1978), contains a detailed overview of El Guaymas's detention and interrogation. The file also includes several photographs, including one of his face when he was on a hospital gurney and one from when he was imprisoned. In addition to detailing what he disclosed during his interrogation, the file includes information on who visited him while in prison.

75. The use of "madrinas" in Mexican policing is also explained in Condés Lara, *Represión y rebelión*, 163.

76. González Villareal, *Historia de la desaparición*, 105.

77. Poniatowska, *Fuerte es el silencio*, 109–10.

78. Gustavo Hirales Móran, *Memoria de la guerra de los justos* (Mexico City: Cal y Arena, 1996).

79. For more on Hirales Morán's political trajectory, see *Proceso*, January 8, 1994.

80. Gustavo Hirales Morán, "Defender lo indefendible," *Nexos en Línea*, no. 323 (October 2004); and "Ecos de la guerra sucia," *Nexos en Línea*, no. 325 (December 2004). See also Gustavo Hirales Morán, *La Liga Comunista 23 de Septiembre: Orígenes y naufragio* (Mexico City: Cultura Popular, 1977); Hirales Morán, *Memoria de la guerra*.

81. Hirales Morán, *Memoria de la guerra*, 16–17.

82. Hirales Morán, *Memoria de la guerra*, 16–26.

83. Hirales Morán, *Memoria de la guerra*, 27–30.

84. Hirales Morán, *Memoria de la guerra*, 69–72.

85. Their torture is also described in Dios Corona, *La historia que no pudieron borrar*, 135–38.

86. AGN-DFS, Versión Pública, Manuel Mondragón y Kalb, Caja 32. For additional information on these activities in April and June 1965, see AGN-DFS, Versión Pública, José Pagés Llergo, Archivos de la Represión, https://biblioteca.archivosdelarepresion.org/item/37574#?c=&m=&s=&cv=.

87. Humberto Padgett, "Mondragón, don camaleón: De medico 'rebelde' a entrenador de la policía política de LEA; de la izquierda al PRI," *Sin Embargo*, January 14, 2013, https://www.sinembargo.mx/14-01-2013/488229. Note that several women interviewed in Méndez Alvarado, "México," 164, stipulate they were tortured with karate kicks to various parts of their body.

88. David Vicenteño, "Perfil Manuel Mondragón y Kalb," *Excelsior*, March 30, 2018, https://www.excelsior.com.mx/nacional/perfil-manuel-mondragon-y-kalb/1229518.

89. Calderón, "Working-Class Heroes," in Pensado and Ochoa, *México Beyond 1968*, 155–74.

CHAPTER 3

1. Comisión de la Verdad del Estado de Guerrero (COMVERDAD), "Anexo 3: Personas participantes en desapariciones forzadas," in *Informe final de la Comisión de la Verdad del Estado de Guerrero (COMVERDAD)*, 2nd ed. (Mexico City: Article 19, 2023), accessed May 11, 2023, https://memoricamexico.gob.mx/swb/memorica/Cedula?oId=cP4zfYgBhkPQL8y2UyvM. The "Lista de Represores" was among the research exhibits generated for the state of Guerrero's Truth Commission. It was released to the public as "Anexo 3: Personas Participantes en Desapariciones Forzadas—Informe del la Comisión de la Verdad del Estado de Guerrero" in February 2023. This document as well as the full report and other supplementary materials for the COMVERDAD can be found at https://articulo19.org/informecomverdad/.

2. Harold Hinds Jr. and Charles M. Tatum, *Not Just for Children: The Mexican Comic Book in the Late 1960s and 1970s* (Westport, CT: Greenwood, 1992), 70–81. Note that Condés Lara, *Represión y rebelión*, 147–50, also draws this comparison. Pensado discusses Rius and his influence on student politics in *Rebel Mexico*, 170–71.

3. Stern, *Remembering Pinochet's Chile*, xxvii.

4. I borrow this analogy from Stern, *Remembering Pinochet's Chile*.

5. Roderic Ai Camp, *Generals in the Palacio: The Military in Modern Mexico* (New York: Oxford University Press, 1992), 88.

6. Here I draw inspiration from Christopher R. Browning, *Ordinary Men: Reserve Police Battalion 101 and the Final Solution in Poland*, 3rd ed. (New York: HarperCollins, 2017), on why Nazis followed orders to kill Jewish people during World War II.

7. Browning, *Ordinary Men*, 234. Browning poses this question too.

8. See, e.g., Joanna Bourke, *An Intimate History of Killing: Face-to-Face Killing in Twentieth-Century Warfare* (New York: Basic Books, 1999).

9. I developed the overview of Nazar Haro presented here from Aguayo Quesada, *La charola*; Castellanos, *México armado*; Gustavo Castillo García, El Tigre de Nazar: "Había que ser fanático como ellos" (Mexico City: Penguin Books, 2023); Carlos Fernando López de la Torre, "Miguel Nazar Haro y la guerra sucia en México," *Revista Grafía* 10, no. 1 (January–June 2013): 56–72; Rafael Rodríguez Castañeda, *El policía: Perseguía, torturaba, mataba* (Mexico City:

Grijalbo, 2013); and Jorge Torres, *Nazar, la historia secreta: El hombre detrás de la guerra* (Mexico City: Debate, 2008).

10. Torres, *Nazar, la historia secreta*, 145.

11. Torres, *Nazar, la historia secreta*, 152.

12. Torres, *Nazar, la historia secreta*, 16, 151–52.

13. Torres, *Nazar, la historia secreta*, 20–21.

14. Seigel, "Objects of Police History"; Rodríguez Castañeda, *El policía*.

15. "De su propria boca: Nazar Haro fue el creador de la Brigada Blanca," *Proceso*, October 29, 2000. For more on Nazar Haro's time at the IPA, see Castillo García, *El Tigre de Nazar*, 171–77.

16. For more on the IPA, see Stuart Schrader, *Badges without Borders: How Global Counterinsurgency Transformed American Policing* (Oakland: University of California Press, 2019).

17. "10 claves para conocer quién fue Miguel Nazar Haro," *ADNPolítico*, January 27, 2021; "De su propia boca," *Proceso*, October 29, 2000.

18. Aguayo Quesada, *La charola*, 125.

19. Aguayo Quesada, *La charola*, 182–84.

20. Torres, *Nazar, la historia secreta*, 26.

21. Castellanos, *México armado*, 265–68.

22. López de la Torre, "Miguel Nazar Haro," 66–70.

23. Torres, *Nazar, la historia secreta*, 118.

24. Torres, *Nazar, la historia secreta*, 118.

25. Torres, *Nazar, la historia secreta*, 118–19.

26. For example, this is gleaned from Carlos Salcedo's observations in his meetings with Nazar Haro at CM-1 during the early 1970s.

27. Lazreg, *Torture and the Twilight*.

28. Lazreg, *Torture and the Twilight*, 138.

29. The AGN has released "curated" collections of DFS files, referred to as "versiones públicas" (public versions), for several of these former DFS agents. While some contain useful information, such as for Gutierréz Barrios, others are anemic at best. Nazar Haro's "version pública" DFS file is slim and contains mostly press clippings on him.

30. Though Nazar Haro was indicted in 2004 through the FEMOSPP, his case was dismissed in 2006. *ADNPolítico*, January 27, 2012; *Proceso*, September 9, 2013.

31. For interviews he gave to the press, see *La Jornada*, February 4, 2009, January 28, 2012, and January 29, 2012; *Proceso*, October 29, 2000. Leigh Payne helps us understand such confessions in *Unsettling Accounts: Neither Truth nor Reconciliation in Confessions of State Violence* (Durham, NC: Duke University Press, 2008), 173–95.

32. Rodríguez Castañeda, *El policía*, 148.

33. Jesús Vicente Vásquez, interview by Camilo Vicente Ovalle, Juchitán, Oaxaca, January 12, 2016.

34. Lazreg, *Torture and the Twilight*, 143.

35. Vicente Ovalle, *[Tiempo suspendido]*, 125.

36. Rodríguez Castañeda, *El policía*, 90.

37. See, e.g., Ai Camp, *Generals in the Palacio*, 66–99. See also Thomas Rath, *Myths of Demilitarization in Postrevolutionary Mexico, 1920–1960* (Durham, NC: Duke University Press, 2013).

38. I discuss the use of guardias blancas in Morelos and Puebla in *Logic of Compromise*.

39. For more on the military's presence in local and regional law enforcement, see Ai Camp, *Generals in the Palacio*; Rath, *Myth of Demilitarization*; and Paul Gillingham, *Unrevolutionary Mexico: The Birth of a Strange Dictatorship* (New Haven, CT: Yale University Press, 2021).

40. There are a number of sources discussing the Batallón Olimpia and its actions surrounding the events on October 2, 1968. See, e.g., FEMOSPP, "Informe Documenta"; Montemayor, *La violencia de estado*.

41. There are a number of sources detailing the activities of the Halcones in the Corpus Christi massacre (at the time referred to as El Halconazo). Several were released to commemorate the fiftieth anniversary of the massacre in 1971. See, e.g., Camilo Vicente Ovalle et al., *A 50 años del Halconazo: 10 de junio 1971*, vol. 2: *Antología de testimonios* (Mexico City: Instituto Nacional de Estudios Históricos de las Revoluciones de México, 2021); Alberto del Castillo Troncoso, *La matanza del jueves de Corpus: Fotografía y memoría* (Mexico City: Instituto Nacional de Estudios Históricos de las Revoluciones de México, 2021).

42. FEMOSPP, "Informe Documenta," 187.

43. For detailed accounts of the role of the Halcones in the Corpus Christi massacre, see Carey, *Plaza of Sacrifices*; Condés Lara, *Represión y rebelión*, 195–205; Vicente Ovalle et al., *A 50 años del Halconazo*, 69–120.

44. FEMOSPP, "Informe Documenta," 234. This is reinforced in the oral histories of Vicente Ovalle et al., *A 50 años del Halconazo*.

45. Pansters, "Zones and Languages of State-Making," 45.

46. Kloppe-Santamaría, *In the Vortex of Violence*.

47. Kloppe-Santamaría, *In the Vortex of Violence*, 8.

48. Kloppe-Santamaría, *In the Vortex of Violence*. Also refer to Aviña, *Specters of Revolution*; Paul Gillingham, "Who Killed Crispín Aguilar? Violence and Order in the Postrevolutionary Countryside," in Pansters, *Violence, Coercion, and State-Making in Twentieth-Century Mexico*, 91–111; Pablo Piccato, *A History of Infamy: Crime, Truth, and Justice in Mexico* (Berkeley: University of California Press, 2017).

49. For a detailed analysis of this group, see Alexander Aviña, "Grupo Sangre: Drugs, Death Squads, and the Dirty War Origins of Mexico's Drug Wars," in Pansters and Smith, *Histories of Drug Trafficking in Twentieth-Century Mexico*, 263–86.

50. The DFS files first report appearances of this group in June 1974, in AGN-DFS, Exp 100-1-16, L 9, H 244.

51. Aviña, "Grupo Sangre."

52. AGN-DFS, Exp 100–10–1, L 63, H 137 (November 19, 1977).

53. AGN-DFS, Exp 100–10–1, L 63, H 137 (November 19, 1977).

54. There is a formidable literature on LC23S by scholars as well as participants in the movement. See, e.g., the 552-page volume edited by Rodolfo Gamiño Muñoz et al., *La Liga Comunista 23 de Septiembre—Cuatro décadas a debate: Historia, memoria, testimonio, y literatura* (Mexico City: UNAM, 2014). The FEMOSPP report includes a snapshot of the volume of DFS and SEDENA documents on the group.

55. Jorge Luis Sierra Guzmán, *El enemigo interno: Contrainsurgencia y fuerzas armadas en México* (Mexico City: Plaza y Valdés, Universidad Iberoamericana, and Centro de Estudios Estratégicos de América del Norte, 2003), 108.

56. Fritz Glockner Corte, "La piel de la memoria," in Gamiño Muñoz et al., *La Liga Comunista 23 de Septiembre*, 243.

57. Arturo Acosta Chaparro, "Movimiento subversivo en México," unpublished manuscript (Mexico City, 1990).

58. Aurora Castillo Mata, interview in *Diario de la Tarde*, April 16, 1977. Quoted in Ortiz Rosas, "La Brigada Especial," 62.

59. Glockner Corte, "La piel de la memoria," 248.

60. For more on this case, see Jorge Fernández Menéndez, *Nadie supo nada: La verdadera historia del asesinato de Eugenio Garza Sada* (Mexico City: Grijalbo, 2006); Glockner Corte, "La piel de la memoria"; Mario Rivera Ortiz and Mario Rivera Guzmán, *El secuestro de José Guadalupe Zuno Hernández: Un capítulo de la lucha guerrillera en el México de 1974* (Mexico City: Medicina y Sociedad, 1992). See also Ramón Pimentel Aguilar, *El secuestro: ¿Lucha política o provocación?* (Mexico City: Editorial Posada, 1974).

61. Several sources discuss the Brigada Roja. See, e.g., Rodolfo Gamiño Muñoz, *Repertorios de una violencia urbana en México: Orígenes de la Liga Comunista 23 de Septiembre* (Saarbrücken: Editorial Académia Española, 2011). José Luis Moreno Borbolla, a member of LC23S, has written about his role in it as well: "La Brigada Roja: Comité Regional de la Liga Comunista," in Gamiño Muñoz et al., *La Liga Comunista 23 de Septiembre*, 283–316.

62. Adela Cedillo, "Violencia, memoria, historia y tabú" in Gamiño Muñoz et al., 343–73.

63. Ortiz Rosas, "La Brigada Especial," 63, cites the figure of 75 officers.

64. Ortiz Rosas, "La Brigada Especial," 63.

65. President Luis Echeverría Álvarez statement. Quoted in Ortiz Rosas, "La Brigada Especial," 70.

66. AGN-DFS, Exp 11–235, L 8, H 13 (June 4, 1976).

67. Rodolfo Gamiño Muñoz, *Guerrilla, represión y prensa en la década de los setenta en México: Invisibilidad y olvido* (Mexico City: Instituto José María Luis Mora, 2011), discusses the interplay between the press's coverage of such events and the government's aim to demonize LC23S through propaganda highlighting its supposed violence.

68. AGN-DFS, Exp 11–235, L 41, H 60 (July 1977).

69. AGN-DFS, Exp 11–235, L 26, H 203 (October 1974).

70. Juan Fernando Reyes Peláez, "El largo brazo del estado: La estrategia contrainsurgente del gobierno Mexicano," in Oikión Solano and García Ugarte, *Movimientos armados*, 2:405–13; Sierra Guzmán, "Fuerzas armadas y contrainsurgencia," in Oikión Solano and García Ugarte, *Movimientos armados*, 361–404; Sotelo Marbán, "El ejército mexicano."

71. For the White Brigade, see "De su propia boca," *Proceso*, October 29, 2000; Reyes Peláez, "El largo brazo del estado," in Oikión Solano and García Ugarte, *Movimientos armados*, 2:406–8; and Sierra Guzmán, "Fuerzas armadas y contrainsurgencia," in Oikión Solano and García Ugarte, *Movimientos armados*, 2:400–403.

72. AGN-DFS, Exp 100–12–1, L 19, H 305–308 (January 4, 1972). For more on Francisco Quiróz Hermosillo's activities, refer to his Versión Pública in Caja 140 from the same collection.

73. AGN-DFS, Exp 11–235, L 38, H 55 (no date on document). Note that the Plan de Operaciones No. 1, "Rastreo," encompasses Exp 11–235, L 38, H 50–55, and includes details of the logistics and support for the White Brigade.

74. Note that chap. 11, "Mecanismos que el Estado utilize para corromper el poder," 22–27, of the FEMOSSPP draft report contains a list naming 162 White Brigade members. This list comes directly from Javier Ramirez et al., "La Brigada Blanca: Expediente complete de sus integrantes," *Bajo Palabras* 2, no. 20 (June 16, 2001). It can also be found in José de Jesús Morales Hernández, "'El aparecimiento con vida de los desaparecios' y 'el juicio y castigo a los responsables,'" in *Noche y neblina: Los vuelos de la muerte: La historia de los campos de concentración en México y los desaparecidos de la guerra en el siglo XX* (Mexico City: Plaza Editores, 2007), https://www.marxists.org/espanol/tematica/guerrilla/mexico/noche/07.htm

75. "De su propria boca," *Proceso*, October 29, 2000. DFS files also provide outlines of the White Brigade in AGN-DFS, Exp 11–235, L 38, H 50; and H 56–57, Plan de Operaciones No. 1, "Rastreo" (no date).

76. AGN-DFS, Exp 11–235, L 38, H 55, Plan de Operaciones No. 1, "Rastreo" (no date).

77. Rodríguez Castañeda, *El policía*, 82–83.

78. AGN-DFS, Exp 11–235, L 38, H 55, Plan de Operaciones No. 1, "Rastreo" (no date).

79. Rodríguez Castañeda, *El policía*, 87–88.

80. AGN-DFS, Exp 11–235, L 38, H 50–52, Plan de Operaciones No. 1, "Rastreo" (no date).

81. AGN-DFS, Exp 11–235, L 38, H 50–52, Plan de Operaciones No. 1, "Rastreo" (no date).

82. AGN-DFS, Exp 11–235, L 38, H 46, Plan de Operaciones No. 1, "Rastreo" (no date).

83. Rodríguez Castañeda, *El policía*, 88–89.

84. AGN-DFS, Exp 11–235, L 39, H 23, 30–31 (August 11, 1976). The agents suspected that the individual's name was Armando Torres Solís.

85. Gustavo Castillo Garcia, "Los guerrilleros, aventureros que querían el poder," *La Jornada*, February 5, 2003, https://www.jornada.com.mx/2003/02/05/018n1pol.php?printver=1.

86. Rodríguez Castañeda, *El policía*, 132–33.

87. Tim Weiner, "Mexico Seizes Official in 'Dirty War' Case of 70's," *New York Times*, February 20, 2004, https://www.nytimes.com/2004/02/20/world/mexico-seizes-official-in-dirty-war-case-of-70-s.html.

88. Rodríguez Castañeda, *El policía*, 133–34.

89. *La Jornada*, February 25, 2003.

90. Weiner, "Mexico Seizes."

91. *El Universal*, July 27, 2005.

92. *El Universal*, July 27, 2005.

93. COMVERDAD, "Anexo 3."

94. AGN-DFS, Exp 80–85 Estado de Guerrero (June 23, 1974), L 1, H 107–8.

95. Acosta Chaparro, "Movimiento subversivo en México."

96. Gustavo Castillo García, "Acosta y Quirós ordenaron asesinar a más de 1500, dice testigo protegido," *La Jornada*, November 18, 2002, https://www.jornada.com.mx/2002/11/18/012n1pol.php?printver=0.

CHAPTER 4

1. AGN-DGIPS, Vol. 2860, Exp 10 (September 11, 1961). For CM-1 in its early years, see Condés Lara, *Represión y rebelión*, 125–90.

2. Condés Lara, *Represión y rebelión*, 125–90.

3. Vicente Ovalle, *[Tiempo suspendido]*, 134.

4. E.g., AGN-DFS, Exp 11-4-69, L 98, H 79–84 (October 23, 1969) lists 200 political prisoners housed in Lecumberri.

5. AGN-DFS, Exp 11–235, L 23, H 211 (January 12, 1974); Exp 100–5, L 32, H 344 (December 20, 1971).

6. AGN-DFS, Exp 100–24, L 24306 (August 25, 1975); Exp 100–117, L 28, H 228 (April 8, 1972); Exp 11–235, L 30, H 15 (June 10, 1975).

7. AGN-DFS, Exp 11–235, L 26, H 81 (April 18, 1975).

8. AGN-DFS, Exp 53–2, L 1, H 65–71 (September 30, 1969).

9. Aguayo Quesada, *La charola*, 184.

10. Aguayo Quesada, *La charola*, 184–85.

11. AGN-DFS, Exp 11–235, L 14, H 50 (May 8, 1974).

12. AGN-DFS, Exp 100–10–28, L 1, H 16 (February 9, 1974).

13. AGN-DFS, Exp 53–2, L 1, H 134 (July 21, 1969).

14. Salvador Castañeda, an original founder of the MAR, relates his experiences as a political prisoner in Lecumberri in *Los diques del tiempo (diario desde la cárcel)* (Mexico City: UNAM, 1991).

15. AGN-DFS, Exp 100–10–16, L 11, H 236 (September 3, 1975).

16. AGN-DFS, Exp 100–10–16, L 11, H 236 (September 3, 1975).

17. This type of bribery was common in prisons throughout Mexico. See, e.g., example, AGN-DFS, Exp 100–12, L 54, H 67 (May 15, 1977).

18. AGN-DFS, Exp 100–5, L 71, H 261 (January 6, 1979). For a similar investigation of the Reclusorio Oriente, see AGN-DFS, Exp 53–2, L 8, H 216 (February 28, 1979).

19. Ulloa Bornemann describes a similar bribery process in *Surviving Mexico's Dirty War*, 138–40.

20. AGN-DFS, Exp 11–233, L 4, H 45 (June 23, 1977).

21. AGN-DFS, Exp 53–2, L 2, H 89 (March 9, 1970).

22. AGN-DFS, Exp 53–2, L 1, H 199–207 (January 3, 1970); Exp 100–10–28, L 1, H 25 (February 25, 1974); Exp 100–15, L 42, H 33 (March 21, 1977).

23. AGN-DFS, Exp 100–12–28, L2, H 71–79 (November 10, 1977). This riot came on the heels of an earlier riot in April 1977 that also included political prisoners; Exp 100–12, L 53, H 133 (April 27, 1977).

24. AGN-DFS, Exp 100–12, L 2, H 74, H 134–41 (October 12, 1977).

25. AGN-DFS, Exp 100–12–28, L 2, H 71 (October 19, 1977).

26. AGN-DFS, Exp 30–72, L 2, H 236 (November 16, 1960). Note that family members used hunger strikes as they became more organized later in the 1970s. Most importantly, the founding members of what would become the Comité Eureka resorted to public hunger strikes beginning in 1978 to pressure the government to disclose information on their missing sons and daughters. See, e.g., Poniatwoska, *Fuerte es el silencio*, 72–112.

27. AGN-DFS, Exp 100–5–1, Exp 28, H 28 (December 12, 1969); H 95 (December 13, 1969); Exp 11–4, L 100, H 86 (December 2, 1969).

28. See, e.g., AGN-DFS, Exp 100–6-1, L 16, H 80 (December 18, 1969, Coahuila), Exp 100–5-1, L 28, H 76 (December 12, 1969, Chihuahua); Exp 100–14-1, L 18, H 272 (December 19, 1969, Michoacán); Exp 100–25-1, L 6, H 350 (January 16, 1969, Tabasco).

29. AGN-DFS, Exp 100–26-1, L 16, H 238 (January 19, 1970).

30. AGN-DFS, Exp 100–10, L 41, H 303 (January 23, 1973); L 43, H 178–182 (July26–27, 1973).

31. E.g., AGN-DFS, Exp 100–15, L 42, H 51 (March 22, 1977).

32. AGN-DFS, Exp 11–12-28, L 1, H 222 (June 18, 1976), describes a failed escape attempt by political prisoners at Oblatos.

33. AGN-DFS, Exp 11–235, L 24, H 280 (January 26, 1975).

34. AGN-DFS, Exp 11–235, L 36, H 2–22 (February 14–15, 1976).

35. AGN-DFS, Exp 100–10-1, L 76, H 60–63 (September 25, 1978).

36. AGN-DFS, Exp 100–235, L 35, H 203 (January 22, 1976); Exp 11–235, L 36, H 76 (March 15, 1976). Several accounts exist of this prison escape. In addition to his interview, Antonio Orozco Michel detailed what happened in *La fuga de Oblatos: Una historia de las LC23S* (Guadalajara: La Casa del Mago, 2007). For more on the escape and conditions inside the prison, see Jesús Zamora, *Los guerrilleros de Oblatos* (Guadalajara: La Casa del Mago, 2010).

37. Marlise Simons, "Help Sought for Long-Ignored Mexican Prisoners," *Washington Post*, March 20, 1977.

38. This refers to the Halcones, described in chap. 3, the paramilitary group that in June 1971 attacked a group of student demonstrators in Mexico City, leaving an unknown number injured or killed.

CHAPTER 5

1. AGN-DFS, Exp 100–12-1, L 42, H 87 (February 7, 1976); Exp 100–12-28, L 2, H 19 (June 26, 1977); L 2, H 26 (September 2, 1977).

2. AGN-DFS, Exp 53–2, L 1, H 257 (January 5, 1970).

3. Armando and Luciano Rentería, interviewer unknown, August 30, 1996, Archivos de la Resistencia / Archivo memoria de la Resistencia en Jalisco (AMRJ), Guadalajara, Jalisco, https://biblioteca.archivosdelaresistencia.org/item/68293#?c=&m=&s=&cv=10&xywh=-446%2C145%2C2701%2C1694. Part of a collection of transcribed interviews with participants of the Frente Estudiantil Revolucionario, la Liga Comunista 23 de Septiembre, Los Vikingos, and the Comité de Familiares de Defensa de Presos Políticos.

4. AGN-DFS, Exp 100–12, L 59, H 101 (October 23, 1977).

5. AGN-DFS, Exp 100–12-1, L 42, H 88 (February 7, 1976).

6. AGN-DFS, Exp 100–12, L 55, H 272 (June 29, 1977).

7. I am not the first to take note of the pattern. See Mendoza García, "La tortura en el marco," 7.

8. COMVERDAD, "Anexo 3," 81–98.

9. Rayas, "Subjugating the Nation," 177. Sierra Gúzman, *El enemigo inferno*, 91, states that members of the White Brigade killed Margarita Andrade Vallejo in an operation in 1977.

10. CNDH, "Informe especial."

11. He does not specify the name of the guerrilla member.

12. Poniatowska, *Fuerte es el silencio*, 108, 111, 113; *Nexos*, October 1993.

13. CNDH, "Informe especial."

14. Calderón and Cedillo, *Challenging Authoritarianism*, 180–81.

15. AGN-DFS, Exp 11–235, L 13, H 46 (August 29, 1978).

16. *Washington Post*, January 5, 2005; *Proceso*, January 16, 2005.

17. Victoria Mendoza Salgado, *México, 1977: Testimonios de tortura* (Mexico City: Sigla Ediciones, 2008), 9–12, 96–100, 115–19.

18. Mendoza Salgado, *México, 1977*, 115–19, 138–39. It is unclear who impregnated her or if she was pregnant when she was detained.

19. Dios Corona, *La historia que no pudieron borrar*, 151–53.

20. Dios Corona, *La historia que no pudieron borrar*, 188–89.

21. Ávila Coronel includes a series of detailed genealogies for the Cabañas family, in *La guerrilla del Partido de los Pobres*, Annex 4. In these, Ávila Coronel maps out the relationships between the various members of Lucio's family who were targeted in the counterinsurgency operations. The trees corresponding to his aunts and uncles as well as those of his cousins, several of whom were interviewed for this book, are especially telling of how the Mexican government targeted family units.

22. Note that part of José Luis's story is used as an opening anecdote in chap. 2.

23. As explained in chap. 1, this is the only instance in any of the interviews collected for this book that I found mention of an American official present at a torture session. No further information exists of who this individual was.

24. AGN-DFS, Exp 100–10–16–4, L 7, H 33–35 (October 25, 1972).

25. AGN-DFS, Exp 100–10–16–4, L 7, H 33–35 (October 25, 1972).

26. For more on Don Petronil, see Aviña, *Spectres of the Revolution*, 162–63.

27. COMVERDAD, "Anexo 3," 81–88.

28. Alicia Mendoza, "Más de 50 años buscando a sus desaparecidos: La lucha de las madres mexicanas víctimas de la violencia," *El Nacional*, May 12, 2022,https://cuestione.com/nacional/marcha-10-mayo-madres-buscan-familiares-victimas-violencia-amlo/. Antonio's daughter tells of what happened to her father and what it has been like to search for her father all these years.

CHAPTER 6

1. This chapter is inspired in part by Ávila Coronel's work on the life stories of various activists involved in Lucio Cabañas's Partido de los Pobres and the community of Atoyac, Guerrero, in *La guerrilla del Partido de los Pobres*. He takes a longer view spanning decades to trace how activism cuts across generations to understand this community's particular experience with social justice. I especially appreciate his framing of gender and family dynamics to give a more nuanced analysis of community activism.

2. Aviña, *Specters of Revolution*, 132–35.

3. James, *Doña María's Story*, 160–66.

4. James, *Doña María's Story*, 166.

5. For more on Carmelo Cortés Castro, see Ávila Coronel, *La guerrilla del Partido de los Pobres*, 249–62.

6. The DFS public version of the files related to the Fuerzas Armadas Revolucionarias contains documents discussing Patricio's capture on June 20, 1970, along with Miguel Flores Leonardo.

7. AGN-DFS, Versión Pública, "Fuerzas Armadas Revolucionarias."

8. The divides within leftist groups of the time, including over guerrilla tactics and ideological differences, are central to many studies of these groups across the long 1970s. For a detailed historiographical analysis of these debates, see Vicente Ovalle, *Instantes sin historia*, esp. 76–98. Pablo Piccato, *Historia mínima de la violencia en México* (Mexico City: El Colegio de México, 2022), 163–213, also unpacks these debates. In *Rebel Mexico*, Pensado unpacks what these debates were like on the UNAM campus in the 1960s.

9. The notion of emblematic memory frameworks comes from Stern, *Remembering Pinochet's Chile*.

CONCLUSION

1. Marlise Simons, "Help Sought for Long-Ignored Mexican Prisoners," *Washington Post*, March 22, 1977.

2. The Comité Eureka files can be accessed at the Centro Académico de la Memoria de Nuestra América (CAMENA), located at the Universidad Autónoma de México, https://selser.uacm.edu.mx/.

3. See, e.g., Elena Poniatowska's chapter detailing Rosario Ibarra's hunger strike in support of her disappeared son and as part of a group of families, in *Fuerte es el silencio*, 72–113. For an account of the founding of the Comité Eureka and this particular hunger strike in 1978, see CNDH, "Huelga de hambre de las madres de desaparecidos políticos en la Catedral Metropolitana,

durante el periodo conocido come la Guerra Sucia," August 28, 1978, https://
www.cndh.org.mx/sites/default/files/documentos/2023–08/FRN_AGO_28-3
.pdf.

4. For more on Gilly, see Tony Wood, "Latin America Has Lost One of Its Last
Great Revolutionaries," *Jacobin*, July 23, 2023, https://jacobin.com/2023/07
/adolfo-gilly-mexican-revolution-prison-argentina-guatemala.

5. Alan Riding, "Mexico Is Pursuing Better Rights Image," *New York Times*,
January 16, 1978, https://www.nytimes.com/1978/01/16/archives/mexico-is
-pursuing-better-rights-image-fights-politicalprisoner.
html?searchResultPosition=1; Alan Riding, "A Mother Leads Crusade in Mexico
for Political Amnesty," *New York Times*, July 27, 1978, https://www.nytimes
.com/1978/07/27/archives/a-mother-leads-crusade-in-mexico-for-political-amnesty-
says-image.html?searchResultPosition=2.

6. AGN-DFS, 100–12, L 64, H 294 (September 1, 1978).

7. González Villareal, *Historia de la desaparición*, 133–40.

8. Vicente Ovalle discusses some of these subsequent acts of political violence
in *Instantes sin historia*. See, e.g., his description of what took place in Hidalgo,
Chiapas, and Oaxaca, 70–71.

9. AGN-DFS, Versión Pública, Francisco Sahagun Baca "[Notas periodísticas
sobre la masacre del Río Tula]," https://biblioteca.archivosdelarepresion.org
/item/87615#?c=&m=&s=&cv=&xywh=-289%2C-97%2C2880%2C1920&m=
&s=&cv=&xywh=-128%2C-214%2C2560%2C2154; José Xavier Návar, "Joya de
la nota roja: Masacre en el río Tula," *El Universal*, March 19, 2022, https://www
.eluniversal.com.mx/opinion/jose-xavier-navar/joya-de-la-nota-roja-masacre-en-
el-rio-tula-0/.

10. Cedillo, "Operation Condor, the War on Drugs."

11. Lazreg, *Torture and the Twilight*, 164–67.

12. Lazreg, *Torture and the Twilight*, 164–67.

13. Bourke, *An Intimate History of Killing*.

14. Payne, *Unsettling Accounts*.

15. Alta Comisión de las Naciones Unidas para los Derechos Humanos
(ACNUDH), "Doble injusticia: Informe sobre violaciones de derechos humanos
en la investigación del caso Ayotzinapa," March 15, 2018, https://www.ohchr
.org/sites/default/files/Documents/Countries/MX/ExecutiveReportMexico_
March2018_SP.PDF.

16. CNDH, "Mecanismo Nacional de Prevención de la Tortura 2018," 2018,
https://www.cndh.org.mx/web/informe-del-mecanismo-nacional-de-prevencion-de-
la-tortura-2018.

17. ACNUDH, "Doble injusticia."

18. Human Rights Watch, "Mexico: Events of 2018," 2019, https://www.hrw
.org/world-report/2019/country-chapters/mexico.

19. CNDH, "Informe especial 2022: Sobre actividades de prevención indirecta del Mecanismo Nacional de Prevención de Tortura," https://www.cndh .org.mx/sites/default/files/documentos/2023–09/IE_01_2022.pdf.

20. Encuesta Nacional de Victimización y Percepción sobre Seguridad Pública (ENVIPE), "Principales resultados," 2023, https://www.inegi.org.mx/contenidos /programas/envipe/2023/doc/envipe2023_cdmx.pdf.

21. ENVIPE, "Principales resultados."

22. Misael Zavala, "Gobierno inaugura memorial del 'Halconazo' en instalaciones de la DFS," *El Universal*, June 10, 2019, https://www.eluniversal.com .mx/nacion/gobierno-inaugura-memorial-del-halconazo-en-instalaciones-de-la-dfs.

23. Abraham Nuncio, Opinion, "Circular de Morelia 8," *La Jornada*, June 20, 2019, https://www.jornada.com.mx/2019/06/20/opinion/018a1pol.

24. Fabiolo Martinez and Nestor Jimenez, "Hay esperanza de llegar a la verdad: Tita Radilla tras reunión con AMLO," *La Jornada*, June 10, 2021, https:// www.jornada.com.mx/notas/2021/06/10/politica/hay-esperanza-de-llegar-a-la-verdad-tita-radilla-tras-reunion-con-amlo/.

25. For the formal annoucement of the truth commission, see Secretaría de Gobernación, "Comisión para Acceso a la Verdad, Esclarecimiento Histórico e Impulso a la Justicia de violaciones graves a derechos humanos de 1965 a 1990," June 23, 2022, https://www.gob.mx/segob/prensa/comision-para-acceso-a-la-verdad-esclarecimiento-historico-e-impulso-a-la-justicia-de-violaciones-graves-a-derechos-humanos-de-1965-a-1990.

26. Gamiño Muñoz, "La memoria ante las polítícas del olvido."

27. Gamiño Muñoz, "La memoria ante las polítícas del olvido," 425–28.

Interviewees

Aguilar Terrez, María De la Luz	April 11, 2018
Abarca Martínez, Patricio	January 9, 2018
Alonso Vargas, José Luis	June 18 and September 26, 2018
Arizaga, Enrique	April 24, 2018
Arroyo, José Luis	January 11, 2018
Barrera, Ambrosia	January 12, 2018
Barrientos Serafín, Humberto	August 26, 2018
Barrientos Serafín, Mariela	August 26, 2018
Barrientos Serafín, Sofia	August 26, 2018
Bello, Guillermo	January 10, 2018
Cabañas Barrientos, Pablo	February 9, 2018
Cabañas Ocampo, Bertoldo	December 2 and 19, 2017
Cabañas, Erasmo	March 12, 2018
Cartagena, Mario Álvaro	August 9 and 22, 2018
Casas Quiroz, Yolanda Isabel	June 15, 22, and 24, 2018
Chacón, Raúl René	March 19, 2018

Condes Lara, Enrique	August 7, 2018
Echeverría Martínez, Rodolfo	December 29, 2017
Esparza, José Luis	March 19 and April 13, 2018
Fuentes, Nicómedes	January 8, 2018
Fuentes de la Fuente, Eduardo	November 17, 2018
Gallegos Nájera, Arturo	January 8 and 9, 2018
Godoy, Adolfo	January 11, 2018
Hernández, Josafath	August 26, 2018
Hernández Hernández, Elia	October 9, 2018
Iriarte Bonilla, Hugo David	November 17, 2018
Laguna Berber, Jaime	April 6, 2018
León Mendiola, Luis	February 24, 2018
Loperena, Adalberto	March 9, 2018
Lorenses, Rigoberto	August 29, 2018
Lorenzana, Cuauhtémoc	February 8 and 10, 2017
Molina Salazar, Manuel	November 17, December 4 and 14, 2017
Morales Hernández, José de Jesús	October 27, November 2 and 9, 2017
Moreno Borbolla, José Luis	May 1, 2, and 3, 2012; March 7, 2018
Orozco Michel, Antonio	November 16 and 23, December 5, 2017
Pérez Aragón, Benjamín	October 23, November 17, 2018
Quiñones, Lourdes	August 4, 2018
Ramírez Estrada, Francisco	March 31, 2018
Ramírez Hernández, Zoilo	November 17, 2018
Rivera Leyva, Humberto	July 28, 2018
Rodríguez González, Ricardo	January 28, 2018
Romo, Miguel	January 31, February 22, 2018
Salcedo, Carlos	May 4 and 6, 2012; April 1, May 29, June 18, 2018

Santiago Díaz, Laurentino	January 12, 2018
Serafín Gervacio, Alejandro	October 5, 2018
Also known as David Cabañas	
Serafín Gervacio, Bartola	August 26, 2018
Silva Valle, Desidor	January 12, 2018
Torres Flores, Eladio	September 30, 2018
Uranga, Lourdes	March 24, 2018
Velasco, Ricardo	October 19, 2018

Periodicals

Animal Político
Excelsior
Jacobin
La Jornada
New York Times
Nexos
Proceso
Reforma
El Universal
Washington Post

Bibliography

Acosta Chaparro, Arturo. "Movimiento subversivo en México." Unpublished manuscript. Mexico City, 1990.

Agamben, Giorgio. *State of Exception*. Translated by Kevin Attell. Chicago: University of Chicago Press, 2005.

Aguayo Quesada, Sergio. *La charola: Una historia de los servicios de inteligencia en México*. Mexico City: Grijalbo, 2001.

———. *1968: Los archivos de la violencia*. Mexico City: Grijablo/Reforma, 1998.

Aguilar Camín, Héctor. *La guerra de Galio*. Mexico City: Cal y Arena, 1991.

Aguilar Terrés, Luz María. "Guerrilleras: Antología de testimonios y textos sobre la participación de las mujeres en los movimientos armados socialistas en México, segunda mitad del siglo XX." Unpublished manuscript. Mexico City, 2014.

———. "Memoria del Primer Encuentro Nacional de Mujeres Exguerrilleras." Unpublished manuscript. Mexico City, 2007.

Aguilera Arévalo, José. "La rebelión de Oblatos." Unpublished manuscript. Guadalajara, 1979.

Aguirre, Carlos. *The Criminals of Lima and Their Worlds: The Prison Experience, 1850–1935*. Durham, NC: Duke University Press, 2005.

Ai Camp, Roderic. *Generals in the Palacio: The Military in Modern Mexico*. New York: Oxford University Press, 1992.

———. *Political Recruitment across Two Centuries: Mexico, 1884–1991*. Austin: University of Texas Press, 1995.

———. *Politics in Mexico*. New York: Oxford University Press, 1993.

Alegre, Robert F. *Railroad Radicals in Cold War Mexico: Gender, Class, and Memory*. Lincoln: University of Nebraska Press, 2013.

Alonso Vargas, José Luis. "Los guerrilleros mexicalenses." Unpublished manuscript. Mexico City, 2004.

Alta Comisión de las Naciones Unidas para los Derechos Humanos (ACNUDH). "Doble injusticia: Informe sobre violaciones de derechos humanos en la investigación del caso Ayotzinapa." March 15, 2018. https://www.ohchr.org /sites/default/files/Documents/Countries/MX/ExecutiveReportMexico_ March2018_SP.PDF.

Álvarez Garín, Raúl. *La estela de Tlatelolco: Una reconstrucción histórica del Movimiento estudiantil del 68*. Mexico City: Itaca, 2002.

Anaya Gallardo, Federico, et al. *Siempre cerca, siempre lejos: Las fuerzas armadas en México*. Mexico City: Global Exchange/CIEPAC/CENCOS, 2000.

Anguiano, Arturo. *Entre el pasado y el future: La izquierda en México 1969–1995*. Mexico City: Universidad Autónoma Metropolitana, 1997.

Angulo Macías, Alfredo. *La hora de los mártires: Apuntes para una historia del movimiento estudiantil y guerrillero de Guadalajara (1970-1977)*. Guad-alajara: La Casa del Mago, 1997.

Aranda Flores, Antonio. "Los cívicos guerrerenses." Unpublished manuscript. Mexico City, 1979.

Armendáriz, Minerva. *Morir de sed junto a la fuente*. Mexico City: Universidad Obrera de México, 2001.

Ávila Coronel, Francisco. *La guerrilla del Partido de los Pobres: Historia social, género, y violencia pólitica en Atoyac de Álvarez, Guerrero (1920-1974)*. Mexico City: Plaza y Valdes, 2022.

———. "La vision official de la guerrilla y el fenómeno de la manificación en el caso de la guerrilla del Partido de los Pobres (PDLP) (Atoyac, Guerrero)." In *Reflejos de la Guerra Sucia en el estado de Guerrero: Historia, literatura, música e imágenes*, edited by Ana María Cárabe, 75–110. Mexico City: Miguel Ángel Porrúa, 2015.

Aviña, Alexander. "Grupo Sangre: Drugs, Death Squads, and the Dirty War Origins of Mexico's Drug Wars." In Pansters and Smith, 263–86.

———. "Mexico's Long Dirty War." *NACLA Report on the Americas* 48, no. 2 (Summer 2016): 144–49.

———. *Specters of Revolution: Peasant Guerrillas in the Cold War Mexican Countryside*. Oxford: Oxford University Press, 2014.

———. "A War against Poor People: Dirty Wars and Drug Wars in 1970s Mexico." In Pensado and Ochoa, 134–52.

———. *A War against Poor People: Dirty Wars, Narcotics and the Cold War Roots of Mexico's Contemporary Drug Violence*. Forthcoming.

———. "We Have Returned to Porfirian Times": Neopopulism, Counterinsurgency, and the Dirty War in Guerrero, Mexico, 1969–1976." In *Populism in Twentieth-Century Mexico: The Presidencies of Lázaro Cárdenas and Luis Echeverría*, edited by Amelia M. Kiddle and María L. O. Muñoz, 106–21. Tucson: University of Arizona Press, 2010.

Balderas Domínguez, Jorge, and Guadalupe Santiago Quijada. "Fundamento ideológico de la acción revolucionaria del grupo armado *Lacandones*." *Nóesis: Revista de Ciencias Sociales y Humanidades* 17, no. 34 (August–December 2008): 66–91.

Barr-Melej, Patrick. *Psychedelic Chile: Youth, Counterculture, and Politics on the Road to Socialism and Dictatorship*. Chapel Hill: University of North Carolina Press, 2017.

Bartra Verges, Armando. *Guerrero bronco: Campesinos, ciudadanos y guerrilleros en la Costa Grande*. Mexico City: Era, 2000.

Bartra, Roger. "Memorias de la contracultura." *Letras Libres*, September 30, 2007. https://letraslibres.com/revista-mexico/memorias-de-la-contracultura/.

Bellingeri, Marco. *Del agrarismo armado a la guerra de los pobres: Ensayos de guerrilla rural en el México contemporáneo, 1940–1974*. Mexico City: Ediciones Casa Juan Pablos; Secretaría de Cultura del Gobierno del Distrito Federal, 2003.

Bonilla Machorro, Carlos. *Ejercicio de guerrillero*. Mexico City: Grupo Editorial Gaceta, 1981.

Borbolla, Carlos. *La guerra sucia: Hechos y testimonios*. Colima: Universidad de Colima, 2007.

Bourke, Joanna. *An Intimate History of Killing: Face-to-Face Killing in Twentieth-Century Warfare*. New York: Basic Books, 1999.

Brennan, James P. *Argentina's Missing Bones: Revisiting the History of the Dirty War*. Oakland: University of California Press, 2018.

Britto, Lina. *Marijuana Boom: The Rise and Fall of Colombia's First Drug Paradise*. Oakland: University of California Press, 2020.

Browning, Christopher R. *Ordinary Men: Reserve Police Battalion 101 and the Final Solution in Poland*. 3rd ed. New York: HarperCollins, 2017.

Buchenau, Jürgen, and Gilbert Joseph. *Mexico's Once and Future Revolution: Social Upheaval and the Challenge of Rule since the Late Nineteenth Century*. Durham, NC: Duke University Press, 2013.

Calderón, Fernando Herrera. "Working-Class Heroes: Barrio Consciousness, Student Power and the Mexican Dirty War." In Pensado and Ochoa, 155–74.

Calderón, Fernando Herrera, and Adela Cedillo, eds. *Challenging Authoritarianism in Mexico: Revolutionary Struggles and the "Dirty War," 1964–1982*. New York: Routledge, 2012.

Campos Gómez, Eleazar, et al. *Lucio Cabañas y el Partido de los Pobres: Una experiencia guerrillera en México*. Mexico City: Nuestra América, 1987.

Canseco Ruiz, Felipe Edgardo, ed. *Lucio Cabañas 20 años después*. Mexico City: Claves Latinoamericanas and Centro de Información y Monitoreo de los Derechos Humanos en México, 1995.

Cárdenas Montaño, Macrina. "La participación de las mujeres in movimientos armados." In Oikión Solano and García Ugarte, 2:129–43.

Carey, Elaine. *Plaza of Sacrifices: Gender, Power, and Terror in 1968 Mexico*. Albuquerque: University of New Mexico Press, 2005.

Carr, Barry. *La izquierda mexicana a través del siglo XX*. Mexico City: Era, 1996.

———. *Marxism and Communism in Twentieth-Century Mexico*. Lincoln: University of Nebraska Press, 1992.

Carrasco Gutiérrez, Leticia, and Hugo Velázquez Villa. *Breve historia del MAR: La guerrilla imaginaria del Movimiento de Acción Revolucionaria*. Guadalajara: Universidad Autónoma de Guadalajara–CUCSH, 2010.

Carrillo Prieto, Ignacio. *Arcana Imperii: Apuntes sobre la tortura*. Mexico City: Instituto Nacional de Ciencias Penales, 1987.

Castañeda, Jorge. *La utopía desarmada: El futuro de la izquierda en América Latina*. Mexico City: J. Mortiz and Planeta, 1993.

Castañeda, Juan Antonio, Rubén Martín, Rafael Sandoval, and Miguel Topete. *Memoria guerrillera, represión y contrainsurgencia en Jalisco*. Guadalajara: Grafisma Editores, 2012.

Castañeda, Salvador. *Los diques del tiempo (diario desde la cárcel)*. Mexico City: Universidad Nacional Autónoma de México, 1991.

———. *La negación del número*. Mexico City: CONACULTA, 2006.

Castillo García, Gustavo. *El Tigre de Nazar: "Había que ser fanático como ellos."* Mexico City: Penguin Books, 2023.

Castillo Troncoso, Alberto del. *La matanza del jueves de Corpus: Fotografía y memoria*. Mexico City: Instituto Nacional de Estudios Históricos de las Revoluciones de México, 2021.

Castellanos, Laura. *México armado 1943-1981*. Mexico City: Era, 2007.

Cedillo, Adela. "Análisis de la fundación del EZLN en Chiapas desde la perspectiva de la acción colectiva insurgente." *Liminar: Estudios Sociales y Humanísticos* 10, no. 2 (2012): 15–34.

———. "La crisis del poder, las guerrillas y el endurecimiento del régimen después de 1968 en México." *Jornadas de Historia de Occidente*, no. 31 (2009): 151–70.

———. *El fuego y el silencio: Historia de las FPL*. Mexico City: Comité 68 Pro Libertades Democráticas, 2008.

———. "Mayoría religiosa, minoría política: El origen de la alianza entre la Diócesis de San Cristóbal y las Fuerzas de Liberación Nacional (1979–1983)." In *Pensar la resistencia y la disidencia social*, edited by César Roberto Avendaño Amador, Víctor Manuel Alvarado García, and Mayra

Eréndira Nava Becerra, 123–46. Mexico City: Universidad Nacional Autónoma de México, 2012.

———. "The 23 of September Communist League's Foco Experiment in the Sierra Baja Tarahumara (1973–1975)." In Pensado and Ochoa, 92–112.

———. "Violencia, memoria, historia, y tabú en torno a la Liga Comunista 23 de Septiembre." In Gamiño Muñoz et al., 343–73.

———. "The War on Drugs, Counterinsurgency, and the State of Siege in the Golden Triangle." In Pansters and Smith, 240–62.

———. "The Operation Condor, the War on Drugs, and Counterinsurgency in the Golden Triangle." Working Paper, Kellogg Institute for International Studies, University of Notre Dame, May 2021.

Cedillo, Adela, and Fernando Herrera Calderón. "Análisis de la producción historiográfica en torno a la 'Guerra Sucia' mexicana." In *El estudio de las luchas revolucionarias en América Latina (1959–1996): Estado da la cuestión*, edited by Véronica Oikión Solano, Eduardo Rey Tristán, and Martin López, 263–88. Zamora: El Colegio de Michoacán, Universidad de Santiago de Compostela, 2014.

Comisión Nacional para los Derechos Humanos–México (CNDH). "Informe especial sobre las quejas en materia de desapariciones forzadas ocurridas en la década de los 70 y principios de los 80." 2001. http://www.cndh.org.mx/sites/all/doc/Informes/Especiales/2001_Desapariciones70y80.pdf.

———. "Informe especial 2022: Sobre actividades de prevención indirecta del Mecanismo Nacional de Prevención de Tortura." https://www.cndh.org.mx/sites/default/files/documentos/2023-09/IE_01_2022.pdf.

———. "Mecanismo Nacional de Prevención de la Tortura 2018." 2018. https://www.cndh.org.mx/web/informe-del-mecanismo-nacional-de-prevencion-de-la-tortura-2018.

Comisión de la Verdad del Estado de Guerrero (COMVERDAD). "Anexo 3: Personas participantes en desapariciones forzadas." In *Informe Final de Actividades de la Comisión de la Verdad del Estado de Guerrero*. 2nd ed. Mexico City: Article 19, August 2021. https://memoricamexico.gob.mx/swb/memorica/Cedula?oId=cP4zfYgBhkPQL8y2UyvM.

Comité Eureka. "Eureka: Historia gráfica, doce años de lucha: México 1977–1989." Unpublished manuscript. Mexico City, 1989.

Condés Lara, Enrique. *Represión y rebelión en México (1959–1985)*. 3 vols. Mexico City: Benemérita Universidad Autónoma de Puebla and Miguel Ángel Porrúa, 2007–9.

Contreras Orozco, Javier. "La guerrilla: Del asalto al cuartel Madera al EPR." Unpublished manuscript. Chihuahua, 1998.

———. *Los informantes: Documentos confidenciales de las guerrillas en Chihuahua*. Chihuahua: Universidad Autónoma de Chihuahua, 2007.

Cowan, Benjamin. *Securing Sex: Morality and Repression in the Making of Cold War Brazil*. Chapel Hill: University of North Carolina Press, 2016.

De la Barreda Solórzano, Luis. "Asesinar por la utopía." *Nexos en Línea*, no. 325 (January 2005).

———. "¿Guerra limpia?" *Nexos en Línea*, no. 323 (November 2004).

———. "¿Justicia o venganza?" *Nexos en Línea* 26, no. 321 (September 2004): 42–48.

Díaz Prieto, Gabriela. "Un exilio venturoso: Chilenos en México (1973–1990)." In Garciadiego and Kourí, 793–815.

Dios Corona, Sergio René de. *La historia que no pudieron borrar: La Guerra Sucia en Jalisco, 1970–1985*. Guadalajara: La Casa del Mago, 2004.

Domínguez, José. "Cuatro hermanos en la guerrilla." *Nexos*, no. 319 (July 2004): 39–43.

Doyle, Kate. "Draft Report Documents 18 Years of 'Dirty War' in Mexico: Special Prosecutor: State Responsible for Hundreds of Killings, Disappearances." National Security Archive, February 16, 2006. http://www2.gwu .edu/~nsarchiv/NSAEBB/NSAEBB180/index.htm.

Ebner, Michael. *Ordinary Violence in Mussolini's Italy*. New York: Cambridge University Press, 2014.

Echeverría Álvarez, Luis. "Fourth Government Report." Speech, opening of Congress, Mexico City, September 1, 1974. https://es.wikisource.org/wiki /Discurso_de_Luis_Echeverría_Álvarez_en_su_Cuarto_Informe_de_ Gobierno.

Encuesta Nacional de Victimización y Percepción sobre Seguridad Pública (ENVIPE). "Principales resultados." September 25, 2018. https://www.inegi .org.mx/contenidos/programas/envipe/2018/doc/envipe2018_presentacion _nacional.pdf.

Esteve Díaz, Hugo. *Amargo lugar sin nombre: Crónica del movimiento armado socialista en México (1960–1990)*. Guadalajara: La Casa del Mago, 2013.

———. *Las armas de la utopía: La tercera ola de los movimientos guerrilleros en México*. Mexico City: Instituto de Proposiciones Estratégicas, 1996.

Evangelista, Agustín. *Carmelo Cortés Castro y la guerrilla urbana: Fuerzas armadas revolucionarias*. Mexico City: Centro de Investigaciones Históricas de los Movimientos Sociales, 2007.

Feitlowitz, Marguerite. *A Lexicon of Terror: Argentina and the Legacies of Torture*. 2nd ed. New York: Oxford University Press, 2012.

Fernández Gómez, Raúl. *Juego político y guerrilla rural en México*. Chilpancingo: UAG-IIEPA-IMA/Quadrivium Editores, 2006.

Fernández Menéndez, Jorge. *Nadie supo nada: La verdadera historia del asesinato de Eugenio Garza Sada*. Mexico City: Grijalbo, 2006.

Fiscalía Especial para Movimientos Sociales y Políticos del Pasado (FEMOSPP). "Informe Documenta sobre 18 años de 'Guerra Sucia' en México." 2006. http://nsarchive.gwu.edu/NSAEBB/NSAEBB180/index2.htm.

Flores Solana, María Teresa. "La lucha por la memoria histórica: El caso de H.I.J.O.S. México." *Aletheia* 3, no. 5 (December 2012): 1–22.

Gallegos Nájera, José Arturo. *La guerrilla en Guerrero: ¡A merced del enemigo!* Mexico City: Centro de Investigaciones Históricas de los Movimientos Sociales, 2009.

———. *La guerrilla en Guerrero: Testimonio sobre el Partido de los Pobres y las Fuerzas Armadas Revolucionarias*. Mexico City: Editorial Lamm, 2004.

———. *¡A merced del enemigo!: Detenciones, interrogatorios, torturas, mazmoras y . . . algo más*. Guadalajara: Centro de Investigaciones Históricas de los Movimientos Sociales, Universidad de Guadalajara, 2009.

Gamiño Muñoz, Rodolfo. *Guerrilla, represión y prensa en la década de los setenta en México: Invisibilidad y olvido*. Mexico City: Instituto José María Luis Mora, 2011.

———. *Repertorios de una violencia urbana en México: Orígenes de la Liga Comunista 23 de Septiembre*. Saarbrücken: Editorial Académica Española, 2011.

Gamiño Muñoz, Rodolfo, Yllich Escamilla Santiago, Rigoberto Reyes, and Fabián Campos. *La Liga Comunista 23 de Septiembre—Cuatro décadas a debate: Historia, memoria, testimonio, y literatura*. Mexico City: Universidad Nacional Autónoma de México, 2014.

Gamiño Muñoz, Rodolfo, and Jesús Zamora, eds. *Los vikingos: Una historia de lucha política social*. Guadalajara: Colectivo Rodolfo Reyes Crespo, 2011.

García, Daniel Carlos. *Fulgor rebelde: La guerrilla en Aguascalientes*. Mexico City: Filo de Agua, 2006.

García Morales, Alfonso, María de los Ángeles Magdaleno Cárdenas, Mario Ramírez Salas, and Américo Meléndez Reyna. "México: La fiscalía especial para movimientos sociales y políticos del pasado." In *Entre la memoria y la justicia: Experiencias latinoamericanas sobre Guerra Sucia y defensa de Derechos Humanos*, edited by Rubén Ruiz Guerra, 221–38. Mexico City: Universidad Nacional Autónoma de México, 2005.

García Sánchez, Liliana. *Judith Reyes: Una mujer de canto revolucionario 1924–1988*. Mexico City: Ediciones Clandestino, 2007.

Garciadiego, Javier, and Emilio Kourí. *Revolución y exilio en la historia de México: Del amor de un historiador a su patria adoptiva: Homenaje a Friedrich Katz*. Mexico City: Era, 2010.

Gil Olivo, Ramón. *Dientes de perro*. Guadalajara: La Casa del Mago, 2006.

Gill, Lesley. *The School of the Americas: Military Training and Political Violence in the Americas*. Durham, NC: Duke University Press, 2004.

Gillingham, James, and Benjamin Smith, eds. *Dictablanda: Politics, Work, and Culture in Mexico, 1938–1968*. Durham, NC: Duke University Press, 2014.

Gillingham, Paul. "Military Caciquismo in the PRIísta State: General Mange's Command in Veracruz." In *Forced Marches: Soldiers and Military Caciques in Modern Mexico*, edited by Ben Fallaw and Terry Rugeley, 210–37. Tucson: University of Arizona Press, 2012.

———. *Unrevolutionary Mexico: The Birth of a Strange Dictatorship*. New Haven, CT: Yale University Press, 2021.

———. "Who Killed Crispín Aguilar? Violence and Order in the Postrevolutionary Countryside." In Pansters, 91–111.

Glockner Corte, Fritz. *Cementerio de Papel*. Mexico City: Ediciones B, 2004.

———. *Memoria roja: Historia de la guerrilla en México (1962–1968)*. Mexico City: Ediciones B, 2007.

———. "La piel de la memoria." In Gamiño Muñoz et al., 233–49.

———. *Veinte de cobre: Memoria de la clandestinidad*. Mexico City: Joaquín Mortiz, 1997.

González, Fernando M. "Algunos grupos radicales de izquierda y de derecha con influencia católica en México (1965–1975)." *Historia y Grafía*, no. 29 (2007): 57–93.

González Ruiz, José Enrique. *El banquito de la foto del recuerdo: El chino y el invidente: Dos cuentos de la guerra sucia*. Mexico City: Tierra Roja, 2003.

González Ruiz, José Enrique, and David Cilia. *Testimonios de la guerra sucia*. Mexico City: Tierra Roja, 2006.

González Villareal, Roberto. *Historia de la desaparición: Nacimiento de una tecnología represiva*. Mexico City: Editorial Terracota, 2012.

Grandin, Greg. *The Last Colonial Massacre: Latin America in the Cold War*. Chicago: University of Chicago Press, 2004.

Herrera Sánchez, Raymundo, and Xavier Talavera Alfaro. *La muerte de un guerrillero: Genaro Vázquez Rojas*. Morelia: Linotipográfica, 1985.

Hinds, Harold, Jr., and Charles M. Tatum. *Not Just for Children: The Mexican Comic Book in the Late 1960s and 1970s*. Westport, CT: Greenwood, 1992.

Hipólito, Simón. *Guerrero, amnistía y represión*. Mexico City: Grijalbo, 1982.

Hirales Morán, Gustavo. "Defender lo indefendible." *Nexos en Línea*, no. 323 (October 2004).

———. "Ecos de la guerra sucia." *Nexos en Línea*, no. 325 (December 2004).

———. "La guerra secreta, 1970–1978." *Nexos en Línea*, no. 54 (June 1982): 34–42.

———. *La Liga Comunista 23 de Septiembre: Orígenes y naufragio*. Mexico City: Cultura Popular, 1977.

———. *Memoria de la guerra de los justos.* Mexico City: Cal y Arena, 1996.

Hodges, Donald. *Mexican Anarchism after the Revolution.* Austin: University of Texas Press, 1995.

Hodges, Donald, and Ross Gandy. *Mexico under Siege: Popular Resistance to Presidential Despotism.* New York: Zed Books, 2002.

Human Rights Watch. "Mexico: Events of 2018." 2019. https://www.hrw.org /world-report/2019/country-chapters/mexico.

Ibarra Chávez, Héctor. *La guerrilla de los 70 y la transición a la democracia.* Mexico City: Ce-Ácatl, 2006.

———. *Juventud rebelde e insurgencia estudiantil: Las otras voces del movimiento político y social en México en los años setenta.* Mexico City: Ediciones Expediente Abierto/Ce-Ácatl, 2010.

———. *Pensar la guerrilla en México.* Mexico City: Ediciones Expediente Abierto, 2006.

James, Daniel. *Doña María's Story: Life History, Memory, and Political Identity.* Durham, NC: Duke University Press, 2001.

Jones, Halbert. "Social Dissolution: Article 145 of the Mexican Federal Penal Code in International Context, 1941–1970." Paper presented at the Boston Area Latin American History Workshop, Cambridge, MA, April 2009.

Joseph, Gilbert, and Jürgen Buchenau. *Mexico's Once and Future Revolution: Social Upheaval and the Challenge of Rule since the Late Nineteenth Century.* Durham, NC: Duke University Press, 2013.

Keller, Renata. *Mexico's Cold War: Cuba, the United States, and the Legacy of the Mexican Revolution.* Cambridge: Cambridge University Press, 2015.

Kenny, Paul, and Mónica Serrano. "Part I: The Background." In *Mexico's Security Failure: Collapse into Criminal Violence,* edited by Paul Kenny, Mónica Serrano, and Arturo C. Sotomayor, 27–86. New York: Routledge, 2012.

Kloppe-Santamaría, Gema. *In the Vortex of Violence: Lynching, Extralegal Justice, and the State in Post-Revolutionary Mexico.* Oakland: University of California Press, 2020.

Knight, Alan. "The Weight of the State in Modern Mexico." In *Studies in the Formation of the Nation State in Latin America,* edited by James Dunkerley, 212–53. London: Institute of Latin American Studies, University of London, 2002.

Knight, Alan, and Wil Pansters, eds. *Caciquismo in Twentieth-Century Mexico.* London: Institute for the Study of the Americas, 2006.

Lagarda, Ignacio. *El color de las amapas: Crónica de la guerrilla en la sierra de Sonora.* Mexico City: Universidad Tecnológica del Sur de Sonora, 2007.

Langland, Victoria. *Speaking of Flowers: Student Movements and the Making and Remembering of 1968 in Military Brazil.* Durham, NC: Duke University Press, 2013.

Lazreg, Marnia. *Torture and the Twilight of Empire: From Algiers to Baghdad*. Princeton, NJ: Princeton University Press, 2008.

Lernoux, Penny. *A Cry of the People: The Struggle for Human Rights in Latin America: The Catholic Church in Conflict with U.S. Policy*. New York: Penguin Books, 1982.

Lira Robles José Alonso. *Guerrilla en Guanatos*. Guadalajara: CONACULTA/Secretaría de Cultura de Jalisco, 2006.

López, Jaime. *Diez años de guerrillas en México*. Mexico City: Editorial Posada, 1974.

López Astrain, Martha Patricia. *La guerra de baja intensidad en México*. Mexico City: Plaza y Valdés and Universidad Iberoamericana, 1996.

López de la Torre, Carlos Fernando. "Miguel Nazar Haro y la guerra sucia en México." *Revista Grafía* 10, no. 1 (January–June 2013): 56–72.

López de la Torre, Saúl. *Guerras secretas: Memoria de un exguerrillero de los setentas que ahora no puede caminar*. Mexico City: Artefacto Editor, 2001.

López Hernández, Gladys. *Ovarimonio, ¿yo guerrillera?* Mexico City: Itaca, 2013.

López Limón, Alberto. *David Jiménez Sarmiento: Por la senda de la revolución*. Mexico City: Centro de Investigaciones Históricas de los Movimientos Sociales, 2006.

———. "Proceso de construcción de la Liga Comunista 23 de Septiembre." *Cuadernos de Marte* 2, no. 1 (April 2011): 177–207.

Lozano Rubello, Gabriela. "Militancia y transgresión en la guerrilla mexicana: Una mirada crítica feminista al caso de la Liga Comunista 23 de Septiembre." *Revista de la Carrera de Sociología Entramados y Perspectivas* 5, no. 5 (2015): 90–111.

Lucero Estrada, Diego. *Sueños guajiros: Diego Lucero y la guerrilla mexicana de los años 60 y 70*. Mexico City: Casa de las Palabras, 2011.

Lugo Hernández, Florencio. *El asalto al cuartel de Madera: Testimonio de un sobreviviente: 23 de septiembre de 1965*. Mexico City: Universidad Autónoma Chapingo, 2006.

Macías Cervantes, César Federico. *Genaro Vázquez, Lucio Cabañas y las guerrillas en México entre 1960 y 1974*. Guanajuato: Universidad de Guanajuato, 2008.

Macías-González, Victor. "Los homosexuales como sujetos peligrosos en la Ciudad de México (1940-1960)." In *Hampones, intocables y pecatrices: Sujetos peligrosos de la Ciudad de México (1940-1960)*, edited by Susana Sosenski, 84–119. Mexico City: Fondo de Cultura Económica, 2019.

Maier, Elizabeth. *Las Madres de los Desaparecidos: ¿Un nuevo mito materno en América Latina?* Mexico City: Universidad Autónoma de México, El Colegio de la Frontera Norte, and La Jornada, 2001.

Mallon, Florencia. "Barbudos, Warriors, and Rotos: The MIR, Masculinity, and Power in the Chilean Agrarian Reform, 1965-1974." In *Changing Men and*

Masculinities in Latin America, edited by Matthew C. Gutmann, 179–215. Durham, NC: Duke University Press, 2003.

Maran, Rita. *Torture: The Role of Ideology in the French-Algerian War.* New York: Praeger, 1989.

Martínez Nateras, Arturo. *La flor del tiempo.* Mexico City: Universidad Nacional Autónoma de México and Universidad Autónoma de Sinaloa, 1988.

———. *¡No queremos apertura, queremos revolución!* Mexico City: Fondo de Cultura Popular, 1972.

———. *El secuestro de Lucio Cabañas.* Madrid: Altalena, 1986.

———. *El tema de la amnistía.* Mexico City: Cultura Popular, 1978.

Maya Nava, Alfonso, ed. *Los movimientos armados en México 1917–1994.* Mexico City: El Universal, 1994.

Maza, Enrique. *Obligado a matar: Fusilamiento de civiles en México.* Mexico City: Proceso, 1988.

McCormick, Gladys I. "The Last Door: Political Prisoners and the Use of Torture in Mexico's Dirty War." *The Americas* 74, no. 1 (January 2017): 57–81.

———. *The Logic of Compromise in Mexico: How the Countryside Was Key to the Emergence of Authoritarianism.* Chapel Hill: University of North Carolina Press, 2016.

———. "Torture and the Making of a Subversive during Mexico's Dirty War." In Pensado and Ochoa, 254–72.

McCoy, Alfred W. "Covert Netherworld: An Invisible Interstice in the Modern World System." *Comparative Studies in Society and History* 58, no. 4 (October 2016): 847–79.

———. *A Question of Torture: CIA Interrogation, from the Cold War to the War on Terror.* New York: Holt Paperbacks, 2006.

———. *Torture and Impunity: The US Doctrine of Coercive Interrogation.* Madison: University of Wisconsin Press, 2012.

Meade, Everard. Introduction to *The Taken: True Stories of the Sinaloa Drug War*, by Javier Valdez Cárdenas, 3–52. Translated by Everard Meade. Norman: University of Oklahoma Press, 2017.

Méndez Alvarado, María de Jesús. "México: Mujeres insurgentes de los años 70: Género y lucha armada." PhD diss., Universidad Nacional Autónoma de México, 2015.

Mendiola-García, Sandra C. *Street Democracy: Vendors, Violence, and Public Space in Late Twentieth-Century Mexico.* Lincoln: University of Nebraska Press, 2017.

Mendoza García, Jorge. "Otra ofensiva gubernamental: La ideologización hacia la guerrilla." *Memoria*, CEMOS 7, no. 149 (July 2001): 18–27.

———. "La tortura en el marco de la guerra sucia en México: Un ejercicio de memoria colectiva." *Polis: Investigación y Análisis Sociopolítico y Psicosocial* 7, no. 2 (2011): 139–79.

Mendoza Salgado, Victoria. *México, 1977: Testimonios de tortura*. Mexico City: Sigla Ediciones, 2008.

Menjívar, Cecilia, and Néstor Rodríguez, eds. *When States Kill: Latin America, the U.S., and Technologies of Terror*. Austin: University of Texas Press, 2005.

Middlebrook, Kevin J. *The Paradox of Revolution: Labor, the State, and Authoritarianism in Mexico*. Baltimore: Johns Hopkins University Press, 1995.

Miranda Ramírez, Arturo. *El otro rostro de la guerrilla: Genaro, Lucio y Carmelo: Experiencias de la guerrilla*. Mexico City: Editorial El Machete, 1996.

Miranda Ramírez, Arturo, and René Cuevas. *La violación de los derechos humanos en el estado de Guerrero durante la guerra sucia: Una herida no restañada*. Saarbrücken: Editorial Académica Española, 2011.

Montemayor, Carlos. *Las armas del alba*. Mexico City: Joaquín Mortiz, 2003.

———. *La fuga*. Mexico City: Fondo de Cultura Económica, 2007.

———. *La guerrilla recurrente*. Mexico City: Editorial Debate, 2007.

———. *Las mujeres del alba*. Mexico City: Grijalbo-Mondadori, 2010.

———. *La violencia de estado en México: Antes y después de 1968*. Mexico City: Debate, 2010.

Mora, Juan Miguel de. *Las guerrillas en Mexico y Jenaro Vasquez Rojas: Su personalidad, su vida y su muerte*. Mexico City: Editora Latino Americana, 1972.

———. *Lucio Cabañas, su vida y muerte*. Mexico City: Editores Asociados, 1975.

Morales Hernández, José de Jesús. *Memorias de un guerrillero*. Guadalajara: Published by author, 2006.

———. *Noche y Neblina: Los vuelos de la muerte: La historia de los campos de concentración en México y los desaparecidos de la guerra en el siglo XX*. Mexico City: Plaza Editores, 2007.

Morales Muñoz, Daniela. "Brasileños asilados en México: Dos casos de excepción." *Historia Mexicana* 70, no. 2 (October–December 2020): 839–91.

Moreno Borbolla, José Luis. "La Brigada Roja: Comité Regional de la Liga Comunista." In Gamiño Muñoz et al, 283–316.

Navarro, Aaron W. *Political Intelligence and the Creation of Modern Mexico, 1938–1954*. University Park: Pennsylvania State University Press, 2010.

Negrete, Juan Manuel. *Canuteros de plomo*. Mexico City: Porrúa, 2003.

Newcomer, Daniel. *Reconciling Modernity: Urban State Formation in 1940s León, Mexico*. Lincoln: University of Nebraska Press, 2007.

Núñez Jara, Alberto. *Las causas: Memorias de un desaparecido político*. Mexico City: Moción, 1985.

Ocaña Martínez, Julio César. "Atoyac, a 25 años de Lucio Cabañas: Una refleción política." Unpublished manuscript. Mexico City, 1995.

Oikión Solano, Verónica. "El Estado mexicano frente a los levantamientos armados en Guerrero: El caso del Plan Telaraña." *Tzintzun: Revista de Estudios Históricos*, no. 45 (January–June 2007): 65–82.

———. "Represión y tortura en México en la década de 1970: Un testimonio político." *Historia y Grafía*, no. 37 (July–December 2011): 115–48.

Oikión Solano, Verónica, and Marta Eugenia García Ugarte, eds. *La guerrilla en la segunda mitad del siglo*. Vol. 2 of *Movimientos armados en México, siglo XX*. 3 vols. Mexico City: El Colegio de Michoacán and CIESAS, 2006.

———. *Movimientos armados en México, siglo XX*. 3 vols. Mexico City: El Colegio de Michoacán and CIESAS, 2006.

———. *Los movimientos de las últimas décadas*. Vol. 3 of *Movimientos armados en México, siglo XX*. 3 vols. Mexico City: El Colegio de Michoacán; CIESAS, 2006.

———. *Visiones y revisiones de la guerilla en la primera mitad del siglo*. Vol. 1 of *Movimientos armados en México, siglo XX*. 3 vols. Mexico City: El Colegio de Michoacán and CIESAS, 2006.

Oikión Solano, Verónica, and Miguel Ángel Urrego Ardila, eds. *Violencia y sociedad: Un hito en la historia de las izquierdas en América Latina*. Morelia: El Colegio de Michoacán; Universidad Michoacana de San Nicolás de Hidalgo, 2010.

Ornelas Gómez, Francisco. "Sueños de libertad." Unpublished manuscript. Chihuahua, 2005.

Orozco Michel, Antonio. "Ayer y hoy: La vida por un ideal (Testimonio)." In Gamiño Muñoz et al., 157–66.

———. *La fuga de Oblatos: Una historia de la LC23S*. Guadalajara: La Casa del Mago, 2007.

Ortiz, Orlando. *Genaro Vázquez*. Mexico City: Editorial Diógenes, 1972.

Ortiz Rosas, Rubén. "La Brigada Especial: Un instrumento de la contrainsurgencia urbana en el Valle de México (1976–1981)." Master's thesis, Universidad Nacional Autónoma de México, 2014.

Padilla, Tanalís. "'Latent Sites of Agitation': *Normalistas Rurales* and Chihuahua's Agrarian Struggle in the 1960s." In Pensado and Ochoa, 53–72.

———. "Rural Education, Political Radicalism and Normalista Identity (in Post-1940 Mexico)." In Gillingham and Smith, 341–59.

———. *Rural Resistance in the Land of Zapata: The Jaramillista Movement and the Myth of the Pax Priísta, 1940–1962*. Durham, NC: Duke University Press, 2008.

———. *Unintended Lessons of Revolution: Student Teachers and Political Radicalism in Twentieth-Century Mexico*. Durham, NC: Duke University Press, 2021.

Padilla, Tanalís, and Louise E. Walker, eds. "Dossier: Spy Reports: Content, Methodology, and Historiography in Mexico's Secret Police Archive." Special issue, *Journal of Iberian and Latin American Research* 19, no. 1 (July 2013).

———. "In the Archives: History and Politics." In "Dossier: Spy Reports: Content, Methodology, and Historiography in Mexico's Secret Police Archive," edited by Tanalís Padilla and Lousie E. Walker. Special issue, *Journal of Iberian and Latin American Research* 19, no. 1 (July 2013): 1–10.

Padrón, Javier. *Los bombazos de 1975: Terrorismo de estado (el rochismo y la guerra sucia)*. Mexico City: Ediciones Ruta Crítica, 2005.

Palacios Hernández, Benjamín. *Héroes y fantasmas: La guerrilla mexicana de los años 70*. Monterrey: Universidad Autónoma de Nuevo León, Facultad de Filosofía y Letras, 2009.

Pansters, Wil G., ed. *Violence, Coercion, and State-Making in Twentieth-Century Mexico: The Other Half of the Centaur*. Stanford: Stanford University Press, 2012.

———. "Zones and Languages of State-Making: From *Pax Priísta* to Dirty War." In Pensado and Ochoa, 33–52.

———. "Zones of State-Making: Violence, Coercion, and Hegemony in Twentieth-Century Mexico." In Pansters, 3–42.

Pansters, Wil G., and Benjamin T. Smith, eds. *Histories of Drug Trafficking in Twentieth-Century Mexico*. Albuquerque: University of New Mexico Press, 2022.

Payne, Leigh. *Unsettling Accounts: Neither Truth nor Reconciliation in Confessions of State Violence*. Durham, NC: Duke University Press, 2008.

Pedraza Reyes, Héctor. "Apuntes sobre el movimiento armado socialista en México (1969–1974)." *Nóesis: Revista de Ciencias Sociales y Humanidades* 17, no. 34 (August–December 2008): 92–124.

Pensado, Jaime M. *Love and Despair: How Catholic Activism Shaped Politics and Counterculture in Modern Mexico*. Oakland: University of California Press, 2023.

———. *Rebel Mexico: Student Unrest and Authoritarian Political Culture during the Long Sixties*. Stanford: Stanford University Press, 2013.

Pensado, Jaime M., and Enrique Ochoa, eds. *México beyond 1968: Revolutionaries, Radicals, and Repression during the Global Sixties and Subversive Seventies*. Tucson: University of Arizona Press, 2018.

Pérez Ricart, Carlos A. "U.S. Pressure and Mexican Anti-Drugs Efforts from 1940–1980: Importing the War on Drugs?" In *Beyond the Drug War in Mexico: Human Rights, the Public Sphere, and Justice*, edited by Wil G. Pansters, Benjamin T. Smith, and Peter Watt, 33–51. New York: Routledge, 2017.

Pérez Rosales, Laura. "Estado, violencia y sociedad en México: Apuntes sobre a importancia de las historias de vida para la historia de los disidentes políticos de los años setenta." *Historia y Grafía*, no. 30 (2008): 115–33.

Pettinà, Vanni. *A Compact History of Latin America's Cold War*. Chapel Hill: University of North Carolina Press, 2022.

———. "Mexican Soviet Encounters in the Early 1960s: Tractors of Discord." In *Latin America and the Global Cold War*, edited by Thomas Field Jr., Stella Kreep, and Vanni Pettinà, 73–99. Chapel Hill: University of North Carolina Press, 2020.

Piccato, Pablo. *City of Suspects: Crime in Mexico City, 1900-1931*. Durham, NC: Duke University Press, 2001.

———. "Comments: How to Build a Perspective on the Recent Past." *Journal of Iberian and Latin American Research* 19, no. 1 (July 2013): 99–110.

———. *Historia mínima de la violencia en México*. Mexico City: El Colegio de México, 2022.

———. *A History of Infamy: Crime, Truth, and Justice in Mexico*. Berkeley: University of California Press, 2017.

Pimentel Aguilar, Ramón. *El secuestro: ¿Lucha política o provocación?* Mexico City: Editorial Posada, 1974.

Pineda Ochoa, Fernando. *En las profundidades del MAR (el oro no llegó de Moscú)*. Mexico City: Plaza y Valdés, 2003.

Poniatowska, Elena. *Fuerte es el silencio*. Mexico City: Era, 1981.

———. *Massacre in Mexico*. Translated by Helen R. Lane. Columbia: University of Missouri Press, 1992.

Portelli, Alessandro. *The Death of Luigi Trastulli and Other Stories: Form and Meaning in Oral History*. Albany: State University of New York Press, 1991.

Los Procesos de México 68: La criminalización de las víctimas. Mexico City: Comité 68 por Libertades Democráticas, 2008.

Radilla Martínez, Andrea. *Poderes, saberes y sabores: Una historia de resistencia de los cafeticultores: Atoyac, 1940-1974*. Chilpancingo: Universidad Autónoma de Guerrero, 1998.

———. *Voces acalladas (vidas truncadas): Perfil biográfico de Rosendo Radilla Pacheco*. Chilpancingo: Universidad Autónoma de Guerrero, 2002.

Radilla Martínez, Andrea, and Claudia E. G. Rangel Lozano, eds. *Desaparición forzada y terrorismo de Estado en México: Memorias de la Represión de Atoyac, Guerrero durante la década de los setenta*. Chilpancingo: Universidad Autónoma de Guerrero and Plaza y Valdés, 2012.

Ramos Zavala, Raúl, et al. *El tiempo que nos tocó vivir y otros documentos de la guerrilla en México*. Mexico City: Tierra Roja, 2003.

Rangel Lozano, Claudia E. G. "La historia oral como método interdisciplinario: La desaparición forzada de personas durante la guerra sucia en Atoyac, Guerrero." In *De la literatura a la política: Seis siglos de transformación social en México (memoria de la décima quinta semana nacional de la ciencia y la tecnología)*, edited by F. Ávila Juárez, 117–142. Mexico City: Universidad Autónoma de Guerrero, 2009.

Rangel Lozano, Claudia E. G., and Evangelina Sánchez Serrano. "La guerra sucia en los setenta y las guerrillas de Genaro Vázquez y Lucio Cabañas en Guerrero." In Oikión Solano and García Ugarte, 495–526.

Rath, Thomas. *Myths of Demilitarization in Postrevolutionary Mexico, 1920–1960.* Chapel Hill: University of North Carolina Press, 2013.

Rayas Velasco, Lucía. *Armadas: Un análisis de género desde el cuerpo de las mujeres combatientes.* Mexico City: Colegio de México, 2009.

———. "Hitos de la memoria guerrillera en México: Creación de espacios memorísticos y de monumentos virtuales." In *Subversiones: Memoria social y género: Ataduras y reflexiones,* edited by Luz Maceira Ochoa and Lucía Rayas Velasco, 267–90. Mexico City: Juan Pablos, FONCA, and INAH, 2011.

———. "Subjugating the Nation: Women and the Guerrilla Experience." In Calderón and Cedillo, 167–81.

Regalis, Darius. *Torture and Democracy.* Princeton, NJ: Princeton University Press, 2009.

Reyes Peláez, Juan Fernando. "Introducción a la historia de la guerrilla en México (1943–1983)." Unpublished manuscript. Mexico City, 2010.

———. "El largo brazo del estado: La estrategía contrainsurgente del gobierno mexicano." In Oikión Solano and García Ugarte, 405–13.

Reyes Serrano, Ángel Custodio. *¡Trinchera . . . ! Lucio Cabañas, Genaro Vázquez y su guerrilla.* Mexico City: Costa-Amic Editores, 1985.

Rico Galán, Víctor. *Escritos políticos (1966–1971).* Mexico City: Ediciones Proletariado y Revolución, 1984.

Rivera Ortiz, Mario, and Mario Rivera Guzmán. *El secuestro de José Guadalupe Zuno Hernández: Un capítulo de la lucha guerrillera en el México de 1974.* Mexico City: Medicina y Sociedad, 1992.

Robin, Marie-Monique, dir. *Escadrons de la mort: L'école française.* DVD. Ideal Audience, 2003.

Robles Garnica, Héctor Guillermo. *Guadalajara, la guerrilla olvidada: Presos en la isla de la libertad.* Mexico City: Ediciones La otra Cuba, 1996.

———. *La guerrilla olvidada.* Guadalajara: La Casa del Mago, 2013.

Rodríguez Castañeda, Rafael. *El policía: Perseguía, torturaba, mataba.* Mexico City: Grijalbo, 2013.

Rodríguez Kuri, Ariel. *Historia mínima de las izquierdas en México.* Mexico City: El Colegio de México, 2021.

Rodríguez Munguía, Jacinto. *Las nóminas secretas de gobernación.* Mexico City: LIMAC, 2004.

———. *La otra guerra secreta: Los archivos secretos de la prensa y el poder.* Mexico City: Random House Mondadori, 2007.

Rosales, José Natividad. *La muerte (?) de Lucio Cabañas.* Mexico City: Editorial Posada, 1975.

———. *¿Quién es Lucio Cabañas?: ¿Qué pasa con la guerrilla en México?* Mexico City: Editorial Posada, 1974.

Rubin, Jeffrey W. *Decentering the Regime: Ethnicity, Radicalism, and Democracy in Juchitán, Mexico.* Durham, NC: Duke University Press, 1997.

Ruiz de Esparza, José Luis. *Luis Echeverría: 2 de octubre 68, 10 de junio 71, la guerra sucia.* Mexico City: Mendizábal, 2001.

Ruiz Guerra, Rubén, ed. *Entre la memoria y la justicia: Experiencias latinoamericanas sobre Guerra Sucia y defensa de Derechos Humanos.* Mexico City: Universidad Nacional Autónoma de México, 2005.

Salas Obregón, Ignacio Arturo. *Cuestiones fundamentales del movimiento revolucionario o manifestó al proletariado: Liga Comunista 23 de Septiembre.* Mexico City: Editorial Huasipungo, 2003. https://ligacomunista23.files.wordpress.com/2015/05/cuestiones09.pdf.

Salcedo García, Carlos. "Grupo guerrillero Lacandones: La luz que no se acaba." Unpublished manuscript. Mexico City, Símbolo Digital, 2004.

———. "Grupo Los Lacandones." In Gamiño Muñoz et al., 183–204.

———. *La luz que no se acaba: Grupo Guerrillero Lacandones.* Mexico City: Editorial Libertad Bajo Palabra, 2022.

Salgado Salgado, Armando. *Una vida de guerra.* Mexico City: Planeta, 1990.

Sánchez Parra, Sergio Arturo. *Estudiantes en armas: Una historia política y cultural del movimiento estudiantil de los Enfermos (1972–1978).* Culiacán: Universidad Autónoma de Sinaloa; Academia de Historia de Sinaloa, 2012.

———. "Violencia política en Sinaloa: El caso de los 'Enfermos' 1972–1978 (Los lugares y medios para la radicalización)." *Historia de la Educación Latinoamericana* 11 (2008): 205–24.

Sánchez Serrano, Evangelina. "Terrorismo de Estado y la repression en Guerrero durante la guerra sucia." In *Desaparición forzada y terrorismo de Estado en México: Memorias de la represión en Atoyac, Guerrero durante la década de los setenta,* edited by Andrea Radilla Martínez and Claudia E. G. Rangel Lozano, 137–78. Mexico City: Universidad Autónoma de Guerrero, 2012.

Santiago Dionisio, Octaviano. *El movimiento estudiantil en Guerrero.* Chilpancingo: Universidad Autónoma de Guerrero, 1981.

Scherer García, Julio, and Carlos Monsiváis. *Los patriotas: De Tlatelolco a la guerra sucia.* Mexico City: Aguilar, 2004.

Schlefer, Jonathan. *Palace Politics: How the Ruling Party Brought Crisis to Mexico.* Austin: University of Texas Press, 2008.

Schrader, Stuart. *Badges without Borders: How Global Counterinsurgency Transformed American Policing.* Oakland: University of California Press, 2019.

Secretaría de Servicios Parlamentarios. *Código Penal Federal.* June 7, 2013. https://www.diputados.gob.mx/LeyesBiblio/pdf/CPF.pdf

Seigel, Micol. "Objects of Police History." *Journal of American History* 102, no. 1 (June 2015): 152–61.

Servín, Elisa. *Ruptura y oposición: El movimiento henriquista, 1945–1954.* Mexico City: Cal y Arena, 2001.

Sierra Guzmán, Jorge Luis. *El enemigo interno: Contrainsurgencia y fuerzas armadas en México.* Mexico City: Plaza y Valdés, Universidad Iberoamericana, Centro de Estudios Estratégicos de América del Norte, 2003.

———. "Fuerzas armadas y contrainsurgencia, 1965–1982." In Oikión Solano and García Ugarte, 361–404.

Sierra Villarreal, José Luis. *Nazar Haro: La guerra sucia en Yucatán.* Mexico City: CEPSA, 2004.

Sorensen, Diana. *A Turbulent Decade Remembered: Scenes from the Latin American Sixties.* Stanford: Stanford University Press, 2007.

Sotelo Marbán, José. "El ejército mexicano y la guerra sucia en Guerrero." Unpublished manuscript. Mexico City, December 2002.

———. *Informe histórico a la Sociedad mexicana: ¡Qué no vuelva a suceder!* Mexico City: Fiscalía Especial para Movimientos Sociales y Políticos del Pasado, 2006.

Stern, Steve J. *Battling for Hearts and Minds: Memory Struggles in Pinochet's Chile, 1973–1988.* Vol. 2 of *The Memory Box of Pinochet's Chile.* Durham, NC: Duke Unviersity Press, 2006.

———. *The Memory Box of Pinochet's Chile.* 3 vols. Durham, NC: Duke University Press, 2004–2010.

———. *Reckoning with Pinochet: The Memory Question in Democratic Chile, 1989–2006.* Vol. 3 of *The Memory Box of Pinochet's Chile.* Durham, NC: Duke University Press, 2010.

———. *Remembering Pinochet's Chile: On the Eve of London 1998.* Vol. 1 of *The Memory Box of Pinochet's Chile.* Durham, NC: Duke University Press, 2004.

Suárez, Luis. *Lucio Cabañas: El guerrillero sin esperanza.* Mexico City: Roca, 1976.

Taibo, Paco Ignacio. *Calling All Heroes: A Manual for Taking Power.* Translated by Gregory Nipper. Oakland, CA: PM Press, 2010.

Teague, Aileen. *"Dirty War" on Drugs: The United States, Mexico, and the Origins of Militarized Policing, 1969–2000.* New York: Oxford University Press, forthcoming.

Topete, Miguel. *Los ojos de la noche: El comando guerrillero Óscar González Eguiarte.* Guadalajara: La Casa del Mago, 2009.

Torres, Jorge. *Nazar, la historia secreta: El hombre detrás de la guerra sucia.* Mexico City: Debate, 2008.

Ulloa Bornemann, Alberto. *Sendero en tinieblas.* Mexico City: Cal y Arena, 2004.

————. *Surviving Mexico's Dirty War: A Political Prisoner's Memoir*. Edited and translated by Arthur Schmidt and Aurora Camacho de Schmidt. Philadelphia: Temple University Press, 2007.

Uranga López, Lourdes. *Comparezco y acuso*. Mexico City: Universidad Autónoma de Chapingo and Plaza y Valdés, 2012.

Velázquez Villa, Hugo. *Biográfica armada*. Guadalajara: Universidad de Guadalajara, 2008.

————. *El 68 como discurso de Estado*. Guadalajara: Sindicato de Trabajadores Académicos de la Universidad de Guadalajara, 2017.

Veledíaz, Juan. *El general sin memoria: Una crónica de los silencios del ejército mexicano*. Mexico City: Debate, 2010.

Vicente Ovalle, Camilo. *Instantes sin historia: La violencia política y de estado en México*. Mexico City: UNAM, 2023.

————. *[Tiempo suspendido]: Una historia de la desaparición forzada en México, 1940–1980*. Mexico City: Bonilla Artigas Editores, 2019.

Vicente Ovalle, Camilo, Daniel Librado Luna Cárdenas, Halina Gutiérrez Mariscal, José Luis Soto Espinosa, Mariana Gómez Godoy, Miguel Ángel Ramírez Jahuey, and Veremundo Carrillo Reveles. *A 50 años del Halconazo: 10 de junio de 1971*. Mexico City: Instituto Nacional de Estudios Históricos de las Revoluciones de México, 2021.

Walker, Louise E. *Waking from the Dream: Mexico's Middle Classes after 1968*. Stanford: Stanford University Press, 2013.

Zamora, Jesús. *Los guerrilleros de Oblatos*. Guadalajara: La Casa del Mago, 2010.

Zolov, Eric. *The Last Good Neighbor: Mexico in the Global Sixties*. Durham, NC: Duke University Press, 2020.

————. *Refried Elvis: The Rise of Mexican Counterculture*. Berkeley: University of California Press, 1999.

Index

Abarca Martínez, Patricio, 108, 130, 171–178, 191–192, 197–198
accommodation, 177–178
Acosta Chaparro, Mario Arturo, 79, 100, 107–108, 166–167
Agencia de Investigación Criminal (AIC; Criminal Investigation Agency), 204
Aguas Blancas massacre of 1995, 200
Aguayo Quesada, Sergio, 32, 118
Aguilar Torres, María de la Luz, 61
Aguirre, Elsa, 163
Alfaro Siqueiros, David, 17
Alonso Vargas, José Luis, 48, 134
Amnesty International, 199
Andrade Vallejo, Margarita, 241n9; detention of family, 141–142
"antirevolutionary war" tactics. See counterinsurgency tactics
Argentina: Cold War politics and, 4; dirty war in, 24; memory sites in, 71, 205–206; state violence in, 4, 71
arrepentidos, 135–137
Arroyo Cabañas, Alejandro, 21–22, 49, 197
Arroyo Castro, José Luis, 152–156
Article 145 of Federal Penal Code ("social dissolution" law), 64
Asociación Cívica Revolucionaria (Civic-Revolutionary Association), 56

Asociación de Padres y Familiares de los Presos Políticos (Association of Parents and Family of Political Prisoners), 139
Atoyac massacre of 1967, 12, 146
Ávila, Coronel, 69
Aviña, Alexander, 68–69
Ayala, Isabel, 164
Ayocac massacre of 1967, 36, 56, 157
Ayotzinapa disappearances, 204

Barreda Moreno, Luis de la, 88–89
Barrientos Serafín, Humberto, 161, 164–165
Barrientos Serafín, Mariela, 160–163
Barrientos Serafín, Sofia, 160–166
Bartra, Roger, 59
Batallón Olimpia, 95–99
Bello López, Guillermo, 127, 136–137
Bornemann, Ulloa, 32, 35
Bourke, Joanna, 201
Brigada Blanca. See White Brigade
Brigada Campesina de Ajusticiamiento (Peasant Brigade for Justice), 172–174
Brigada Quince of the División de Investigaciones para la Prevención de la Delincuencia (DIPD), 199
Brigada Roja (Red Brigade), 100–101
Britain, 25

Brownding, Christopher, 84
bureaucratization of torture, 26, 202

Cabañas, Celerina, 133
Cabañas, Lucio, 17–18, 56, 115, 129, 145;
  complaints on behalf of, 197; death of,
  151, 162; detainment and torture of fam-
  ily members, 133, 139, 145–166,
  241n21; followers of, 171; as political
  prisoner, 17–18. *See also* Partido de los
  Pobres
Cabañas Barrientos, Pablo, 37–38, 91, 115,
  128–130, 146, 149–152, 197; release of,
  133, 194
Cabañas Ocampo, Bertoldo, 119–120, 137,
  156–158
Cabañas Ocampo, Isaías, 157
Cabañas Ocampo, Luis, 120
Calderón, Felipe, 203
Calderón, Fernando, 8–9, 57, 203
Camarena, Enrique "Kiki," 17
Campaña López, Francisco Juventino,
  33–34
Campo Militar-1 (CM-1; Military Base
  Number 1), 30, 103, 115; communication within, 120; detainment/torture of
  family members in, 143, 148–149, 157–
  158, 159, 161; disappearances from,
  137; torture of prisoners in, 37–38,
  43–44, 46, 115
Cárdenas, Lázaro, 17
Cartagena López, Álvaro Mario "El Guaymas,"
  24, 117; *arrepentidos* and, 136; detainment and torture of, 35, 40–41, 71–72,
  232n74; escape attempts and, 131–132;
  family visits to, 138; as political prisoner,
  117, 123, 127
Casas Quiroz, Yolanda Isabel, 42, 61, 90–91,
  111, 187–193
Castellanos, Laura, 88
castration, 47–48, 91–92, 180
Castro Hernandez, Don Petronilo, 157
Castro Velásquez, Isaías, 154–156
Catholic movements, 70–71; liberation theol-
  ogy, 56, 71; right-wing political organiza-
  tions, 63; torture of priests, 71
Cedillo, Adela, 8–9, 45, 101
Celis Gutiérrez, Alfredo, 107
Central Intelligence Agency (CIA), 49–51;
  Nazar Haro and, 106
Centro de Investigación y Docencia
  Económica (CIDE; Center for Economic
  Research and Teaching), 203–204

Centro de Investigación y Seguridad Nacional
  (CISEN; Center for Investigation and
  National Security), 17
Centro de Readaptación Social (CERESO;
  Social Rehabilitation Center), 128–129,
  151
Chacón López, Saúl René, 135
Chiapas, 200
children, torture of, 142–143
Chile, 4, 71; memory sites in, 205–206
Cienfuegos, Salvador, 209
circuito concept, 22–23
Circular de Morelia 8, 205–212
Ciudad Madera: assault on army barracks,
  12, 88
clandestine prisons, 1–2, 5–6, 81, 111–112,
  114–117, 216n7; collaboration in,
  72–73; communication within, 119–
  120; contrasted with formal prisons,
  111–112; detainment/torture of families
  in, 141, 148–149, 167; establishment of,
  5; investigation of, 197; map of, xvii–
  xviii; as memorial, 205–212; military
  bases as, 83, 119; public knowledge of, 2,
  6, 23, 80–81, 139; as spaces of exception,
  6; torture of prisoners in, 26–27, 33,
  36–37, 72, 85, 108, 115–116, 175, 182;
  US involvement in, 49. *See also* Campo
  Militar-1
CM-1. *See* Campo Militar-1
CNDH. *See* Comisión Nacional de Derechos
  Humanos
Cold War, 3; cognitive science and, 51; counterinsurgency tactics and, 12, 16, 39, 97;
  "dirty war" tactics and, 7–8; extralegal
  violence and, 97; 1970's Mexico and, 4–7
collaboration, 66, 73–76
Comisión Nacional de Derechos Humanos
  (CNDH; National Human Rights Commission), 9, 28, 204–205, 208, 221n41
Comisión para Acceso a la Verdad, Esclarecimiento Histórico e Impulso a la Justicia
  de violaciones graves a derechos humanos
  de 1965-1990, 208
Comité Eureka de Desaparacidos, 70, 195–
  196, 232n71, 239n26, 242n2
Comité Pro-Presos Políticos, 125
Condés Lara, Enrique, 19
conjugal visits, 127
Corpus Christi massacre of 1971, 13, 14–15,
  50, 63, 169, 220n38; memorialization of,
  208; paramilitary groups and, 14, 83, 96,
  98, 235n41

Corral, Salvador, 74
Cortés Castro, Carmelo, 172–174
counterculture movement, 55, 58–59, 62, 66–67; political opposition to, 63
counterinsurgency tactics, 2–3, 7, 11, 217n10; bureaucratization of, 23; Cold War and, 12, 16, 39, 97; counternarcotics operations and, 50, 68, 199–200, 220n36; DFS use of, 15–17, 54; Echeverría Álvarez and, 13; end of in Mexico, 15, 199; extralegal violence and, 97–98; against families of "subversives," 138, 142, 145–146, 241n21; Hirales Morán and, 74; institutionalization of torture, 23; narcotrafficking and, 17; Nazar Haro and, 85–88; paramilitaries and, 15, 95, 97–98; Plan Telaraña as, 67–68; selection of officers, 85; "subversive" identity and, 58, 82, 84, 555; torture as central strategy, 3, 23, 26, 28, 38, 82–83, 93–94, 202; US involvement in, 49–50, 87, 200; White Brigade and, 103–105. See also "dirty war" tactics
counternarcotics operations, 68, 179, 199–200, 220n36; torture and, 203–205; US involvement in, 50
covert war, 82, 85. See also counterinsurgency tactics; unconventional warfare
Cuba, 63, 192, 216n6; Cold War politics and, 4–5; PRI presidents and, 13
culture of fear, 6–7, 14, 18, 25–26, 69–70, 101, 146–147

Danzos Palomino, Ramón, 125
de la Luz Aguilar, María and Raul, 144
del Río, Eduardo "Ruis," 80
depth interrogation, 89, 91
DFS. See Dirección Federal de Seguridad
Díaz Escobar, Manuel, 50
Díaz Ordaz, Gustavo, 5, 14, 115; Tlatelolco massacre and, 13, 53, 63
Dirección Federal de Seguridad (DFS; Federal Security Directorate), 15–17, 101–102; counterinsurgency methods of, 13; creation of, 12; dissolution of, 17; families of detainees and, 155–156; Group C-047 and, 88, 102; headquarters as memorial, 205–212; hunger strikers and, 125; identification of subversives and, 65; informants and, 72–74, 88; LC23S and, 100–102; lexicon of torture, 28; location of torture centers, 114–115; Nazar Haro and, 88–89; relationship with military,

83, 94; as space of exception, 5–6; surveillance activities of, 69; surveillance and, 83, 88; torturers employed by, 80; White Brigade of, 82–83, 102–105. See also Campo Militar-1
"dirty war" tactics, 5, 7–10, 12, 106, 168–169, 192–193, 217n10; clandestine detention centers and, 116; in contemporary Mexico, 200; disappearances and, 161; end of, 13, 199; family members and, 140, 145, 150, 154, 165–167; individuals responsible for, 107; lexicon of, 24; memorialization of, 205–208; resistance to, 71; state terror and, 8–9, 201; success of, 201; Truth Commission and, 107; women and, 156, 195. See also counterinsurgency tactics
disappearances, 15, 22–25, 28, 57, 137, 168, 176, 194, 221n41; after dissolution of DFS, 17, 200; Ayotzinapa case, 204; at CM-1, 137, 149; commemoration of, 206–207; of family members, 138, 166; Grupo Sangre and, 98; of LC23S members, 100, 106; of political prisoners, 119; self-erasure and, 151; Truth Commission and, 107; White Brigade and, 103
Drug Enforcement Agency (DEA), 13, 17, 200

Echeverría Álvarez, Luis, 5, 58, 87, 101, 199, 209, 231n70; lack of opposition to, 70, 179; state repression and, 13–15
Ejército Zapatista de Liberación Nacional (EZLN; Zapatista Army of National Liberation), 74, 200
El Corral, 117–118
Los Enfermos, 57, 99
Escamilla García, Rodolfo, 71
escape attempts, 130–133, 183
escuelas normales, 56, 66
Esparza, José Luis, 48, 60, 110, 117, 135
Espino Barros, Humberto, 171
Estrada Ramírez, Domingo, 32
extralegal violence, 97

family members, 138–141, 166–167; arrest and torture of, 114, 133, 139–166; Cabañas family, 133, 139, 145–166, 241n21; complaints on behalf of, 197; following release, 190–191, 193; hunger strikes and, 239n26, 242n3; intergenerational trauma and, 14, 154, 163–165;

family members (*continued*)
  political action by, 71, 139–140, 148,
    152–153, 163–164, 182, 195–196, 199;
    release of, 148, 151; torture of children,
    142–143, 201; visits from, 18, 110,
    117–118, 124, 126–127, 138, 148,
    176, 196
Federación Estudiantil Revolucionario (FER;
  Revolutionary Student Federation), 57,
  77
Federal Specialized Torture Investigations
  Unit, 204
Feitlowitz , Marguerite, 24, 28
FEMOSSP. *See* Fiscalía para Movimientos
  Sociales y Políticos del Pasado
Fernández del Real, Carlos, 195
Fiscalía para Movimientos Sociales y Políticos
  del Pasado (FEMOSSP; Special Prosecu-
  tor for Social and Political Movements of
  the Past), 9, 106–107, 149, 165, 208,
  218n16
Flores Jiménez, Agustín, 157
Fox, Vicente, 10, 165, 197, 209; Nazar Haro
  and, 106
France, 25, 89; antirevolutionary war and, 7,
  217n10
Frente Estudiantil Revolucionario (FER;
  Revolutionary Student Front), 43
Frente Revolucionario Armado del Pueblo
  (FRAP; Armed Revolutionary Front of
  the People), 2, 58; detainment/torture of
  members, 33–34, 117
Frente Urbano Zapatistas, 99
Fuerzas de Liberación Nacional (FLN), 99

Gallegos Najera, José Arturo, 30–31, 39–40,
  47, 89
García Barragán, Marcelino, 108
Garcia Cabañas, Manuel, 159–161, 164
García Nájera, Juan, 107
García Paniagua, Javier, 89, 108
Garza Sada, Eugenio, 100
General Law on Torture, 204
Gillingham, Paul, 97
Gilly, Adolfo, 196
Godoy Cabañas, Adolfo, 37–38, 72–73, 119–
  120, 146–149
Godoy Cabañas, Felicito, 147–148
Godoy Cabañas, Marcial, 154–155
Gómez Serafín, Eugenio, 159
González Villareal, Roberto, 72, 199
Gortari, Eli de, 125
Group C-047, 88, 102

Grupo Jaguar, 199–200
Grupo Sangre (Blood Group), 95, 98–99
Guadalupe Soto, Thelma, 176
guerrilla organizations, 56–63; *arrepentidos*
  and, 135–136; concept of sickness and,
  88–89; conflicts between, 242n8; controversial memories of, 196–197; counterculture movement and, 58–59; covert
  war against, 85; criminalization of members, 68; DFS and, 101–103; drug war
  and, 68; gender and, 60–62; infiltration
  of, 14, 62, 66–67, 88, 95–96; scope of,
  227n10; student organizations, 57;
  urban-rural divide, 57–58, 67; White
  Brigade and, 102–105; women in, 111,
  229n28. *See also* subversives; individual
  organizations
Guevara, Ernesto "Che," 5, 49; as icon,
  62–63, 117, 129
Gutiérrez Barrios, Fernando, 88–89, 234n29

Halcones (Hawks) paramilitary group,
  14–15, 50, 95–99, 235n41, 240n38
Henriquéz Gúzman, Miguel, 12, 87
Hernández, Virgilio de la Crúz, 176
Hernández Hernández, Elia, 46, 61, 110,
  134, 143–144
Hernandez Hinojosa, Julio, 47, 167
Hernández Ríos, Josafath, 35, 37, 145, 167
Herníquez Guzmán, Miguel, 87
Hirales Morán, Gustavo, 9, 73–74, 76
homosexuality, 67, 231n70
hunger strikes, 125, 126, 139, 196, 239n26,
  242n3

Ibarra, Rosario, 195–196, 199, 242n3
impunity, 3–4, 10, 69, 80–81, 85, 135, 202–
  205; challenges to, 194; clandestine prisons and, 2; concept of "subversives" and,
  5; in contemporary Mexico, 201, 203–
  205; counternarcotics operations and,
  203–205; detainment of family members
  and, 143, 165–167; of DFS, 17, 206;
  national security and, 19; of paramilitary
  groups, 14, 96–97, 200; silence as, 76; of
  White Brigade, 105
infiltration, 14, 62, 66–67, 88, 95–96; in
  prisons, 118
informants, 72–76
institutionalization of torture, 3, 23, 28, 71,
  84–85
Instituto Politécnico Nacional, 52–53
International Police Academy (IPA), 87

interrogation, 23, 25, 72–76, 105; CIA and, 50–51; depth interrogation, 89, 91; of families of "subversives," 147–150, 159; gender and, 60, 92–93; interrogation techniques, 38, 50, 75–76, 85, 88–89, 93; Nazar Haro and, 89–91; on-the-job training, 80, 93–94; of political prisoners, 119–120; professionalization of techniques, 76, 88; as psychological torture, 42; torture as purpose of, 22–23, 72
Iriarte Bonilla, Hugo David, 39
Islas Marias Federal Penal Colony, 117

James, Daniel, 170
Jaramillo, Rubén, 12

Keller, Renata, 50
Kennedy, William, 106
Kloppe-Santamaría, Gema, 96–97
Kubark Counterintelligence Interrogation handbook, 50–51

Los Lacandones, 57, 99, 187–188
Laguna Berber, Jaime, 105, 121–122, 126–127, 178–187, 195–197; release of, 134
"last door" metaphor, 107–109, 201
Lazreg, Marnia, 25–26, 28, 46, 89, 201, 216n4; definition of torture, 216n4; on subversion, 227n5
LC23S. *See* Liga Comunista 23 de Septiembre
Lecumberri penitentiary, 116–117, 121, 123–126, 139
León massacre of 1946, 12
lexicon of torture, 24, 28, 223n18
liberation theology, 56, 71
Liga Comunista 23 de Septiembre (LC23S; September 23 Communist League), 2, 57–58, 99–105; *arrepentidos* and, 136; detainment/torture of members, 30, 44–45, 100, 106, 116–117, 144, 179, 212; DFS campaign against, 65–66; disappearances of members, 100, 106; dissolution of, 186; escape attempts and, 131–132; founding of, 99–100; Laguna Berber and, 179–180, 182; members as political prisoners, 129; political prisoners and, 18; violence committed by, 101; White Brigade and, 102–105
Liga Comunista Espartaco, 187
López de la Torre, Saul, 32
López Mateos, Adolfo, 13
López Obrador, Andrés Manuel "AMLO,"

178; memorialization of torture survivors and, 9, 206–209
López Portillo, José, 13, 89, 199–200; lack of opposition to, 70; state repression and, 14
López Uranga, Lourdes, 19
López Valenzuela, David, 73, 76
Lorenzo López, Rigoberto, 34, 61
Lugos, Alejandro, 162
Luis Sierra, Jorge, 99

Mayoral, Rubén, 118–119
McCoy, Al, 17, 23, 38, 50–51; on psychological torture, 41–42
memorialization of torture survivors, 205–212
memory sites, 205–206
Méndez Alvarado, María de Jesús, 46
Méndez Arceo, Sergio, 70–71
Mendoza Salgado family, 140, 143
Mercado Espinoza, Francisco, 126
methodologies of torture, 37–45; use of electricity, 41; use of rape, 45–48; use of water, 40; witnessing as torture, 41–45
Miyazahua Alvarez, Jesús, 89
La Mojonera, 114
Molina Salazar, Manuel, 43–44
Mondragón y Kalb, Manuel, 73, 75–76
Morales, Jesús, 32
Morales Gervacio, Abelardo and Moisés, 159
Moreno Borbolla, José Luis, 19, 31–33, 35, 46, 116, 120–124, 137, 141–142; descriptions of torturers, 89
Mothers of the Plaza de Mayo, 71
Movimiento Armado Revolucionario, 99
Movimiento de Acción Revolucionaria (MAR; Movement for Revolutionary Action), 57, 122, 212

"narcos" threat, 13
narcotics, 124–125, 127–128. *See also* counternarcotics operations
narrative storytelling, 170
Natividad Rosales, José, 123
Nazar Haro, Miguel, 15, 28–31, 33–34, 46, 74, 79–80, 82, 86–92, 137; disappearances and, 137; early life of, 86–87; interrogation style of, 88–92; memorials and, 206–207; paramilitary groups and, 98–99; professionalization of torturers and, 88; resignation and later life of, 106–107; torture of families and, 144; training of in US, 50–51, 87; White Brigade and, 30, 82–83, 95, 99, 102, 104

Nazi Germany, 84
Nixon, Richard, 68
non-state actors, 97
normalization of torture, 3–4, 8, 84, 97
North Korea, 63

Oblatos prison, 72, 116–118, 123–124,
    139–140; escape from, 131–133
Ojeda Paullada, Pedro, 133
Okión Solano, Verónica, 8
Olympics (Mexico City, 1968), 4, 9, 53–54;
    Batallón Olimpia and, 96; counterinsur-
    gency tactics and, 12–13. *See also* Tlate-
    lolco massacre of 1968
Onofre Barrientos, Antonio, 159, 163
Operation Condor, 200
Orozco Michel, Antonio, 19, 44–45, 131–
    132, 198

Padilla, Tanalís, 57
Pansters, Wil, 11
paramilitary groups, 14–15, 50, 95; Corpus
    Christi massacre and, 14, 83, 96, 98,
    220n38, 235n41; Halcones (Hawks)
    paramilitary group, 14–15, 50, 95–99,
    235n41; impunity of, 14, 96–97, 200
Parque de la Memoria, 205–206
Parra Ramos, Ana María, 212
Partido de Acción Nacional (PAN; National
    Action Party), 10
Partido de la Revolución Democrática (PRD;
    Party of the Democratic Revolution), 196
Partido de la Revolución Institucional (PRI;
    Institutional Revolutionary Party), 18,
    81; political prisoners and, 18; protests
    against, 52; state violence and, 10–11,
    13–14, 52, 207; voted out of office, 10,
    15, 200
Partido de los Pobres (Party of the Poor), 2,
    145, 242n1; detention/torture of party
    members, 27–28, 30, 153; founding of,
    56; government actions against, 67; para-
    military groups and, 98. *See also* Cabañas,
    Lucio
Partido Revolucionario de los Trabajadores
    (PRT; Revolutionary Workers Party), 196
Partido Socialista (Socialist Party), 177
Pasco, Roberto, 196
patriarchy, 93
Payne, Leigh, 202
Pensado, Jamie, 62, 71
Pérez Mora, Enrique "El Tenebras," 131
Picatto, Pablo, 97

Pie de la Cuesta base, 119, 147–148; as
    space of exception, 5–6
Piedra Ibarra, Jesús, 106, 196
Plan Telaraña (Plan Spiderweb), 67–68
political prisoners, 17–19, 110–112, 186,
    194; attempts to obtain justice for, 197–
    199; clandestine prisons and, 115–116;
    communication between, 119–120, 124;
    daily lives of, 121–130; decrease in num-
    bers of, 137; disappearances of, 119,
    137; escape attempts by, 130–133; fami-
    lies of, 139–140; formal acknowledgment
    of, 199; hunger strikes and, 125, 126;
    legal advocacy for, 195–196, 199; "nar-
    cos" and, 127–128; political conflicts
    among, 128–129; public support of, 125;
    regrets faced by, 135–137; relationships
    with common prisoners, 124–125, 129–
    130; release of, 133–135, 176–177, 199;
    separated from common prisoners, 117–
    118, 127–128; solidarity among, 186,
    190; violence against, 120–121; visibility
    of, 111; women as, 111
Poniatowska, Elena, 32, 73
Portillo, José López, 5
PRI. *See* Partido de la Revolución
    Institucional
Los Procesos, 99
professionalization of torturers, 81–82, 86,
    88
psychological torture, 175–176, 185, 200–
    201, 216n4; castration as, 47; contrasted
    with physical torture, 89, 91; depth inter-
    rogation as, 89; effects of, 92; re-telling
    as, 165–166; torture of family members
    as, 43, 144–145, 153, 201; witnessing
    as, 41–45

Quiñones, Lourdes, 34, 42–43, 61, 111, 134
Quiñones, Rigoberto, 42–43
Quinto, Carlos, 46
Quirós Hermosillo, Francisco, 89, 102, 108

Rabasa, Emilio, 50
Rangel, Claudia, 8
Rangel Escamilla, Manuel, 87, 89
Rangel Medina, Salvador, 98
rape of torture survivors, 45–48, 51, 60,
    143–144, 189, 201, 204
Reclusorio Oriente, 116
regrets, 135–137
Rentería Castillo, Armando, 34, 139
Rentería Castillo, Luciano, 139

La revolución interrumpida (The Interrupted
    Revolution) (Gilly), 196
Revueltas, José, 125
Reyes Crespo, Rodolfo, 143
Rivera Leyva, Humberto, 27–28
Rodríguez, Lourdes, 90
Rodríguez Kuri, Ariel, 8

Salas Obregón, Ignacio Arturo, 106
Salcedo, Carlos, 19, 28–30, 32–33, 35, 45;
    Casas Quiroz and, 188, 190; countercul-
    ture movement and, 59–60; descriptions of
    torturers, 85–86, 89; "last door" metaphor
    and, 107–109, 201; Los Lacandones and,
    188; torture of, 47, 91–92, 116, 200–201
San Andrés neighborhood (Guadalajara),
    76–77
Sánchez, Evangelina, 8
Santa Martha Acatitla prison, 185–186, 196
Santa Martha de Acatitla penitentiary,
    121–122
School of the Americas (SOA), 50
self-erasure, 151
Serafín Gervacio, Bartola, 158–166
Serafín Gervacio, David, 159–162, 164
Sheinbaum, Claudia, 208–209
Silva Valle, Desidor, 36–37
Simons, Marlise, 133–134, 194–195
Sitios de Memoria (Sites of Memory) website,
    207
6/a Brigade of Special Services of the Division
    of Investigations for the Prevention of
    Delinquency, 102
"soft" authoritarianism, 18, 81
Soviet Union, 63
spaces of exception, 6, 92
Special Investigations Group C-047, 88
Special Prosecutor's Office, 197
state violence, 10–15; attempts to investigate,
    197; cumulative effects of, 22; against
    family members, 145, 166–167; intergen-
    erational effects of, 164; memorialization
    of, 205–212; ongoing nature of, 199,
    202–203; opposition to, 70–71; periodi-
    zation of, 12–15; state making and, 3, 11,
    16; Tlatelolco massacre of 1968 and, 54;
    torture as state terrorism, 200–201
Stern, Steve, 81
student movements, 57, 62–63, 78; infiltra-
    tion of, 96; surveillance of, 66; Tlatelolco
    massacre of 1968 and, 52–53
subversives, 5–7, 82; ambiguous identity of,
    6; commemoration of, 77; countercul-

ture movement and, 55, 58–59, 66–67,
    78; criminalization of, 64–65, 68, 169,
    197; deaths of, 48; defined as "enemy," 5,
    55, 63–71; denial of civil rights/due proc-
    ess, 6, 11, 115; DFS campaign against,
    65–66, 75; disappearances and imprison-
    ment of, 24–25, 116; erasure of, 74; fam-
    ilies of (*See* family members); gender and,
    60–62; homosexuality and, 67, 231n70;
    Lazreg on, 227n5; self-image of, 62; as
    social degenerates, 58. *See also* guerrilla
    organizations
surveillance, 16, 69, 83, 147; DFS and, 83,
    88; of families, 140; inside prisons, 112,
    118–119, 125

Tarín Chávez, Gustavo, 108
Tlatelolco massacre of 1968, 4, 9, 11, 53–56,
    169, 179; aftermath of, 58–59, 63, 188;
    Batallón Olimpia and, 96–97; counterin-
    surgency tactics and, 12; effect of on
    guerrilla organizations, 57
Topo Chico prison, 64, 116
Torres, Eliado, 30
Torres, Moi, 80
Torres, Olivares, 74
Torres Castrejón, Jesús, 189
transitional justice, 201, 208
transition to democracy, 197
trauma: collective, 10, 165; intergenerational
    trauma, 14, 154, 163–165; Tlatelolco
    massacre and, 54; of torture survivors,
    3, 135
Truth Commissions, 107–109, 161;
    in contemporary Mexico, 208–209,
    244n45

unconventional warfare, 4–5, 85, 92, 105,
    202. *See also* counterinsurgency tactics;
    "dirty war" tactics
Unión del Pueblo (UP; Union of the People),
    57
United States, 25; Drug Enforcement Agency
    of, 13, 17, 200; involvement in Mexico's
    torture program, 48–51, 87, 153; rela-
    tionship with Mexico, 225n65; "war on
    drugs," 68
Universidad Nacional Autónoma de México,
    52–53
Uranga, Lourdes, 134

Valdez Rodríguez, Alicia, 118
Valdez Valdovinos, Clemente, 155

Vallejo, Demetrio, 17
Vázquez, Alfonso, 72–73, 76
Vázquez, Genaro, 15, 56, 72, 120, 148–149, 168; followers of, 170
Velasco, Ricardo "Richard," 1, 80, 112–114
Vicariate of Solidarity, 71
Vicente Ovalle, Camilo, 8, 22–24, 57, 92, 116
Vicente Vásquez, Jesús, 90
Vietnam, 4, 7
Los Vikingos (the Vikings), 57, 77
Von Clausewitz, Karl, 123

Walker, Louise, 58–59
waterboarding, 40, 116
White Brigade, 82–83, 94, 95, 102–105, 180; detention of families by, 141; dis-
banding of, 199; memorialization of, 206–207; Nazar Haro and, 30, 82–83, 95, 99, 102, 104; precursors of, 95–99
witnessing as torture, 41–45
Woldenberg, José, 9
women, 170, 225n55; "dirty war" tactics and, 156, 195; guerrilla organizations and, 60–62, 229n28; memorials and, 212; as political prisoners, 111, 162–163; pregnancy/birth while detained, 142–143; rape of torture survivors, 45–48, 51, 60, 143–144, 189, 201, 204; story of Casas Quiroz, 187–191. See also family members

Zapatistas, 156, 200
Zorrilla Pérez, José Antonio, 89

Founded in 1893,
UNIVERSITY OF CALIFORNIA PRESS
publishes bold, progressive books and journals
on topics in the arts, humanities, social sciences,
and natural sciences—with a focus on social
justice issues—that inspire thought and action
among readers worldwide.

The UC PRESS FOUNDATION
raises funds to uphold the press's vital role
as an independent, nonprofit publisher, and
receives philanthropic support from a wide
range of individuals and institutions—and from
committed readers like you. To learn more, visit
ucpress.edu/supportus.

www.ingramcontent.com/pod-product-compliance
Lightning Source LLC
LaVergne TN
LVHW091522230525
812061LV00002B/174